American Government

A Wiley Brand

American Government

by Marcus A. Stadelmann, PhD

American Government For Dummies®

Published by: **John Wiley & Sons, Inc.**, 111 River Street, Hoboken, NJ 07030-5774, www.wiley.com

For general information on our other products and services, please contact our Customer Care Department within the U.S. at 877-762-2974, outside the U.S. at 317-572-3993, or fax 317-572-4002. For technical support, please visit https://hub.wiley.com/community/support/dummies.

Wiley publishes in a variety of print and electronic formats and by print-on-demand. Some material included with standard print versions of this book may not be included in e-books or in print-on-demand. If this book refers to media such as a CD or DVD that is not included in the version you purchased, you may download this material at http://booksupport.wiley.com. For more information about Wiley products, visit www.wiley.com.

Library of Congress Control Number is available from the publisher.

ISBN 978-1-394-37574-5 (pbk); ISBN 978-1-394-37577-6 (ebk); ISBN 978-1-394-37575-2 (ebk)

Contents at a Glance

Table of Contents

Introduction

Currently almost 90 percent of all U.S. junior and high school students must take an American government course. In addition, 20 percent of all U.S. college and university students are required by law to take the course.

Most students do not take American government because they believe it is a fun course and that they will enjoy it; they take it because it is required to graduate. That's where this book comes in. It is designed to make the course more enjoyable and easier to understand.

It is imperative for our citizens to understand not just how our government works but also how to participate in it and impact future policy decisions. Our founding fathers designed a representative democracy for us, in which we have the power to select who will make decisions on our behalf. This allows us to also control what type of decisions are made by our policymakers. This is a privilege unavailable in many forms of government. Most people in the world have no political power, cannot shape policy, and must abide by decisions made elsewhere. U.S. citizens have political power and can force policymakers to make policy they agree with. If they disagree, citizens can just vote them out of office.

American government courses are designed to bring about true citizens with knowledge and willingness to politically participate in this democracy.

This book is designed to help students in American government or civics courses to understand concepts and materials in an easy and fun way. Many American government textbooks are full of jargon and scientific terminology students do not know or readily understand. Students can get confused or frustrated and just give up on the study of American government. This book is designed to achieve the opposite: to get students interested in American government, understand concepts and historical events, and get involved in government. The hoped-for end result of taking an American government course and reading this book is an educated citizen ready to participate in American government.

To quote Thomas Jefferson: "With all the imperfections of our present government, it is without comparison the best existing, or that ever did exist."

By reading this book and becoming a student of American government, you will acquire the necessary tools to become familiar with, study, and hopefully become interested in both American political institutions and public policymaking. This book makes it easier to pass an American government class and create an interest in American politics resulting in an educated citizen ready to participate in our political world.

This book is intended as an introduction to American politics. I assume no prior knowledge of American political institutions and policymaking. It is also important to point out that while writing this book I have striven to be nonpartisan, meaning that I did not write with any type of political ideology in mind and did not attempt to push certain ideas and concepts while ignoring others.

I would like for the reader of this book to come to their own conclusions, become informed, and participate in the political process. Citizens need to be educated on the political issues of the day and must be informed and willing to participate in the political process.

I designed this book to provide a solid foundation for the field of American government. It will prove to be helpful whether you are trying to pass a high school or college class, writing a paper, or reading just to expand your knowledge. I tried to make the book entertaining, adding certain little-known titbits on many topics. So, whether you are an American government student or just someone interested in the field, this book is for you. My hope in publishing this book is that everyone understands that politics matters and everyone needs to get involved in it.

I modelled this book on the most widely used textbooks in American government. American government courses are usually structured in a similar fashion and so are textbooks on American government. The *American Government For Dummies* textbook is structured in a similar fashion to make it easy for students to use for help in the classroom, especially when it comes to the chapter topics and material location. This allows students to easily follow their class lectures and materials using this book.

I foresee students using this book to study for tests and to look up certain concepts and facts they might have missed in class. I foresee the casual reader discovering how American political institutions have developed over time and how policymaking has changed.

To be able to accomplish all of this, this book explains the history of Congress, the presidency, the bureaucracy, and the judiciary. It analyzes domestic and foreign policymaking and shows the reader the roles political parties, interest groups, the media, and public opinion play in U.S. politics.

Conventions Used in This Book

The information in some chapters is relevant to more than just one chapter. When this is the case, I include cross-references to these chapters by chapter number. For example, I discuss voting rights in Chapter 8 on civil rights but also mention them in Chapter 12 on voting.

Icons Used in This Book

As you read and enjoy this book, you will see three different icons that alert you to specific aspects related to American government, its structures, concepts, and major writers and politicians.

TIP

When you see this icon you are dealing with interesting, sometimes unique information, that might come in handy in class or everyday life.

REMEMBER

This icon points out important information you need to be aware of as you read this, the chapter or the book. The remember icon covers material which might just be on an exam you have to take. This icon covers the most important events, people, and issues.

TECHNICAL STUFF

Historical information, often case-specific, including treaties, constitutional changes, important presidential actions, and other relevant materials or events have this icon beside them. This information is not necessary for grasping certain concepts but is required to do well in a class, be a well-educated citizen or for becoming a political scientist.

Beyond the Book

In addition to what you're reading right now, this book also comes with a free, access-anywhere Cheat Sheet that includes a list of major political events and documents as well as important concepts, and more. To view the Cheat Sheet, simply go to www.dummies.com and type **American Government For Dummies Cheat Sheet** in the Search box.

Where to Go from Here

Feel free to start with any chapter in the book that interests you or is being covered in your high school or college class. Keep in mind that all the chapters are nonlinear, so you can start with any topic in any chapter.

Happy reading!

1
Setting the Foundation for a New Nation

Discover the reasons why the colonists were unhappy with British rule and started a revolution.

Examine the Declaration of Independence and see why the new form of government, created by the Articles of Confederation, was not feasible.

Observe the process of writing a new constitution and study the subsequent debate over ratification of the document.

Understand why a Bill of Rights had to be added to the Constitution and become familiar with how the Constitution can be changed.

Become familiar with the concept of federalism and see how federalism has changed in the U.S. over time.

Chapter **1**

Designing a New Country and a New Constitution

Throughout the 17th and 18th century, thousands of people migrated to North America. Most came for greater economic opportunities than they could find in Europe; others came for religious freedom. The British Empire took interest in the American continent in the 16th century. In 1587, the first English settlement was set up at Roanoke Island in North Carolina. It was established by Sir Walter Raleigh and disappeared under mysterious circumstances. In 1607, the English tried again, and this time established a colony in Jamestown, Virginia. The colony developed for almost a century but had to live under harsh conditions, constantly fighting the native population. Jamestown did leave the country an important legacy. The colonists established a representative assembly to govern their own affairs, a precedent the country later followed.

Creating Colonies

By 1732, all 13 colonies were in place. There was local self-government, but the colonies were controlled by the British crown. With the British little interested in the colonies, they enjoyed quite a bit of self-rule. Soon, the 13 colonies had their own legislatures set up, and passed laws and even levied taxes. Each of them also had a document similar to a constitution in place.

For example, Pennsylvania had a document called a Frame of Government and Massachusetts had one entitled the Body of Liberties. Great Britain did not stop the colonies from self-rule as long as they remained a part of the empire and were economically profitable to trade with.

Relations between the British Empire and the colonies remained friendly until the middle 1750s, when the French and Indian War broke out. Britain not only had to fight the French Empire but also various Indian tribes in the war over control of parts of North America. Even though the British won the war, it almost bankrupted the country. Being broke, the British needed revenue badly, so they turned to the American colonies for money. They decided to tax the colonies directly, which had never been done before.

Fighting the French and cracking down

The French and Indian War, fought between Britain and France and various Indian tribes from 1754 until 1763, changed everything. The French, headquartered in Canada, fought the British for control of North America. The Treaty of Paris, which settled the conflict in 1763, gave Britain control over most of North America. However, the war had cost Britain $130 million pounds, which it now had to recoup.

Britain decided to make the colonies help pay for the war by imposing taxes on them. The Sugar Act, passed in 1764, increased the tax on refined sugar and molasses. The colonists were outraged; how could they be taxed if they were not represented in the British Parliament? So, between 1765 and 1766, the colonists attacked tax agents of the British and boycotted British goods. Suddenly, British merchants were hurt by the boycotts and protested to their home government, and the whole Act was repealed by 1766.

Taxing the colonies

Beginning in 1763, the British Parliament began imposing a series of taxes on the colonies and placed new import duties (tariffs) on textiles, coffee, wine, and other goods.

Among these taxes were the Sugar Act, the Townshend Acts, and the Quartering Act. The taxes culminated with the Stamp Act of 1765, which raised taxes on all printed materials, including newspapers, legal documents, and even playing cards. In other words, the British Empire began taxing the colonies heavily.

To make matters worse, many Americans had fought with the British against the French and now expected to claim free land in the west, which used to be owned by the French Empire. The British blocked them by passing the Proclamation of 1763, prohibiting settlers from moving westward to prevent a new war with Indian tribes. The settlers figured they could just ignore the British, like they had for decades, but this time it was different. After fighting the French, the British army was now in the U.S., and thousands of soldiers stayed. The British now had the manpower to enforce British law. To take care of its soldiers, the British Parliament had passed the Quartering Act in 1765, which required colonial assemblies to house British troops in barns and warehouses. Finally, the British allowed the Americans to trade only with the British Empire and no other empire, such as France or Spain. So profitable trade with the French and Spanish Empires became illegal. The colonists were furious.

Not surprisingly, the colonies reacted to the imposition of taxes. The rallying cry became "No taxation without representation." The colonists began to boycott British products, and the British government gave in and repealed the Stamp Act. However, the colonists had now seen that the British Empire was not as powerful as they had thought. They would give in to the colonists' demands if the colonies resisted. This resulted in the infamous Boston Tea Party in 1773.

Responding to tyranny

The same day it repealed the Stamp Act, the British Parliament passed the Declaratory Act, which stipulated that the king and Parliament had full power to enact laws binding on the colonies. So, Parliament continued to pass acts raising revenue from the colonists for the British crown.

The Townshend Acts passed in 1767, imposing duties on items such as tea, glass, and paper, created a Board of Customs Commission to enforce the new tax laws and collect the duties. Britain was now able to collect taxes instead of having to rely on the colonial governments to raise taxes on their behalf and then hand over the money, which rarely happened. The Townshend Acts further suspended the New York State Assembly for refusing to house British troops. Riots broke out in Boston, and the British brought in thousands of troops to quell them. In the subsequent Boston Massacre, panicked British troops starting shooting at demonstrators, killing several. Now more and more colonists started to support a rebellion against the British Empire.

Again, the colonists at first boycotted British goods, and the British Parliament responded by repealing parts of the taxes imposed by the Townshend Acts in 1770; with one exception: the tax on tea.

Then, in 1773, the Tea Act was passed by the British Parliament. It was passed to help the British East India Company, which was about to go bankrupt. The Tea Act allowed for the East India Company to have a monopoly over the tea trade globally, which put small colonial traders out of business. The East India Company further started to sell tea in the colonies at a lower price than native merchants, in turn destroying native tea merchants. On December 16, 1773, colonists disguised as Mohawk Indians boarded three British ships in Boston Harbor and threw their cargo, 342 chests of tea, overboard in turn destroying it. This event is pictured in Figure 1-1.

REMEMBER

Tea was one of the most sought-after products in the world back in the 18th century. The 342 chests of tea had a market value of 9,600 British pounds. That would be about $2.5 million today.

THE DESTRUCTION OF TEA AT BOSTON HARBOR.

FIGURE 1-1:
The Boston
Tea Party.

N. Currier/Library of Congress/Public domain

The outraged British Parliament in turn passed the Intolerable Acts in 1774. These were designed to punish the colonists. The Acts closed Boston Harbor until the colonists paid for the products they had destroyed, weakened the Massachusetts colonial government by abolishing town meetings, and required that colonists not only harbor British soldiers in their own homes but also feed them. Massachusetts was now under British military control. This was the last straw for the colonists.

Inciting a rebellion

In September 1774, 56 leaders from 12 colonies got together in Philadelphia to respond to the British actions. This was called the First Continental Congress. It denounced British policy and organized a boycott of British goods. It further called upon the colonial militia to arm itself and began to hoard weapons in an arsenal in Concord, Massachusetts. The British governor of Massachusetts sent troops to seize the weapons stored in Concord. The troops were attacked by a small militia of colonists. They called themselves minutemen, because they claimed that they could be ready for military duty at a minute's warning. They were subsequently defeated by the British troops. The British did reach Concord and destroyed the weapons cache, but on the way back they were attacked by more militia. By the time they made it back to Boston, they had lost several hundred men. A revolution had begun.

Fighting a Revolution

In the beginning, most colonists figured that a solution with the British was possible. They assumed that the colonies would receive some local autonomy but remain part of the British Empire. However, things soon changed. At the Second Continental Congress held in 1775, a delegate for Virginia called for the first time for independence from Great Britain, and the Congress commissioned a declaration to discuss not only the grievances against the British but also a reason for independence from Britain. A committee was appointed, and a Declaration of Independence was commissioned. A small committee was formed, consisting of Thomas Jefferson, John Adams, Roger Sherman, Robert Livingston, and Benjamin Franklin. Jefferson was asked to compose the declaration.

TECHNICAL
STUFF

The Second Continental Congress was a convention of members from all 13 colonies. It became the national government during the Revolutionary War.

On July 2, 1776, the committee presented its draft of a declaration of independence to the full Congress. After a few small changes, the Congress adopted the Declaration of Independence on July 4, 1776, as depicted in Figure 1-2. The Declaration stated:

"We hold these truths to be self-evident, that all men are created equal, that they are all endowed by their creator with certain inalienable rights, that among these are life, liberty and the pursuit of happiness."

FIGURE 1-2:
Signing of the
Declaration of
Independence.

Based on the ideas of John Locke, the document then continued to argue that whenever government fails its people, the people have the right to change or even abolish a government.

REMEMBER

The Declaration of Independence accomplished three things:

>> It provided a justification for independence by outlining the concept of individual rights and stated that governments receive their power from the consent of the governed.

>> It listed grievances against King George III and the British Empire.

>> It severed ties with the British Empire.

Now having declared its independence, the colonies knew that a war with the British Empire was about to start.

Winning a war

At first the British government dismissed the Declaration of Independence. There was no concern; what could a few thousand disorganized militiamen do against Britain's well-trained professional army? In the beginning, they seemed to be proven right. The U.S. militia, consisting of farmers and small shopkeepers, suffered one defeat after another. The British army was better trained and equipped, and it showed. The Continental Army came close to defeat. The war did not end until 1781 when General Washington was able to defeat the British General Cornwallis at Yorktown in Virginia. The British then decided to ask for peace and the Revolutionary War ended after six bitter years.

Battling the British

George Washington was named commander in chief of the Continental forces in July of 1775. He took his troops to Massachusetts, and subsequently liberated Boston in the spring of 1776. In the summer of 1776, British General Howe landed with 30,000 troops on Long Island, New York, to put the rebellion down. They took New York City, and Washington had to retreat. By the winter of 1776, it looked like the war was over. There was no financial support from the Continental Congress, mass desertions happened, and George Washington rejected his salary and pledged to use his own money to pay his troops. It was his victory at Trenton, New Jersey, where he crossed the Delaware River at night, seen in Figure 1-3, and surprised the British Army, mostly consisting of German mercenaries, who did not want to be fighting in the U.S. anyway, that changed the war.

FIGURE 1-3: George Washington crossing the Delaware.

Leutze, Emanuel/Library of Congress/Public domain

By summer of 1777, Washington won battles at Germantown and Brandywine. It was the battle of Saratoga that saved the day. After his victory there, the French government decided to join in the war and help the U.S. forces. However, before the French could arrive, Washington had to spend a miserable winter at Valley Forge in Pennsylvania. While he was waiting for the French, the British moved south and conquered parts of Georgia and South Carolina.

When the French finally arrived, Washington was able to move. In the summer of 1781, he launched a massive attack on British forces at Yorktown, Virginia. On October 19, 1781, the British surrendered to Washington, and the Revolutionary War was over. The British Parliament, over the objections of King George III, decided it was time to end the war and let the colonies go free. Finalizing the peace took two more years, and in September 1783, a peace treaty was finally signed.

Creating a new government

After declaring independence, a new government for the colonies had to be created. So, the Second Continental Congress drew up a written statement and principles to guide the new government in 1777. This statement was called the Articles of Confederation. It took until 1781 for all 13 colonies to ratify the Articles of Confederation, so a new government was not put in place until 1781. The Articles of Confederation created a league of friendship between the colonies where power was retained at the state level.

A *confederation* is a form of government where power rests at the state level, not the national level.

The Continental Congress renamed itself the Congress of the Confederation. It was a unicameral legislature, with one house and each one of the 13 states had one vote in it. This of course gave smaller states, such as Rhode Island, more power than larger states such as Virginia. To pass legislation, 9 out of 13 states had to approve, and there was no federal executive or judiciary around. The Congress lacked some basic powers, such as regulating foreign trade or levying and collecting taxes. So, it did not have the money or power to create an army. To change the Articles of Confederation, a unanimous vote in the Congress was necessary.

The most significant policy successes the Congress of the Confederation could brag about were regulating westward expansion, including the selling of farmlands to settlers and the admission of new states. The Land Ordinances of 1785 and 1787 (referred to as the Northwest Ordinance) established guidelines on how to acquire property in the West and allowed areas with a set number of settlers to apply to become a new state.

Having problems

Without the power to tax, the national government was not able to raise an army to protect the country against foreign powers. At this time, the British Empire was not the only danger. The Russian and Spanish Empires were also present on the North American continent, presenting a constant threat. For example, the Spanish Empire closed the Mississippi to American ships, and pirates seized U.S. ships in Africa. The national government could not do anything about it.

Without tax monies, the new confederate government could not redeem war bonds, referred to as *continental loan certificates* at the time, which were used to finance the war against Great Britain. Many patriotic Americans had bought war bonds, expecting them to be redeemed. However, the new government had no money to redeem the war bonds, and many Americans lost their life savings. Obviously, they were not pleased.

To make matters worse, states negotiated with themselves and with foreign powers without informing or taking the new national government into account. How can you create a new country if its members impose trade restrictions against each other? The United States of America looked more like the Disunited States of America back in the 1780s.

The final straw was Shays's rebellion. Captain Daniel Shays led a rebellion consisting of thousands of farmers protesting high taxes and interest rates in Massachusetts in August 1786. Local state militia either deserted or refused to fight, and the national government could not step in. It had no army. Finally, the governor of Massachusetts had to hire mercenaries to put down the rebellion. It was time to act.

By the mid-1780s, the situation got so dire that many prominent Americans and the Congress itself became worried and wanted changes. They recognized the new government created by the Articles of Confederation was not working, so a national Congress was needed to change the Articles of Confederation. In February 1787, Congress called for a convention to amend the Articles of Confederation. This meeting, also referred to as the Constitutional Convention, convened in May of 1787 in Philadelphia. It lasted until September of 1787, and instead of revising the Articles of Confederation, it created a new constitution for the United States.

REMEMBER

The Constitutional Convention called for in Philadelphia in 1787 was only supposed to revise the Articles of Confederation, not to write a brand-new constitution.

Writing a Constitution

The Constitutional Convention, depicted in Figure 1-4, began on May 25, 1787. Fifty-five delegates from 12 states participated. Rhode Island was the only state that did not send any delegates. It continued to believe in a confederation. The delegates in attendance selected George Washington to preside over the convention. Although there was agreement over the issues of foreign threat and economic problems, there was wide disagreement over what type of government to create. The larger states wanted a legislature based on population whereas the smaller states preferred a government based on the concept of one vote per state.

FIGURE 1-4: The Constitutional Convention in Philadelphia.

The Indian Reporter/Wikimedia Common/Public Domain

Soon, two plans emerged for the new government. The first one was the Virginia Plan. Devised by James Madison, it would have created a bicameral legislature with both houses seeing representation based on population. This would have given the larger states control over the new government. The legislatures would have further chosen the executive and members of the judiciary.

To counter this plan, the smaller states came up with the New Jersey Plan. It advised for the creation of a unicameral legislature with only one house, and representation would be based on equality. Each state, regardless of population, would have the same number of votes. This one house would have the power to select the executive and the judiciary.

By July 1787, the debate over the type of legislatures nearly ended the convention. It is at this time Roger Sherman, a delegate for Connecticut, came up with the Great Compromise, also called the Connecticut Plan. Under it, a bicameral legislature would be created with two houses; one, the House of Representatives, would be based on population, and the second, the Senate, where representation would be based on equality with each state sending two senators. Also, all revenue bills had to originate in the House of Representatives.

One of the hottest topics under discussion in Philadelphia was what type of executive the country should have. Some delegates wanted a strong executive; some wanted a weak executive at the mercy of Congress. Some wanted a president elected by the people, some wanted one appointed by Congress. Under the New Jersey Plan, there were even two executives proposed.

Finally, the convention agreed to have the executive elected by an Electoral College. Instead of having the people directly elect the executive, an Electoral College, where each state chose how to select electors, picked the president (for a discussion of the Electoral College, see Chapter 4). This allowed the states, which picked the actual electors, to change the public's selection if necessary. Keep in mind that most of the delegates attending the Constitutional Convention looked down on the average person, believing that they could not make an informed choice for president.

REMEMBER

The current presidency is based on a proposal by James Wilson, a delegate at the convention from Pennsylvania. He based his proposal on how the New York and Massachusetts state constitutions structured the executive.

Discussing slavery

The issue of slavery proved to be a controversial one at the convention. Forty-five percent of the delegates owned slaves themselves. The four largest slave states, with a population of more than 100,000 slaves, were Virginia, North and South Carolina, and Maryland. Maine and Massachusetts, on the hand, had already banned slavery. So, what to do about the slave population? Should they be included for representation when the total U.S. population was counted for representation in the House of Representatives? If they were fully counted, slave states would be overrepresented in the new House of Representatives. If they were excluded, the slaveholding states would not approve the new constitution.

REMEMBER

Both Georgia and South Carolina threatened to walk out of the Constitutional Convention if the institution of slavery was threatened.

A compromise was found. It was referred to as the Three-Fifths Compromise.

Delegates from Southern states wanted enslaved people to be fully counted to increase their representation in the House of Representatives. Northern delegates, many from states where slavery was limited or abolished, opposed this, because it would give disproportionate power to slaveholding states. The Three-Fifths Compromise stipulated that for every five enslaved individuals, three would be counted toward a state's population. If a state had 100,000 slaves, for example, 60,000 were counted for purposes of representation in the House of Representatives. This allowed slaveholding states to wield greater influence in Congress and the Electoral College.

TECHNICAL STUFF

In 1790, 43 percent of the population in South Carolina were slaves; in Virginia, the number was 39.1 percent, whereas in New Hampshire it was 0.1 percent.

The Convention further agreed not to ban the import of more slaves for the next twenty years and stipulated that escaped slaves had to be returned to their owners. It was not until 1808 that importing slaves became illegal in the U.S. The reason then was not pressure from Northern states but the fact that the slave population in the Southern states was growing fast enough that no new slaves were needed to be imported.

To avoid offending the slaveholding states and to assure ratification of the Constitution, the document itself did not address the issue of slavery.

Ratifying a new constitution

Finally, on September 17, 1787, after four months of negotiations and bargaining, all twelve state delegations in attendance approved the Constitution. Now it had to be ratified by 9 out of the 13 states to go into effect.

TECHNICAL STUFF

The Constitution of the United States is the oldest written constitution in the world today. It is also one of the shortest constitutions, with only 7,500 words, which includes the 27 amendments which have been added. India has the longest constitution in the world with 146,385 words, and the Kingdom of Monaco has the shortest with 4,543 words.

Ratification was not assured. There were many in the U.S. who opposed the document, preferring a weaker national government with more power at the state level. To make it easier to ratify the Constitution, the Framers had decided that only nine out of the 13 states had to approve the Constitution for it to go into effect, which proved to be a wise choice.

In addition, the Constitution called for special sessions in each state to vote on the Constitution and not for the state legislatures to be able to ratify the document. The Framers were afraid that the state legislatures would vote the document down, because they had the most to lose. In the 1780s, the U.S. was run by state legislatures, and they would lose many of their powers with the new Constitution.

In addition, the Constitutional Convention agreed on the rule of secrecy. Meetings on ratification were not open to the public but were held behind closed doors. The rule of secrecy also forbade the participants to discuss what had been said in the secret meetings. The hope was that secrecy allowed all participants of the conventions to debate and discuss their points freely.

The Framers further pushed for quick conventions in all states to ratify the new Constitution and made sure they were held in winter. Four states ratified the Constitution before the opposition, the Anti-Federalists, had even organized.

It was tough to travel back then, especially during wintertime, and the hope was that city dwellers could easily attend conventions whereas people living in rural areas would have a tough time to make it to the ratification conventions. People living in cities were more likely to support the Constitution whereas people living in rural areas were more opposed to it.

Favoring or opposing the ratification

Soon two camps developed. The people favoring the Constitution were called the Federalists, and the ones opposing it, the Anti-Federalists. Both sides began to publish essays and gave speeches in support of or against the Constitution. Today, the papers supporting ratification of the Constitution, known as the Federalist Papers, represent some of the most important and discussed writings in U.S. history. They were written by James Madison, Alexander Hamilton, and John Jay. The two essays that stand out are Federalist Papers 10 and 51, both written by James Madison.

REMEMBER

The Federalist Papers consisted of 77 essays in support of the Constitution. The essays were written under the pseudonym Publius and were published in major newspapers and magazines. They discussed the benefits of the new Constitution and tried to alleviate the fear people had of it. In Federalist Paper No. 10, James Madison created the theory of pluralism (see Chapter 15) and in Federalist Paper No. 51, Madison showed how the new Constitution prevented a government from abusing its citizens. His arguments were that the many parts of government would constantly check on each other, preventing one part becoming dominant and that people would organize and bargain and compromise.

The Anti-Federalists were led by Patrick Henry, John Hancock, future president James Monroe, and George Mason. They also published a set of essays. The major concern of theirs, shared by Thomas Jefferson, was that the Constitution did not contain a Bill of Rights and that U.S. citizens therefore were not protected from a new and stronger government. This was a concern that was later remedied by a Bill of Rights being added to the Constitution.

The Anti-Federalists published their views under the pseudonym Brutus. They argued that the government created by the Constitution was too powerful and could limit freedom in the U.S. They were especially afraid of the new government's power to tax and the fact that the Constitution lacked a Bill of Rights to guarantee individual liberties in the U.S.

They also did not like the position of president. They believed that the executive resembled a king. They further rejected the idea of a national army, believing in state militias instead.

The one thing they got out of the debate was a Bill of Rights and that is exactly what they had wanted the most.

Ratifying the Constitution

The first state to ratify the Constitution was Delaware on December 7, 1787. Soon afterwards, New Jersey, Georgia, and Connecticut followed. A battle broke out in Pennsylvania over the lack of a Bill of Rights in the Constitution, and only the promise of adding one got the Constitution ratified. The same happened in Massachusetts. After Maryland, South Carolina, and New Hampshire ratified the Constitution, it had met the nine states threshold, but the Framers knew that the two most powerful states, Virginia and New York, were needed for the new Constitution to succeed. In Virginia, it took a personal appeal from George Washington and a promise of a Bill of Rights from James Madison to get the Constitution approved. With Virginia's approval, New York fell in line and the Framers decided to implement the new Constitution with 11 out 13 states having ratified it.

On September 9, 1789, the House of Representatives voted to submit a Bill of Rights to the states to amend the Constitution. Ten were ratified by the required nine states by December 15, 1791, and the Constitution now had a Bill of Rights. North Carolina did not ratify the Constitution until a draft for a Bill of Rights was introduced in the newly assembled Congress. The last state to ratify the Constitution was Rhode Island. It ratified the Constitution on May 29, 1790, after George Washington had already been elected president.

Adding a Bill of Rights

During the ratification debate, the issue of whether a Bill of Rights was needed came to the forefront. Even Federalist supporters of the Constitution had acknowledged that a Bill of Rights needed to be added. So, one of the first acts of Congress and the new President George Washington was to add a Bill of Rights in 1789. All ten amendments to the Constitution were fully ratified by 1791. The first ten amendments to the Constitution are referred to as the Bill of Rights. They contain the most important civil liberties granted to U.S. citizens (for a detailed discussion of the Bill of Rights and civil liberties, see Chapter 7). They are listed below.

The Bill of Rights

Amendment 1: Freedom of Religion, Speech, Assembly, and the Press

Congress shall make no law respecting an establishment of religion or prohibiting the free exercise thereof; or abridging the freedom of speech, or of the press; or the right of the people peaceably to assemble, and to petition the government for a redress of grievances.

Amendment 2: The Right to Bear Arms

A well-regulated Militia, being necessary to the security of a free State, the right of the people to keep and bear Arms, shall not be infringed.

Amendment 3: The Housing of Soldiers

No soldier shall, in time of peace, be quartered in any house without the consent of the owner, nor in time of war, but in a manner to be prescribed by law.

Amendment 4: Protection from Unreasonable Searches and Seizures

The right of the people to be secure in their persons, houses, papers, and effects, against unreasonable searches and seizures, shall not be violated, and no Warrants shall issue, but upon probable cause, supported by Oath or affirmation, and particularly describing the place to be searched, and the persons or things to be seized.

Amendment 5: Protection of Rights to Life, Liberty, and Property

No person shall be held to answer for a capital, or otherwise infamous crime, unless on a presentment or indictment of a Grand Jury, except in cases arising in the land or naval forces, or in the Militia, when in actual service in time of War or public danger; nor shall any person be subject for the same offense to be twice put in jeopardy of life or limb; nor shall be compelled in any criminal case to be a witness against himself, nor be deprived of life, liberty, or property without due process of law; nor shall private property be taken for public use, without just compensation.

Amendment 6: Rights of the Accused in Criminal Cases

In all criminal prosecutions, the accused shall enjoy the right to a speedy and public trial, by an impartial jury of the State and district wherein the crime shall have been committed, which district shall have been previously ascertained by law, and to be informed of the nature and cause of the accusation; to be confronted with the witnesses against him; to have compulsory process for obtaining witnesses in his favor; and to have the Assistance of Counsel for his defense.

Amendment 7: Right of Trial by Jury

In Suits at common law, where the value in controversy shall exceed twenty dollars, the right of trial by jury shall be preserved, and no fact tried by a jury, shall be otherwise reexamined in any court of the United States than according to the rules of the common law.

Amendment 8: No Excessive Bail, Excessive Fines, and Cruel and Unusual Punishment

Excessive bail shall not be required, nor excessive fines imposed, nor cruel and unusual punishments inflicted.

Amendment 9: Other Rights Kept by the People

The enumeration in the Constitution of certain rights, shall not be construed to deny or disparage others retained by the people.

Amendment 10: Powers Kept by the States

The powers not delegated to the United States by the Constitution, nor prohibited by it to the States, are reserved to the States respectively, or to the people.

Amending the Constitution

REMEMBER

It is important to point out that many constitutional amendments have made our political process more democratic. The 13th Amendment prohibited slavery, the 15th Amendment gave former slaves the right to vote, the 17th Amendment allowed for the popular election of U.S. senators, the 19th Amendment gave women the right to vote, the 24th Amendment barred poll taxes, and the 26th Amendment lowered the voting age to 18.

How are amendments passed? There are two ways to propose amendments to the Constitution:

>> **An amendment can be formally proposed by the U.S. Congress.** This requires a two-thirds vote in both houses, the House of Representatives, and the Senate.

>> **An amendment can be proposed by two-thirds of the state legislatures.** This method has never been used.

Next, the amendment proposed by Congress goes to the states. There it has to be ratified by seventy-five percent of the states. Today, this equals 38 states approving. A second way to approve an amendment is to have it approved in special conventions in three-quarters of the states. This method has only been used once, in 1933, to repeal prohibition.

Two amendments cancel each other out. The 18th Amendment implemented prohibition in 1919, making it illegal to sell and consume alcohol, whereas the 21st Amendment repealed the 18th Amendment in 1933.

It is difficult to change the U.S. Constitution. Since ratification by the states, close to 11,000 amendments have been proposed. Only 27 have passed. Of the 27 amendments that were added, 10, known as the Bill of Rights, were added in 1791.

Having a New Constitution

A *constitution* is defined as the basic principles and laws according to which a country, state, or organization is organized.

Constitutions are written documents that outline the structure of a political system. They determine what type of legislature, executive, and judiciary a country has and what form of government a country possesses. This could be a democracy, monarchy, and so on. Constitutions set rules for governments. Besides setting the structure of government, constitutions also provide for rights and obligations of citizens.

A constitution does not only set up the structures for a government but also outlines the vision for society. It places limits on the power a government has over its citizens and establishes rights for these citizens. Constitutions both empower and limit governments. Constitutions are the highest law of the land, and leaders must follow and abide by the rules constitutions set.

Most constitutions consist of several parts. First, many contain preambles. These are symbolic statements indicating the values of a nation. They are not required and have no legal meaning but express the writers' intention and motives. They further preview the basic principles of a constitution. The U.S. Constitution contains the following preamble:

"We the people of the United States, in order to form a more perfect union, establish justice, insure domestic tranquility, provide for the common defense, promote the general welfare, and secure the blessing of liberty to ourselves and our posterity, do ordain and establish this constitution for the United States of America."

Next come articles and clauses. They contain the actual meat in a constitution. They contain the foundation of the political structures as well as specific rights and obligations citizens possess. The U.S. Constitution contains seven articles that outline the new form of government, its relations with the states, and the process by which the Constitution can be changed.

Structuring the Constitution

Article I is the longest in the Constitution. It consists of ten sections. It establishes Congress, lays out qualifications for serving in the House of Representatives and the Senate, discusses elections for both bodies, discusses procedures for operating both houses of Congress, and, most important, discusses congressional powers (see Chapter 3).

Article II discusses the presidency (see Chapter 4). It only consists of four sections. Section 1 mentions presidential elections and the Electoral College whereas section 2 talks about the powers of the presidency (see Chapter 4). The last two sections discuss the State of the Union address and impeachment procedures.

Article III establishes the judicial system (see Chapter 5). It allows for a Supreme Court and lower federal courts as established by Congress. It further mentions lifelong terms for judges and discusses the impeachment process for the federal judiciary. Finally, it elaborates on the crime of treason and possible punishment, which includes death.

Article IV describes the relationship between the national government and the states (see Chapter 2), and Article V authorizes amendments to the Constitution and discusses in detail how the amendment process works. Article VI makes the Constitution the supreme law of the land, and Article VII outlines the ratification process for the Constitution.

TIP

Every constitution contains an amendment process, telling the reader how to change or alter a constitution. In the U.S. Constitution, Article V outlines the amendment process.

Analyzing the Constitution

The new Constitution introduced the concept of separation of powers to the U.S. The concept was based on the works of the French political philosopher Baron de Montesquieu, who argued that if the executive, legislative, and judiciary are separate, powers cannot be easily abused. By being independent of each other, the three branches could not be controlled by another branch and in addition could check on each other.

REMEMBER

Charles-Louis de Secondat, Baron de La Brede et de Montesquieu, just known as Montesquieu, was a major political theorist impacting the structure of the U.S. government. He came up with the concept of separation of powers by which government is divided into various branches that constantly check on each other. He advocated for three branches of government, a legislative, an executive and a judiciary, which are independent of each other and check each other.

The new Constitution set up a system of checks and balances where the three branches must work together to make policy while at the same time, they can also check on each other to make sure no abuse occurs. For example, the president nominates Supreme Court judges, but they must be ratified by the Senate. The Supreme Court in turn can declare acts of Congress and the executive unconstitutional.

In addition, the Constitution develops a federal system in which both the new national government and the states share power (for a full discussion of federalism, see Chapter 2). The Constitution further lists the powers the federal government should have. These are called enumerated powers and are discussed in Chapter 2. All powers not mentioned in the Constitution were supposed to be left to the states.

The U.S. Constitution is a brief constitution. It provides for a structure of government but does not go into much detail when it comes to societal matters. It is vague and open for interpretation, which has led the U.S. Supreme Court to come in to interpret it many times.

For this reason, the U.S. Constitution is called a living constitution, meaning it is short, vague, and easily adaptable to changing times.

IN THIS CHAPTER

» **Explaining federalism**

» **Comparing federalism to other forms of government**

» **Understanding how federalism has evolved over time**

» **Dealing with grants**

» **Fighting with the states**

Chapter **2**

Dividing Powers to Establish Federalism

Currently, about 90,000 governments (national, state, and local) exist in the U.S. Of course, there is only one national government and 50 state governments. The rest are local governments, such as city, town, and county governments. About 3.4 million people work for the federal government (including the U.S. armed forces), but 5.5 million work for state governments, and 14.4 million work for local governments. Clearly, federalism in the U.S. has resulted in many levels of government being active and employing millions of people.

Not surprisingly, the number of employees at all levels, local, state, and national, has increased over time, mostly at the local level. The federal level has seen the fewest increases, and occasionally even decreases, in past decades.

Figure 2-1 depicts the changes in employment at all levels (national, state, and local) since 1939.

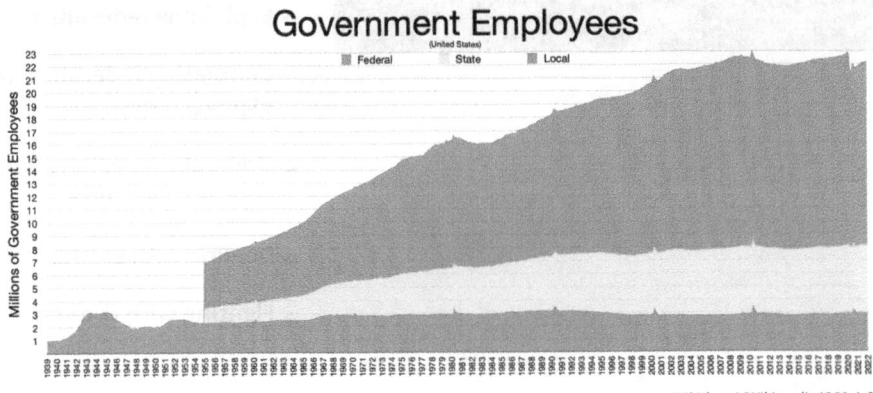

FIGURE 2-1: Government employees.

Government Employees
(United States)

■ Federal State ■ Local

Millions of Government Employees

Explaining Federalism

The term *federalism* originally comes from the Latin *foedus*, which roughly trans-lates to an agreement linking different entities. Thus, a federal system is one where different levels of government are linked together and whose powers are divided among the different levels. The various types of government, national, state, and local, are linked to provide the best and most efficient political outcome for a nation. Federalism requires at least one subnational governmental structure, such as a state in the U.S., or a Land in Germany, and one central government.

Dividing powers

The Founding Fathers implemented the concept of federalism to save the country that was falling apart economically under the Articles of Confederation and was threatened by outside forces (see Chapter 1). In addition, federalism made it easier for the original 13 states to approve the Constitution because it guaranteed states' power and did not make them inferior to the national government in the newly created United States of America. To assure equality, the Constitution lists powers for both the national and the state governments.

First, there are *enumerated* or *delegated powers*. These are powers given to Congress in Article I, Section 8, in the Constitution. Overall, the Constitution lists nineteen powers explicitly given to Congress. They include the power to regulate foreign commerce, borrow money, conduct foreign affairs, coin money, establish a federal court system, declare war, establish post offices, raise and support an army, and admit new states to the union.

At the same time, the Constitution also outlines powers given specifically to the states. They are called *reserved powers*. Reserved powers, given to the states in the

10th Amendment to the Constitution, include the power to regulate a militia, the power to set up a police force and establish prisons, the power to conduct elections and decide who is qualified to vote, the power to regulate health, public safety, and morals, and the power to ratify amendments to change the Constitution.

Finally, the Constitution mentions *concurrent powers*. These are powers shared by the federal government and the states. They include the power to spend money on general welfare, to regulate interstate commerce, to come up with bankruptcy laws, to lay and levy taxes, to establish courts, to establish highways, and to take private property for public purposes with fair compensation.

Looking at the Constitution, national economic policy, foreign policy and war-making were matters left to the national government whereas many local or internal state matters were left to the states.

The Tenth Amendment, the final amendment of the Bill of Rights, solidifies federalism in the U.S. by basically saying that any matter not given in the Constitution to the federal government is reserved for the states. Just looking at the Constitution, it seems the states got a better deal, having more powers. Subsequent court rulings, however, changed this drastically.

Being necessary and proper

Clause 18 of Article I, Section 8 — the Necessary and Proper Clause — within the Constitution authorizes Congress to make any laws necessary and proper to carry out its delegated powers. It is also known as the elastic clause because it can be used to justify just about any Congressional action. This coupled with the concept of implied powers, powers that can be implied from the Constitution but are not necessarily mentioned by it, has allowed for the federal government to take any action that is not specifically prohibited by the Constitution.

The case of McCulloch v. Maryland in 1819 set the precedent for the Necessary and Proper Clause being used to enhance federal powers. The state of Maryland tried to tax a federal bank in Maryland, but the bank refused to pay the tax, arguing that a state could not tax an institution created by Congress. After state courts sided against James McCulloch, the cashier of the bank (today, this position would be referred to as bank manager) and the federal government, for failing to pay the tax, the national government appealed all the way to the Supreme Court. The U.S. Supreme Court sided unanimously with McCulloch and the federal government. It argued that although the Constitution does not explicitly state that the federal government can set up a bank, it mentions that the federal government had the power to collect taxes, coin money, borrow money, and pay off debt. These activities necessitate a banking structure. Thus, chartering a bank was necessary and proper for Congress. Having the federal government have the power to charter a bank made it unconstitutional for a state to try to tax a federal structure.

REMEMBER

The Necessary and Proper Clause states that Congress has the authority to exercise the necessary and proper powers to carry out its designated functions.

Being supreme

Other parts of the Constitution discuss federal powers in more detail, establishing the possibility of a strong federal government. Even though on paper the states have real powers, especially in internal state matters, the federal government can easily infringe upon these powers by using the following clauses.

>> *The Supremacy Clause* is mentioned in Article VI, Section 2, of the Constitution. It states that laws and treaties passed by the federal government are the supreme law of the land. This means that federal law overrides state law if in conflict, provided the power outlined in the federal law is granted to the federal government. States must abide by acts of Congress and the U.S. Supreme Court's interpretations of laws.

>> *Inherent powers* are not mentioned in the Constitution and cannot be implied from it but are necessary for the president and Congress to function properly.

>> The *Commerce Clause* is found in Article I, Section 8, Clause 3 in the Constitution. It gives Congress the power to regulate commerce with foreign nations, between states, and with Indian tribes. In Gibbons v. Ogden in 1824, the Supreme Court ruled that the power to regulate commerce includes the power to regulate navigation. This ruling was later used by Congress to regulate railroads, freeways, and even television and radio.

>> *The Full Faith and Credit Clause* states that each state must recognize and uphold laws passed by the other states. For example, the state of Nevada must accept an Arizona driver's license and a married couple from Indiana is also considered legally married in Illinois.

>> Finally, there is the *Privileges and Immunity Clause* contained in Article IV of the Constitution. This clause guarantees that citizens of one state have all the privileges and immunities of the state they reside in if they travel to another state. This means that citizens of one state who, when moving or travelling to another state, have the same legal rights as the residents of the state they are moving or travelling to. They can enter into contracts, open businesses, and have the same access to the court system. In addition, the clause mentions that if a criminal in one state flees to another state and is captured there, the criminal has to be returned to the state in which the crime was committed.

A few exceptions are allowed, such as out-of-state students paying higher tuition or out-of-state travelers paying higher fees for public services.

Comparing Federalism to Other Systems of Government

One of the fundamental aspects of a state is the distribution of power among its parts and various levels of government. This is referred to as *systems of government*. The amount of power held by the national government determines the system of government a state has. Among the various levels of government making up a state are three major systems of government distributing power: a *unitary system*, a *federal system*, and a *confederation*.

Being unitary

In a unitary system, most power is located with the national government. Often, lower levels of government, such as states, counties, or departments, exist, but they do not have independent powers. All power comes from the national government. Lower levels of government implement policy made at the national level. They cannot change or even question these policies.

France is a great example of a unitary system. It has lower levels of government called *departments*. The departments have limited powers. Their major function is to implement policies made by the central government in Paris. So, although France looks on paper like a federal system, it is unitary because the departments have no independent powers.

A good example of how a unitary system works is the French educational structure. The Department of Education in France sets the high school curriculum for the whole country. In the U.S., on the other hand, education varies by state and is different depending on the state a person lives in. Everybody in France knows that at 11:00 am, all students in 10th grade study, say, algebra in every school in every region of France. In the U.S., this varies by state.

The same goes for bureaucratic rules and regulations. There are no variances between Northern France and Southern France when it comes to these. Everybody in France knows what to expect from laws and regulations and nobody can be surprised. They are the same for the whole country. Other examples of unitary systems include the Netherlands and Japan.

Going federal

There are reasons to set up or join a federation. First, smaller states facing a common foreign threat can join in to become more powerful and protect each other.

One can make a good argument that one of the major reasons the thirteen original American colonies came together to create the United States of America was because they faced a common threat from several European powers, especially Great Britain, France, and Spain. By combining resources, the thirteen colonies were suddenly able to establish a viable economy, implement a system of taxation and create a common military force to face any future threats.

Second, federalism can be a prerequisite to create a new nation-state. It is implausible that the thirteen original states would have joined a unitary system. A federation allowed each to maintain its own way of doing things. In other words, both local culture and the power of local leaders were protected by federalism. Local autonomy makes it easier for previously independent states to join a new federation.

Preferring federalism

In a federalist state, subnational levels of government not only exist but they also have independent powers. These powers are mentioned and reserved in a constitution and cannot be taken away by the central government. The U.S. Constitution, for example, mentions both delegated powers reserved for the national government and reserved powers reserved for the states. Often, lower levels of government are represented at the national level in upper houses of government; a good example is the U.S. Senate.

The central government usually maintains full power over the military policy, monetary policy, and foreign policy, but the lower levels of government do have important powers. In the United States, the states have power over school curricula, police matters, the speed limit, and, most recently, whether to legalize recreational drugs.

Now comes the big question. Which system of government, a federalist or a unitary system, is better suited for a country? What are the advantages and disadvantages of each?

Evaluating federalism

A federal form of government works best in large, diverse countries like the United States or Brazil. These countries are so large that people live thousands of miles from the capital and are quite isolated from their government. There is no close contact between citizens and their government. Most people agree that government should be close to the people, so that people can participate and check on their representatives, and that therefore local government is the best form of government. Local government and even state government bring people close to their elected representatives, making sure that their policy preferences are implemented by their representatives. It is easy to go to a city council meeting, sit in, listen to your representative, and make sure you are represented by the city council member you elected.

For this reason, local government encourages increased political activity. Citizens are more likely to participate if they feel that they can make a difference and observe the results of their actions. Giving a speech in a city council meeting or circulating a petition for a local issue can accomplish this. Voting for someone in Washington, D.C., whom you will never meet and who does whatever he/she wants will not. The further away a government is located from most of its population, the more difficult it becomes to check on it.

Also, federalism is better for a large, diverse nation. How can a central government truly represent the many different groups making up the United States? In the United States, many local and regional differences coexist. Local and state government is much more likely to represent these differences compared to a central government thousands of miles away. Federalism therefore allows for diversity in the United States to be better reflected than a strong all powerful central government. The state government of Louisiana, for example, is much more likely to be aware of and reflect Cajun culture than the central government in Washington, D.C., thousands of miles away.

Unitary governments, on the other hand, can ignore diversity in a country. A central government makes all decisions, ignoring local differences. This results in citizens being opposed to central governmental policies because they are not reflective of their values. Not surprisingly, unitary forms of government are better suited for less diverse and more homogenous nations. Without minority groups, policies reflect the will of the majority, which controls the central government. This explains why it works so well in France or the Netherlands.

Federalism encourages state constitutions to be more detailed and longer, because states have actual power in many public policy areas. State constitutions discuss issues from public education to healthcare and social welfare, even managing water supplies. This allows state governments to come up with quicker decisions and speedy resolutions to disputes on issues.

Finally, federalism allows states to become laboratories for democracy. Here, states can try out different policies and react differently to problems. This allows the federal government and other states to observe whether the policies succeed, and when they do, they can adopt them. If they fail, at least few resources were wasted on them. This saves time and money.

Evaluating unitary systems

Are there any advantages to unitary systems? Yes, there are. The major advantage of a unitary system is its uniformity, which makes it easier to predict economic or political outcomes. The same type of policies, be they economic or social, apply to every part of a nation. A good example involves taxation. In a unitary system, taxes (personal income, sales, and property) are the same throughout the country. There is no reason to move to another part of France to avoid paying higher taxes.

In the United States. taxation is high in some states and low in others. Because they are able to set their own rates for income, sales, and property taxes, some states are more expensive to live in than others. This has led to a mass exodus from high-tax states to low-tax states. Today, California and New York, states with the highest tax rates, are losing population, whereas Texas and Florida, low tax states, are gaining people rapidly.

Finally, unitary systems do better with public education. The central government sets high standards for the whole nation, and nobody is allowed to deviate from it, because the central government provides funding for education. Today, both France and Japan, countries with unitary systems in place, have some of the highest educational standards in the world.

Figure 2-2 shows the distribution of unitary and federal forms of government in the world today.

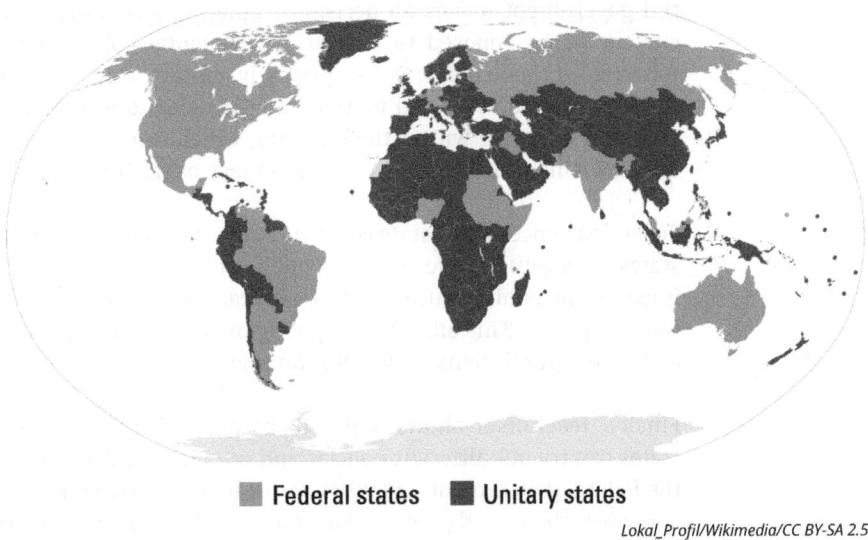

FIGURE 2-2:
Global distribution of federal and unitary forms of government.

■ Federal states   ■ Unitary states

Studying confederations

Confederations have become a rarity. A *confederation* is a very loose organization of localities or states. In a confederation, these localities and states hold all the political power. The central government itself has no or only a few powers.

A great example is the first government created by the United States after the Revolutionary War was won. During the Articles of Confederation, all powers were held by the original thirteen states, whereas the central government around the Continental Congress held few powers.

Without the power to tax or regulate commerce, the new Continental Congress did not have the monies necessary to create a military to defend the country, and trade between the states was chaotic. For this reason, a new constitution with a federal form of government was written and ratified. (See Chapter 1 for a discussion of the Articles of Confederation).

Evolving over Time

Since the creation of the U.S. government back in 1789, different types of federalism emerged in the U.S. The reasons are a shifting pattern of state-federal governmental relations and the emergence of new issues such as foreign policy and international trade, which are federal matters. Two world wars and a Cold War, in addition to global economic relations, brought the federal government to the forefront. Added to this, emerging technologies, such as cell phones, artificial intelligence, and global interconnectedness called for federal government regulations. When the pandemic happened in 2020, nobody looked for action from the California or Texas governor, but everybody looked to the U.S. president.

Based on these developments, federalism in the U.S. went through the phases discussed below.

State-centered federalism (1789–1819)

The Constitution made it very clear that the federal government has a limited role to play in U.S. politics. Article I mentions that the federal government had control over military, foreign, and some domestic affairs, such as setting up a federal judicial structure and coin money, and that was about it. Everything else was left to the states.

For this reason, during the early years of the republic, the national government held limited power relative to the states. Its influence began to grow in the 1790s through key initiatives like Alexander Hamilton's economic plan, which included the federal assumption of state debts and the creation of a national bank. This expansion of federal authority was later reinforced by Supreme Court decisions, particularly under Chief Justice John Marshall, which interpreted the Constitution in ways that favored stronger national power.

National supremacy (1819–1837)

This period was defined by a growing federal presence in American politics. Interestingly, it was the U.S. Supreme Court and its Chief Justice John Marshall who was responsible for this. In 1801, outgoing Federalist President John Adams appointed John Marshall Chief Justice of the U.S. Supreme Court. He singlehandedly increased federal power in the U.S. in the case McCulloch v. Maryland (1819), discussed in the section "Being necessary and proper," earlier in this chapter. John Marshall even stated that the Supreme Court's duty was to protect national power against state encroachment, in turn creating the doctrine of national supremacy.

REMEMBER

National supremacy, or the Supremacy Clause, states that the Constitution and federal law are the supreme law of the land, taking precedence over state law. When federal and state law are in conflict, federal law prevails.

Dual federalism (1837–1933)

Beginning in the 1830s, the question of states' rights became a hot issue. The question was whether states had the right to leave the union over the issue of slavery. Southern states argued that federalism allows a state to leave a federation. Supporters of the federal government denied states that right. A Civil War had to decide this question. After the Civil War, the federal government, headed by the Supreme Court, made sure that states knew that federal law was superior.

The concept of *dual federalism* was now established. It basically stated that states retained authority over many economic matters, including manufacturing and the health and safety of workers. The U.S. Supreme Court even struck down federal laws outlawing child labor and some of FDR's New Deal programs as unconstitutional violations of states' rights.

REMEMBER

Dual federalism referred to a clear division of authority between federal and state governments. It is also called *layer cake federalism*. Each level of government was now supreme within its area of authority.

The federal government dominated international politics. It committed troops into hostile situations and conducted foreign policy. It further dominated in the creation of an interstate infrastructure and conducted monetary policy. Finally, the federal government regulated commerce and settled disputes between the states.

The states, in turn, oversaw just about everything occurring within their borders. They regulated education, marriage, police and crime, even building prisons. This all changed in the next phase.

Cooperative federalism (1933–1981)

After the Supreme Court struck down FDR's legislative agenda in the mid-1930s, the president grew impatient and frustrated. So, he decided to target and change the Supreme Court. FDR proposed what is called court packing, where the Congress increases the number of Supreme Court justices. The idea was to expand the size of the Supreme Court from 9 to 15, appointing many friendly judges who could then support FDR's agenda. With this threat, and with public opinion favoring FDR's policies, one justice changed his mind and started to support FDR's agenda. When FDR was able to appoint one more judge to replace a retiring judge, he suddenly had a majority on the Supreme Court. Now FDR controlled the court and changes like court-packing were unnecessary.

With the Supreme Court in line, FDR was now able to implement his New Deal agenda. This started the era of cooperative federalism, which alludes to a far more active and powerful federal government. Often called *marble cake federalism,* where federal and state authority overlap and are swirled together, the responsibilities of all levels of government are now mingled.

REMEMBER

Cooperative federalism refers to the federal government enlisting states' officials to implement federal policies. In this type of federalism, the federal government passes money to the states and asks them to implement a certain policy.

For example, states receive grant-in-aid funds to build roads, bridges, hospitals, and make welfare payments to their residents, but the federal government tells the states how to exactly spend the money. The federal government thus provides not only the money to states and local governments but also the rules on how and where to spend it. The federal government also possesses oversight of the process of how the money was spent.

Loving and hating grants

Grants-in-aid are federal government funding given to states and local governments with specific instructions on how to spend the funds.

Grants-in-aid go back to the 19th century. They started out as land grants. Many universities, including Ohio State and Michigan State, were established due to land grants being given by the federal government to the states. By the 20th century, grants changed from land to money being given. The program expanded during FDR's New Deal policies and the Great Society programs during the Johnson presidency in the 1960s, which established Medicare and Medicaid (see Chapter 9).

Grants work the following way. Congress establishes a grant for a specific purpose, such as job training or highway safety, and then the states apply for the money. If they get a grant, that must accept federal rules on how to use the money and how programs are administered. Grants allow Congress to set policy throughout the states and compel the states to follow federal policy. When the Reagan administration passed the National Minimum Drinking Age Act of 1984, which increased the drinking age in the U.S. from 18 to 21, states that did not comply with the new drinking age saw their federal funds reduced by 10 percent.

Coercive federalism

In the 1960s, we see the establishment of *coercive federalism*. Coercive federalism refers to the federal government exercising power over states and local governments through mandates, often unfunded grants-in-aid and preemption of state laws. In other words, the federal government tells states and local government what policies to implement and often does not provide funding for them. If state or local law and rules conflict with the policy requested, it is preempted or overridden by federal law. Key characteristics of coercive federalism include the imposition of federal rules and regulations on states, replacing state authority through preemption and the use of grants with strict conditions to achieve federal objectives.

TECHNICAL STUFF

Unfunded mandates started to be used on a regular basis in the 1960s. An *unfunded mandate* is basically a federal law or regulation imposed on state or local government without any funding attached to it. In other words, the federal government tells a state or city to do something and then gives them no money to do it.

A good example is the American with Disabilities Act of 1990. It mandated that existing and new facilities, such as restrooms, be made accessible to people with disabilities, such as those confined to a wheelchair. At the same time, no federal monies were provided to bring about this accessibility, and state and local governments had to pay to make this happen.

New federalism (1981–2009)

In the 1980s, the Reagan administration started a new era of federalism, called new federalism. *New federalism* refers to a continuation of cooperative federalism but with less government intervention or oversight by the federal government.

The government still provides the funds, but states and local governments have more freedom to use them. The Reagan administration further began to use *block grants*, federal funding to state and local government with few restrictions on spending. Block grants were first introduced in 1966 and leave a program's details to state and local government instead of being dictated by the federal government. So, what is the difference between grants-in-aid and block grants? Grants-in-aid provide unlimited federal funding for states. An example is every eligible person getting food stamps. Block grants, on the other hand, provide a limited amount of funds, and when a state or local government uses those funds, they are gone. With a block grant, federal government funding is given to the states and local governments with no restrictions on how to spend the funds.

REMEMBER

New federalism refers to a version of cooperative federalism with less government oversight. State and local government exercise more control over federal monies in this version of federalism.

Progressive federalism (2009–2017)

Progressive federalism was introduced by the Obama administration in 2009. Here, the federal government sets a goal or objective and tasks the states or local governments to achieve it. The states or local government then come up with ideas on how to achieve the task and compete with themselves for federal monies to achieve the objective.

The Trump administration is currently trying to move back to the New Federalism, abandoning progressive federalism in the process.

Federalism today

Today, federalism has become a partisan battlefield. Federal administrations often feud with states and the other way around. During the Biden administration (2021–2025) many states, especially border states, denounced his immigration policies, wanting stricter policies put in place. Lawsuits were filed by states to change federal policies.

During the first Trump administration (2017–2021), when the U.S. pulled out of the Paris Climate Accords, democratic states filed lawsuits and pledged to abide by the accords even if the federal government withdrew from them. Again, lawsuits were filed and not much was accomplished.

2

Developing Political Structures

IN THIS PART . . .

Study the structure of Congress, see how a bill becomes law, and then examine the evolution of Congress. Be surprised to see how Congress dominated American politics until the Great Depression and then observe how Congress lost many of its powers to the president.

Discover the powers of the presidency and see how the presidency became the dominant institution in U.S. politics. Observe the roles the president plays in the U.S. political system and learn how the Electoral College works.

Observe the creation of a federal judiciary and find out how the Supreme Court received the power to declare laws of Congress and acts of the president unconstitutional. See how justices are appointed to federal court and how their decisions can be kept in check.

Discover the need for a professional bureaucracy and see how the federal bureaucracy has slowly changed and expanded over time.

Chapter **3**

Convening a Congress

T he U.S. Congress is one of the oldest legislatures in the world. Article I of the U.S. constitution discusses Congress first, and this was by design. James Madison, one of the Founding Fathers involved in writing the Constitution, even called it the first branch of government. Its major purpose is to enact new laws.

Congress has not just been widely studied but also emulated around the world, especially in Latin America. It is a part of one of the two major democratic forms of government called a *presidential system*. The other is the *parliamentary* form of government.

Comparing Democratic Forms of Government

When studying democracies, two possible legislative structures are found. There is a parliamentary system, as found in Great Britain and many former British colonies. In a parliamentary democracy, a fusion of powers exists, where the legislature is elected by the people and then in turn picks the executive, usually a prime minister or chancellor. In a presidential system, the voters elect both the executive and the legislature separately. This is the system we find in the U.S. and most of Latin America, with president and a Congress elected separately.

Going with a parliamentary system

In a parliamentary system the executive gets picked by the legislature. This means that the executive will most of the time have a majority in parliament. If not, they would not have gotten picked. In addition, the executive is the leader of the majority party in parliament and will always be able to rely on a majority to pass legislation. Often, political parties pass executive legislation without questioning it.

REMEMBER

In some parliamentary democracies, coalition or even minority governments are common. That means that a political party is lacking an absolute majority in parliament. In that case, it needs a coalition partner or political parties that will tolerate a minority government. This happens frequently in Israel or Italy. In these cases, a government can be quite unstable.

For this reason, prime ministers and chancellors can act like all-powerful leaders. They know in advance that most of their legislative proposals will get passed by a friendly parliament controlled by their own political party.

Going with a presidential system

In a presidential system, the executive is independently selected by the voters. So, instead of a fusion of powers, as found in parliamentary systems, there exists a separation of powers. The two institutions, Congress and presidency, constantly check on each other. This is called having a system of checks and balances in place with no institution being dominant.

Presidential systems take longer to make policy and react to crises because the two institutions must bargain and compromise before deciding. The Founding Fathers imagined that this constant bargaining and compromising results in moderate policies, acceptable to most everybody.

Being bicameral or unicameral

Today, most democracies are *unicameral* in nature, having only one legislative chamber. Unicameral democracies are usually found in smaller countries with a small homogeneous population. Examples include Bulgaria, Croatia, and Finland. About 40 percent of all democracies are bicameral, which means that they have two legislative chambers, one lower and one upper house.

Being bicameral

The U.S. had no choice but to become bicameral. The Founding Fathers had to find a compromise between the states when it came to national representation. The larger states were already overrepresented in the House of Representatives and the smaller states were calling for a body where they would also have political power. This would be the Senate (for a discussion of the Great Compromise, see Chapter 1).

Being bicameral makes passing legislation slow and cumbersome. Both chambers have to debate and pass new laws, and if they are not exactly the same, they have to start over. The Founding Fathers had exactly this in mind. They wanted a system of checks and balances in which each chamber checked on the other, where the two legislative structures had to bargain and compromise, and the resulting policies were moderate and acceptable to everybody. Radical new policies cannot be enacted quickly by a bicameral structure.

Being unicameral

Unicameral political structures have certain advantages over bicameral structures. First, they are more cost-effective. This is common sense. Having one legislative house instead of two saves money. A country has to pay the salaries for parliamentarians and for the bureaucratic upkeep of a legislature. A unicameral political structure can cut the costs of running the legislature in half. Congress, with its two houses, costs the American taxpayer $13 million a day, which equals to about $ 6 billion a year. Cutting one of the houses could save the American taxpayer billions a year.

Not surprisingly, unicameral legislatures are more efficient. Instead of having legislation debated in two houses, only one house has to do it. The same goes for voting. In a unicameral legislature, only one house debates bills and then votes on them. That's it, it's over. In a bicameral structure, after one house passes legislation, it goes to the second house to debate and vote on the bill. If it does not pass the bill exactly as is, the two have to meet to discuss a compromise. This can be a long cumbersome process.

So which structure is better? The answer depends on the political structure found in a country. A small country with a small homogeneous population is better off with a unicameral, unitary system, having one national parliament with all the power. However, a large diverse country such as the U.S. is better off with a federal system (see Chapter 2) where subnational levels of government are represented in a second legislative chamber, usually called a Senate. This is not surprising. If lower levels of government with independent powers exist, they expect to be represented at the federal level in policymaking.

Studying Congress

The U.S. Constitution dedicates more space to Congress than the presidency or judiciary. Being familiar with and admiring the British legislative structure, the Founding Fathers modelled Congress on it. Britain has a lower and upper house of parliament, called the House of Commons and the House of Lords. This is a so-called bicameral structure. So, the Founding Fathers copied it and created a House of Representatives and a Senate.

Each had its own purpose. The House of Representatives was elected by the people and could be held accountable by the people. The Senate, on the other hand, was appointed by state legislatures and represented the states' interests. It could block policies by the House of Representatives. Keep in mind our Founding Fathers did not fully trust the people. For this reason, they created an Electoral College to elect the president (see Chapter 4), and had state legislatures appoint the Senate. The Senate was given the power to block the will of the people if deemed irrational. This did not change until 1913 when the 17th Amendment passed, and U.S. senators began to be elected by the people and not appointed by the states.

TIP

Prior to 1913, U.S. senators, appointed by the states, represented both the states and the citizens within the states. Often, demands from the two groups were not the same. Today, elected by the people, U.S. senators are more likely to represent the will of the people and not just state government.

Scholars consider the Senate the more powerful of the two institutions because it possesses some powers the House of Representatives does not possess. The Constitution calls these powers *advise and consent powers*. For example, senators must confirm U.S. Supreme Court justices and ambassadors to foreign countries as well as the president's cabinet. Most important, all treaties negotiated and signed with foreign countries by a president must be ratified by the Senate.

Other powers given to the Senate include the power to remove members of the executive branch after they have been impeached by the House of Representatives.

This includes not just members of the cabinet and the federal judiciary, but even the president himself.

REMEMBER

The 17th Amendment in 1913 provided for the direct election of senators by the people. Interestingly, no great change in the composition of the Senate happened. Most senators who had been selected by state legislatures stood for reelection and easily won in a popular contest.

Structuring Congress

The first Congress of the United States met in 1789. It consisted of 65 members of the House of Representatives and 26 senators, two from each of the original 13 former colonies. Today, this number has grown quite a bit. We now have 435 members in the House of Representatives and 100 senators, two from each of the 50 states making up the U.S. Why this number? Is there a formula for how many congresspeople the U.S. can have and who came up with it?

TECHNICAL STUFF

Each house is the sole judge of the elections and qualifications of its members. For this reason, only Congress can decide disputed Congressional elections and, with a two-thirds vote, they can exclude or even expel a member.

The Senate is easy. Each state can send two senators to the Senate. Currently the U.S. is made up of 50 states, so the Senate has 100 members.

The House of Representatives is more complex. The size of a state's delegation to the House of Representatives is based on the population of a state. The more people live in a state, the more representatives the state has in the House. Originally back in 1789, a House member represented about 30,000 residents living in the district. Over time, the U.S. population grew, and Congress decided to pass the Permanent Apportionment Act of 1929.

The Permanent Apportionment Act of 1929 capped the maximum membership of the House of Representatives at 435 and established a permanent method for apportioning seats after each census. So, now a representative represents about 761,000 people in the district.

Getting into reapportionment

The size of the Senate and the House do not change often, but the number of members of the House from a state can change every ten years. The process is called *reapportionment*.

Although the number of seats in the House of Representatives is fixed at 435, every ten years a reapportionment occurs. During the ten-year period, some states gain population whereas others lose population. Accordingly, states will either gain or lose seats in the House of Representatives. Currently, states such as Texas and Florida are gaining population and have thus gained seats in the House of Representatives. On the other hand, states like Illinois and New York have seen a declining population. For this reason, they have lost seats in the House of Representatives.

REMEMBER

Reapportionment is based on the census taken once every ten years, as required by the Constitution. Afterwards, redistricting can take place. States that have grown in population receive additional seats, whereas states that have lost population lose seats. Keep in mind the number of House districts can never exceed 435 unless Congress passes a law to change that number.

Gerrymandering a district

Every ten years, after a census has been taken, states get to redraw Congressional districts in their states. This allows for the party in power in a state to redraw districts to favor one political party over the other. This is called *gerrymandering*. To be able to gerrymander, the same party must control both houses of the legislature and the governorship in the state. Although gerrymandering is common in many states, some states such as California use independent commissions to redraw districts.

Gerrymandering refers to redrawing districts to favor one political party. The term is named after former Massachusetts Governor Elbridge Gerry, who authorized the redrawing of districts in Massachusetts to favor his party, the Democratic-Republicans. One of the districts looked like a salamander so the opposition Federalists called his plan *gerrymandering*. The term stuck and is still used today. As a side note, gerrymandering did not work out well for Governor Gerry; he lost his bid for reelection.

Tracing the Evolution of Congress

In the beginning, Congress was the dominant institution in American politics. Although the presidents were prominent men legitimizing the newly established government, Congress, mainly the House of Representatives, made policy. This would last until Andrew Jackson became president in 1828, for the first time challenging Congress (see Chapter 4). Jackson began to veto legislation, and Congress became split over the issue of slavery. The Democratic Party even broke apart into Northern and Southern Democrats.

After the Civil War, Congress began to reassert itself. Presidents deferred to Congress and allowed it to take the lead in policymaking. Strong Speakers such as Thomas Reed in 1889 began to establish a powerful Speakership. He was the first Speaker to handpick committee chairs and members. By chairing the Rules Committee, he was able to control what would be debated and who was allowed to debate and what bills would be voted on in Congress.

REMEMBER

The Speaker of the House of Representatives is the leader and the presiding officer of the House. The Speaker is selected by the majority party in the House and is second in line to succeed the President of the United States.

In 1910–1911, there was a revolt against Speaker Joe Cannon. Unhappy members decided that it was time to challenge the Speaker. They were furious, having lost most of their power to the Speaker, and so they changed the rules on him. They removed him from the Rules Committee and took away his power to appoint committee chairs. That power was given to the party caucus, all members of one party in the House, and the chairs of the standing committees.

After the 1974 midterm election, the Democratic Party found itself with a majority in Congress, gaining 49 seats. Voters punished the Republican Party for the Watergate scandal and the subsequent pardoning of President Nixon by President Ford. Many of the new members were to the left of the party leadership and resented the old seniority system in place. The seniority system rewarded the longest-serving members of the House with the best committee assignments. Most of them came from the South, were very conservative, and many had supported segregation. Not surprisingly, the new members were dissatisfied with the old leadership and rebelled against it.

Instead of picking committee chairmanships based on seniority, the new rules stipulated that they were now selected by the party caucus dominated by more liberal Northern members of the party. Chairpersons could no longer refuse to hold meetings on topics they did not want to discuss, and committee meetings became open to the public.

In addition, subcommittees were created. Congress only has about 20 standing or permanent committees. Committees are a source of power; they can facilitate policymaking and can be used to gain interest-group support. The House created literally over a hundred subcommittees, and just about everybody from the majority party got to chair a committee. Now everybody had power.

With every member of the majority party suddenly having power, it became tougher to make legislation. Previously, a powerful leadership forced everybody in line and things got done. Now, the incessant bargaining and compromising meant nothing got accomplished. Another change was needed.

Beginning in 1995, when the Republican Party won the House back and Newt Gingrich became Speaker, changes came. First, the number of committees, especially subcommittees, were reduced, and the Speaker regained the power to appoint committee chairs and dominate the Rules Committee.

Serving in the House of Representatives

The Founding Fathers decided that because the House of Representatives represented the people, it should be held accountable frequently. For this reason, the terms for members of the House are only two years. Members of the House have to be attentive to the opinions in their districts. They are constantly running for reelection.

The first Congress had 65 members. Article I of the Constitution states that each state has to have at least one house member. The largest state, California, currently has 53 members in the House, whereas a state with one of the smallest populations, Wyoming, has just 1 member.

REMEMBER

Article I of the Constitution stipulates that members of the House of Representatives have to be at least 25 years old and must be citizens for at least seven years. They also must live in the states they represent, but do not necessarily have to live in the district they represent.

Leading the House of Representatives

The Constitution is very vague when it comes to leadership in the House of Representatives. Article I, Section 2, only states: "The House of Representatives shall choose their Speaker and other Officers." No more information is provided. So, every two years, when a new Congress convenes after an election, a new Speaker is chosen by the full House. In reality, the candidate for Speaker has already been picked by the majority caucus, which meets before the full vote for Speaker on the floor of the House occurs.

In the beginning of the republic, the Speaker's position in the House was quite weak. The Speaker was considered to be more of a procedural leader and not a political leader. This changed in the late 19th century with the election of the first strong Speakers, Republican congressmen Thomas B. Reed from Maine and Joe Cannon from Illinois.

Both Reed and Cannon (see Figures 3-1 and 3-2) singlehandedly turned the Speaker's office into what it is today. They skillfully used the Rules Committee to their advantage, giving them power in the House. Uncle Joe, as Cannon was called, used the Rules Committee to determine who could speak on the floor of the House and personally made sure that only legislation he approved of would clear the Rules Committee and thus could be voted upon. In addition, the two staffed the most powerful committees in the House with their supporters.

FIGURE 3-1: Speaker of the House Thomas B. Reed.

FIGURE 3-2: Speaker of the House "Uncle" Joe Cannon.

Today, the Speaker is the most powerful member of the House, exercising many powers to keep the House in line. Some of the Speaker's powers include:

>> The Speaker assigns bills to Congressional committees. This allows the Speaker to assign bills to friendly or unfriendly committees, which can impact the outcome of a committee vote on the bill. An unfriendly committee can vote a bill down or "table" it, refusing to let it out of committee so that the whole house cannot vote on it and possibly pass it. This power allows the Speaker to set the agenda for Congress.

>> The Speaker can pick the representatives who speak on the floor of the House. Without a debate, bills will not pass. So, by shaping the debate, allowing some members of House to speak and denying others, the Speaker can shape the way a bill is debated on.

>> The Speaker has the power to appoint members to serve on special committees. Special committees include conference committees, which are committees including House and Senate members to iron out differences in two bills on the same topic.

>> The Speaker can assign members to House committees, such as *standing committees*, which are permanent and the most powerful committees in the House. Being friendly with the Speaker and being a good party member will earn you better committee assignments.

>> Finally, and most importantly, the Speaker decides which bills the House gets to vote on and which bills are delayed or never brought to the House. This allows the Speaker to dominate the legislative agenda in the House.

Figure 3-3 shows Sam Rayburn, a Democrat from Texas, who was one of the most powerful Speakers in recent times. He is the longest-serving Speaker in U.S. history.

Being majority leader and majority whip

The *majority leader* is the floor leader of his party and principal assistant to the Speaker. His party's caucus elects the majority leader at the beginning of each two-year session. He is responsible for creating party unity and making sure that the Speaker's agenda is supported by his own party members. He also assists the Speaker with committee assignments, scheduling debates, and overseeing the legislative process. The majority leader is usually the Speaker-in-waiting.

The minority party caucus elects the *minority leader*, whose functions are quite similar, to maintain unity and support or oppose the majority parties' policies.

Finally, there are both majority and minority whips. As the term implies, party whips are supposed to whip their party members in line when voting for or against policies. They count votes and pressure members into voting a certain way.

Joining caucuses

Beginning in the 1950s, it became fashionable to join *caucuses* in Congress. These caucuses are more like clubs where members can form alliances and discuss issues. They are open to both parties. There are more than 100 caucuses in Congress today. They are based on economic, ideological, regional, ethnic, or social characteristics. For example, there are the Congressional Black and Hispanic Caucuses, the Blue Dog Democrats, a collection of moderate and conservative Democrats, the Freedom Caucus, consisting of conservative Republicans, and so on.

Caucuses allow for like-minded members of Congress to get together and discuss policy and to just socialize with each other. Caucuses are issue-based, and many caucuses are related to relations with foreign countries or specific social and economic causes. There is even a Korea caucus, an Uzbekistan caucus, as well as seafood, arthritis, and ski and snowboard caucuses.

Serving in the Senate

The Founding Fathers were concerned that the people could be too radical when it came to policymaking, so they created a body to balance out the House, called the Senate. By sharing power with the House, the Senate could slow down the House and be more deliberate, which could also protect the country from popular tyranny.

In addition, state legislatures, not the people, chose the senators from each state. Therefore, the Senate was more likely to represent state issues. This was another measure to make sure that the Senate was not a body that supported radical irrational change demanded by the public.

Article I of the Constitution requires that there are two senators from each state. Beginning with 26 senators from the original 13 colonies, the number grew to 100 in 1959 when both Alaska and Hawaii became states. No new states have been admitted since then, so the number of senators in the Senate is still 100.

REMEMBER

The minimum age to be a senator is 30 and a senator must have been a citizen for nine years and must be a resident of the state they represent. Senators serve six-year terms, staggered so that one-third of the Senate is up for reelection every two years.

During an average session of Congress, the Senate must approve thousands of presidential appointees. They include ambassadors, federal judges, Supreme Court justices, cabinet members, and many other executive branch officials. Over the course of a single Senate term, a senator might be involved in up to 3,500 military and civil appointments by a president.

When it comes to approving executive appointees, the Senate follows the rule of Senatorial Courtesy. This means that the senator from the home state of a nominee must support that nominee for the nominee to get confirmation. If they do not, it is unlikely the nominee will be approved by the whole Senate.

TECHNICAL STUFF

Since 1789, the Senate has rejected only 21 treaties submitted for ratification by a president. The most infamous is the Treaty of Versailles, negotiated by President Wilson, which the Senate rejected twice in 1919 and 1920. For this reason, the U.S. did not join the League of Nations.

Leading the Senate

The Senate is a lot less formal when it comes to leadership. Being a lot smaller than the House, most senators know each other by name and are on friendly terms.

The vice president is the presiding officer of the Senate. He holds the title *president of the Senate*. The only function a vice president has is to cast a vote if there is a tie in a Senate vote. So, the vice president rarely shows up in the Senate and while the vice president is away, the Senate is presided over by the *president pro tempore*. (*Pro tempore* is Latin and means for "for the time being," indicating that the position was originally a temporary replacement, used in the vice president's absence.) This is the senator who holds the longest tenure from the majority party. It is a largely ceremonial position with only one function. The president pro tempore is third in line to become president of the United States after the vice president and the Speaker of the House.

The longest serving senator in the history of the U.S. Senate was the late Democratic Senator Robert C. Byrd from West Virginia, depicted in Figure 3-4. He served for 51 years and died in office in 2010.

FIGURE 3-4: Robert C. Byrd, senator from West Virginia.

United States Senate/Wikimedia Commons/Public domain/https://simple.m.wikipedia.org/ wiki/File:Robert_Byrd_official_ portrait.jpg/Last accessed on October 10, 2025.

Although the vice president and the president pro tempore are empowered to preside over Senate sessions, they rarely do so. The real leaders in the Senate are the majority and minority leaders, who are elected by their respective party's caucuses. So are the two whips. The majority leader's powers include the right to recognize members to speak. This allows the majority leader to control debate on the Senate floor by recognizing or not calling on senators to speak or make amendments to bills. The majority leader further controls committee assignments and appoints conference committees with the House.

Chairing a committee

Similar to the House, the Senate also has permanent standing committees where most business takes place. Standing committee members are also elected by majority caucuses, but seniority still matters in the Senate. Senior members of the majority party get better committee assignments, such as chairmanships. Currently, the Senate has 24 committees, but their size and importance vary with each new Congress.

Talking an issue to death

Since the first Congress in 1789, the Senate has had a tradition of unlimited debate. Within this tradition is a tactic is called a *filibuster*. A filibuster is an endless speech or speeches by one or many members of the Senate. Senators go on and on and do not stop speaking, and do not allow for a vote on the issue. It is more than just talking; senators can also call for *points of order*, drawing attention to a possible rules violation, and offer irrelevant amendments to delay a vote. It is an effective tool to delay legislation or to bargain on a bill, especially if it's late in a Congress, meaning the Congress is about to adjourn. The only way to break a filibuster is a vote of cloture, where 60 senators must vote to favor ending debate. After a vote of cloture is passed, senators have another 30 hours to talk until a vote can be taken.

The most infamous filibuster occurred in 1957 when Strom Thurmond, the late senator from South Carolina, filibustered the Civil Rights Act for speaking for a little over 24 hours. The current record is held by Senator Cory Booker from New Jersey, who condemned the second Trump administration in a speech lasting 25 hours and 5 minutes in 2025.

Impeaching a president

How does impeaching a president or any other federal executive work? Both houses of Congress participate in impeaching and removing members of the executive. The House of Representatives starts the impeachment process by investigating a member of the executive branch, including the president. If they find any wrongdoing, they can proceed to impeach this member of the executive. To impeach a member of the executive, only a simple majority is needed in the House of Representatives. After a vote to impeach, the Senate springs into action. The Senate now acts as a judge and jury for the impeached person, while a few select members of the House of Representatives act as the prosecutor. After the case is presented, the Senate takes a vote on whether to remove the accused. It takes a two-thirds vote to remove a member of the executive, including the president.

TECHNICAL STUFF

Three U.S. presidents have been impeached in U.S. history. The first was Andrew Johnson, President Lincoln's successor, in 1868. The second one was Bill Clinton in 1998, and finally, President Trump was impeached twice by the House of Representatives in 2019 and 2021. In all four cases, the Senate refused to remove the president, and he was allowed to finish out his term. In President Trump's case, the president was even reelected by the American people in 2024.

Getting Work Done in Congress

Most work done in Congress happens in committees. Committees today have become specialized, focusing on specific issues. Most members serve on two standing committees and several subcommittees. There are four types of committees in Congress today.

Serving on standing committees

Standing committees are the most powerful committees in the House today. They are permanent committees, and their size varies. Most standing committees focus on a specific policy area, such as transportation, foreign affairs, or the federal budget. Today, 19 standing committees exist. Some of the most powerful are the Appropriations Committee, Armed Services Committee, Budget Committee, International Relations Committee, Judiciary Committee, Ways and Means Committee, and of course the Rules Committee. Standing committees matter because they report legislation out of committee, after the committee passes legislation, and the full House or Senate cannot debate and vote on a bill unless it has been positively reported out of committee.

Committee membership is determined by seniority, party loyalty, being friendly with the leadership, the importance of a member in the House, the needs of a member's district, and finally the candidate's knowledge or expertise in the policy area covered by the committee. For example, a House member who represents a rural district will want to sit on the agriculture committee. In addition, committee membership allows representatives to send benefits back home to their district. This so-called *pork-barrel legislation* is what will get members reelected.

REMEMBER

Pork-barrel legislation is legislation that gives benefits to constituents in districts or states in hope of winning reelection. It is national funding for local projects benefitting a district. Public Works Projects, military funding, and agricultural subsidies are examples. Members are bringing home the bacon, and this gets them reelected.

Committee membership, especially being a chairperson, signals to everybody in Congress how powerful a member of the House is. When a member has a coveted post on an important standing committee, they have a future in the House.

Being a part of select or special committees

Select committees are temporary committees tasked to deal with a specific problem. After they are done researching and investigating, they are disbanded. They produce no reports and do not propose any legislation. Good examples are the Watergate and Iran-Contra select committees. Most recently, in 2009, the Democratic leadership established two select committees on global warming. When the Republicans won back Congress, they disbanded the two committees.

Being appointed to a joint committee

Joint committees are committees that are composed of both members of the House of Representatives and senators. They usually deal with administrative matters pertaining to Congress and do not generate legislation. Instead, they recommend certain administrative changes.

Ironing out differences

Conference committees are also composed of House members and senators. Whenever there are two versions of a bill, one from the Senate and one from the House, conference committees iron out the differences between the two versions and come up with one version with a standardized language in it.

Being a committee chair

Being a committee chair does have certain perks attached to it. The chair gets to hire the committee staff and appoint chairs and members of subcommittees. The chair further is in control of the committee's budget. When the Republican Party took over Congress in 1994, it implemented term limits for chairs. A chair can only chair a committee for three terms (six years) and then has to give up the chairmanship. However, the member can then become the chair of another committee.

Having real powers — The Rules Committee

The Rules Committee is one of the most powerful committees in Congress. It has the power to deal with legislative debate. This refers to the ability to determine how long a bill can be debated and what kind of amendments can be added to the bill. There are three *rules*, or the procedure under which the bill is debated, that can be attached to a bill. They are

>> An *open rule*. which allows for any type of amendment to be added to the bill, which can totally change a bill. Often, after amendments have been added, a bill has been changed to a point where its own author withdraws it. In addition, debate is not limited, which can kill a bill when after hours of debate no vote has been called.

>> A *closed rule*, which prohibits any type of amendments and limits the amount of debate that can happen on a bill on the floor of the House. A closed rule guarantees a vote on the bill as-is. Most sponsors of a bill hope for a closed rule attached to their legislation.

>> A *modified* or *restrictive rule*, which allows for amendments to some parts of the bill but not to others.

Playing Many Roles

So, what do congresspeople do all day? There is a perspective that they are over-paid, do not do much, and are bankrolled by lobbyists and interest groups. Nothing could be further from the truth.

Being a congressperson is tough work. A congressperson has to get up early to meet with their staff to discuss pending legislation. Then they have to attend committee and subcommittee hearings, meet with constituents, lobbyists, and interest group leaders. They have to debate on the floor of the House or Senate and then cast a vote on issues they most likely know little about. If it is an important piece of legislation, they must explain their vote to the media and then to their constituents. When the day is finally ending, they really go to work. They have to attend fundraising dinners, make phone calls to supporters and contributors, and then, on the weekends, travel back to their home district to attend local events. There is little time for family and fun.

Voting is the major function of a legislator. Members of Congress cast thousands of votes each session, most on procedural matters. Only a few are on important issues, which are publicized, and it is these that legislators will be judged upon by the voters in their district.

When casting a vote in Congress, a legislator must decide how to vote. There are three explanations for how a legislator votes.

>> The *representational* view, which states that representatives base their votes on the wishes of their constituency. For example, if the constituency favors gun control, then the representatives support gun control legislation. Most often representatives agree with their constituency on the issues, but even if they personally disagree, they will still vote with the constituency against their own personal beliefs. The reason is that they feel that they are representatives of the public and will vote with the public on issues.

>> The *organizational* explanation, which states the representatives base their vote to please their party and the party leadership. In turn, they get rewarded with better committee assignments and electoral help, such as monetary support during reelection. The president matters quite a bit with this explanation. Presidents contact their party members in Congress often and exert influence on them. Currently, threatening to fund a primary challenger against an incumbent is the threat elected officeholders fear the most. Usually, after being threatened by the president, they fall in line and support the president's agenda. Here, *logrolling* comes in. The term refers to a member of Congress voting for another member's bill, expecting some kind of benefit in return.

>> The *trusteeship* view. Here, legislators base their votes and what they think is right, even if it conflicts with their constituency's wishes or the party leadership preferences. These types of lawmakers do not last long because they upset their constituency and the party leadership, which results in electoral defeat.

Voting is important in serving your constituency, but helping individuals in your home district often matters more. Often, constituents contact their lawmakers and ask for help on issues. Congresspeople are expected to help when it comes to attracting businesses and creating jobs in the district. This can be achieved through pork-barrel legislation. In addition, they might be asked to help out with personal matters, such as helping someone to get disability benefits or the correct amount of social security benefits.

Becoming a Law

It is tough for a bill to become a law. The whole legislative system is designed to make sure as few bills as possible make it all the way. From the president to the Speaker of the House to the Senate majority leader, there are many steps to kill a bill. Congress on average introduces about 10,000 bills per session and only about 10 percent become law. Furthermore, most bills are amended during the approval process, so it is rare that a bill becomes law without being changed. So how does the process work?

First, a bill is introduced in either the House or the Senate. As a side note, tax or revenue bills have to originate in the House. Ironically, most bills introduced are not written by a member of Congress. They come from the executive branch, lobbyists, constituents, or even businesses. The member of Congress who introduces the bill is just a vessel to do so. All they do is submit the bill to the House or Senate clerk, who gives the bill a number. Now the bill goes to the Speaker of the House or the Senate majority leader.

The Speaker of the House or the Senate majority leader then sends the bill to a standing committee. The Speaker and Senate majority leader can send the bill to a friendly committee that will pass it or to an unfriendly committee that will kill it, or they can just table it and not send the bill to any committee, which also means that the bill has been killed.

Most bills die in committee. They are either ignored, not discussed at all or voted down. If the bill is lucky, it gets assigned to a subcommittee that will hold hearings on it, call witnesses to testify, and debate the bill. The subcommittee prepares a final version of the bill and sends it back to the full committee for a vote. If the bill is passed, it moves on to the Rules Committee.

The Rules Committee now decides when the bill is debated on the floor of the House (if at all), how much time is allocated for debate, and whether amendments can be added.

In the Senate, the Senate majority leader decides whether to bring a bill up for a vote on the floor of the Senate. At the end of the debate, the House or Senate vote on the bill. If the bill passes with a simple majority vote, it moves on to the other house for passage.

If there are two versions of a bill, one from the House and one from the Senate, a conference committee is appointed by the leaders of both houses to discuss the differences. If they agree to a common version of the bill, it goes to the president for signature.

The president can now sign the bill or veto it (see Chapter 4). If the president signs a bill, it becomes law. If he vetoes it, both houses of Congress can override the veto with a 2/3 vote. If Congress does override the president's veto, the bill becomes law. If the president decides not to act on a bill, it becomes law, unless Congress is within ten days of adjournment, then the bill is vetoed. This is called a *pocket veto*.

Besides passing bills, Congress can also pass *resolutions*. Resolutions are opinions or decisions proclaimed by Congress. They are a way to impact public policy and deal with issues without enacting laws. Here are three types of resolutions:

>> **Simple resolutions:** These express an opinion in either the House or the Senate to settle a procedural matter.

>> **Concurrent resolutions:** They are passed by both houses to express an opinion on procedural matters.

>> **Most importantly, joint resolutions:** Joint resolutions are similar to bills and authorize specific actions to be taken. They must be approved by both Houses of Congress and signed by the president. After approval, they have the force of law. For example, joint resolutions have been used in the past to declare war.

Voting in Congress

For Congress to be able to vote on bills on the floor of the House or Senate, a *quorum* has to be present. All that means is that half of all the members of the House or Senate (218 members in the House or 51 in the Senate) must be present to vote. There are various methods of voting Congress uses, including

>> **Voice votes:** Here, members of Congress just yell *yea* to signal approval or *nay* to signal disapproval. Then the Speaker or presiding officer in the Senate decides who won the vote. This method is quick and is usually employed for bills that are not very important or are backed by the full House or Senate. Results are not recorded, so nobody knows how a member of Congress voted.

>> **Division votes:** Here, instead of yelling, members stand up from their seats to signify approval. Then they are counted. After they sit back down, the members who disapprove get up to be counted. Again, this vote is quick, and individual members' names are not recorded.

>> **Roll call votes:** Since 1973, the most common method of voting for important bills is the roll call vote. It is done electronically and must be requested by one-fifth of the members present. Roll call votes are tabulated electronically by name, and there is a record of how a member voted. Thus, constituents can check how their representatives voted on important issues.

Getting into Congress

Why would anyone want to run for Congress? It is hard work, time consuming, and tough on a family. Besides accruing political power, the job has some economic benefits. In 2025, a Congressional salary is $174,000 annually. Senior leaders make a little more, with the Speaker of the House making $223,500 in 2025.

This does not sound like much, especially if you have to live in Washington D.C., one of the most expensive cities in the U.S. However, there is more. In addition to your base salary, a congressperson also receives free healthcare for life and generous retirement benefits. They receive a large office and an office allowance, about $1 million, to hire their congressional staff. They further receive an allowance to travel back to their district and can send out mail for free (franking privilege).

REMEMBER

Congress has certain privileges, such as privilege of speech. This means that members of Congress cannot be sued for anything they say if it is related to their legislative duties.

Based on that, what type of person runs for Congress? Most members of Congress share certain characteristics; they are primarily white, male, and protestant. The top profession of members of Congress is a lawyer.

The 119th Congress, convened in 2025, is the most racially diverse Congress in history. Currently it has 66 African-American House members, 53 Hispanic house members, 21 Asian American members and 4 Native American/Alaska native members. 74 percent of congresspeople are white, compared to 58 percent of the U.S. population. Although the number of African Americans serving in Congress is proportionate to the number of African Americans in the population, Hispanics are underrepresented. They make up 20 percent of the population but only 11 percent in Congress. Asian Americans are 6 percent of the population and 4 percent of the Congress.

The most underrepresented group in Congress are women. Although women make up a little over 50 percent of the population, they make up only 28 percent of all members of Congress.

TECHNICAL STUFF

Jeannette Rankin, a Republican from Montana and a committed pacifist, became the first woman elected to the U.S. Congress in 1916 — four years before the 19th Amendment granted women nationwide the right to vote. During her first term in the House of Representatives, she voted against U.S. entry into World War I, a stance that contributed to her defeat in a bid for the U.S. Senate in 1918. She returned to Congress in 1940, once again representing Montana in the House. In 1941, Rankin cast the lone dissenting vote against the declaration of war on Japan following the attack on Pearl Harbor, a decision that led to widespread criticism and her retirement from politics after her term ended in 1943.

Staying in Congress

Winning a seat in the House of Representatives is one of the most difficult jobs to accomplish. Not surprisingly, when you have won your seat you want to keep it. For this reason, members of the House run constantly for reelection. The reelection rate is over 90 percent in the House and 70 percent in the Senate. Thus, incumbency matters.

In the late 19th century, over half of all members of Congress were first-term congresspeople, and many left after one term. Being a politician was not considered a career, and people went back to their real jobs after serving for a brief period in Congress. This changed after WWII, when serving in Congress became a career. Suddenly, over 90 percent of all congresspeople ran for reelection. Most Americans began calling for term limits on congresspeople. Close districts disappeared, with most House members winning reelection by ten or more points. Marginal districts, where the winner gets less than 55 percent of the vote, have declined and safe districts are on the increase. Causes for these high reelection rates include incumbency, name recognition, fundraising advantages, advantages of the office, pork-barrel legislation, and gerrymandering.

Chapter **4**

Focusing on the Presidency

The U.S. president today is the most powerful politician in the world. He is the center of attention of not just the American media but the media globally. The president represents the U.S. abroad. When he talks, the world listens. His speeches can impact world politics and the world economy within minutes. Just about every person in the world is aware of the U.S. president and often judges the U.S. by the kind of person Americans have elected as president. This was not always the case.

The following section compares two types of executives, the prime minister or chancellor and the president to show how unique the U.S. presidency is.

Analyzing Types of Executives

In a representative democracy such as in the U.S. or Germany, citizens do not make policy directly. Instead, they vote for a representative, a legislator, or executive who then makes policy on their behalf. If the representatives follow the people's wishes, they will get reelected, and if they don't, the people will vote them out of office.

Representative democracies are well suited for larger countries with a large population. Smaller countries with a small population, in turn, could choose a direct democracy where the people themselves make policy without a need for a representative to make policy on their behalf.

Two types of representative democracies exist today, a parliamentary democracy, headed by a prime minister, and a presidential democracy, headed by a president.

Studying a prime minister

Parliamentary democracies are very common in Europe and most former British colonies, such as Australia, India, and New Zealand. They are based on the British system of democracy where the people elect their executive, a prime minister or chancellor, indirectly. The people cast a ballot for a member of a political party for the legislature and whichever political party wins the most seats in the legislature gets to pick the executive. It is usually the majority political party that gets to pick the executive.

Because the majority party or majority coalition always chooses the executive, the executive always controls the legislature. Therefore, no divided government exists. In a parliamentary system, we find a fusion of power where the executive controls the legislature. No separation of powers exists here.

This fact makes parliamentary democracies very efficient. Having control of the legislature allows the executive to respond quickly to a changing political crisis. No time-consuming bargaining and compromise is necessary. For this reason, parliamentary democracies are very efficient, react quickly, and can implement new policies almost overnight.

Looking at a president

Presidential democracies are more common on the American continent. Examples are Mexico and Brazil. The separation-of-powers concept exists in a presidential democracy because citizens choose the legislature and the executive separately. In the U.S., voters cast different ballots for Congress and the president. So, the president is independently selected. The two institutions, Congress and presidency, constantly check on each other. There is a system of checks and balances in place where none of the institutions can become dominant. Presidential systems take longer to make policy and react to crises because the two institutions must bargain and compromise before making a decision. On the bright side, this bargaining and compromising usually results in a more moderate policy, acceptable to most citizens.

Being checked

The system of checks and balances is unique to the United States. The delegates at the national convention in Philadelphia, drawing up the U.S. Constitution, were afraid of a powerful executive. They had just experienced executive tyranny by an English king and wanted to make sure that this would never happen again. At the same time, they also did not believe in legislative supremacy. So, they established a system of balance of power where each branch of government checks upon the others. A good example is foreign policy (see Chapter 11). Whereas the president negotiates treaties and nominates ambassadors, the Senate has to ratify his choices. Congress and the Supreme Court have the power to check the president by either overriding a veto, ruling an executive act unconstitutional, or, in extreme cases, even impeaching and removing him from office.

Creating the Presidency

When the office of the presidency was created in the 18th century, it was designed by the U.S. Founding Fathers to be weak in comparison to other executives of the times, such as the kings of England or France.

Still being afraid of a powerful executive, such as a monarch, the Founding Fathers designed the Constitution with a weak presidency in mind. At the Constitutional Convention in Philadelphia, the first question was whether the new republic should even have a president. Being afraid of a powerful executive, such as King George of England, many Founding Fathers believed that an executive was needed but should be weak. So, stipulations were in put in place to make sure the president of the U.S. could not rule by himself but was checked and held accountable by other institutions, namely Congress and the court system.

REMEMBER

The president of the U.S. has to be a natural-born citizen, who has lived in the U.S. for at least 14 years and must be at least 35 years old.

The next question at the Constitutional Convention was whether there should be term limits for the new executive. Alexander Hamilton, one of the Founding Fathers, argued for a lifelong term. Others preferred 4-, 6-, and even 15-year terms. The delegates finally agreed on a 4-year term with no term limits.

TECHNICAL STUFF

The 22nd Amendment to the Constitution, ratified in 1951 by the states, limited the number of terms a president can serve to two. Until FDR (1933-1945), who served four terms, presidents had voluntarily abided by George Washington's precedent of voluntarily stepping down after two terms.

The final question was how to select the new president. Some wanted the people to elect the president; others feared that the average American was not smart and savvy enough to pick the country's leader. Keep in mind that back in 1787, less than two percent of all Americans had a high school degree and most were illiterate. For this reason, the delegates opted for the Electoral College, an indirect way of selecting the president with the possibility of overturning a dreadful choice by the people.

Creating an Electoral College

The Electoral College, established by the Constitution in Article II, consists of electors, selected by the states, who have the power to choose the president and vice president every four years. The first Electoral College, which met in 1789, consisted of representatives from all the states that ratified the Constitution. Depending on the state, either the people or the state legislatures choose the respective delegates for the Electoral College.

The number of Electoral College votes each state possesses depends on the size of the state's congressional delegation, which in turn is determined by the size of the population of a state. A state's congressional delegation equals the number of senators (2) plus the number of members of the House of Representatives for the state. For example, Texas has two senators and 38 representatives in the House of Representatives, so it gets 40 Electoral College votes. Wyoming has 3 Electoral College votes, two senators and one House member. The only exceptions to this rule are found in Maine and Nebraska, where one electoral vote goes to the winner of each Congressional district in the state and two votes go to the presidential candidate who carries the state.

Today, there are 538 total votes in the Electoral College, and a candidate must win 270 to become president. If nobody has a majority in the Electoral College, the vote goes into the House of Representatives.

TECHNICAL
STUFF

A current member of the Senate or House of Representatives cannot be an elector in the Electoral College.

In the first three Electoral College votes, each delegate casts two ballots. Whoever wins the most votes became the president of the United States; the runner-up is named the vice president. This system was confusing because electors could not differentiate between voting for president or vice president. Nobody ever foresaw the possibility of a tie. However, that happened in 1800.

Thomas Jefferson and Aaron Burr received the same number of votes in 1800, even though most electors favored Jefferson for president and Burr for vice president.

The 12th Amendment fixed the system in 1804 by mandating separate ballots for the president and vice president.

In 1961, the 23rd Amendment allowed the District of Columbia to cast three votes in the Electoral College.

Getting technical

Today, the electors in the Electoral College represent all 50 states and the District of Columbia. The electors are chosen by their respective state legislatures or the people of the state. Each party, Democrats and Republicans, draws up a list of electors. Whichever party wins the state in the presidential election gets to use its list in the Electoral College. The electors meet in their respective state capitals between December 14 and December 20 and cast a ballot for their candidate. The votes are then sent to Congress, which counts the votes in a joint session of Congress, consisting of the Senate and all members of the House of Representatives, and announces the results in January. The meeting is presided over by the current vice president. If there is no winner, no candidate receiving an absolute majority of the vote, the election goes into the House of Representatives where each state will get to cast one vote. This has happened only once in U.S. history in 1824, where Congress picked John Quincy Adams over Andrew Jackson even though Jackson had received more Electoral College votes, but not an absolute majority.

Receiving Official Powers

The U.S. Constitution does not spend much time on presidential powers in comparison to Congressional powers. Article 1 contains 54 paragraphs on Congressional powers whereas Article 2 has only 13 paragraphs on presidential powers. Article 2 also outlines the Electoral College.

Having constitutional powers

The few presidential powers mentioned in the Constitution are in Section 2 and Section 3 of Article II. They are referred to as *expressed powers*. These expressed powers are listed below.

>> **Commander in chief of the armed forces:** This power has caused much debate. Many presidents have interpreted it to mean that they have the power to make war. Congress, on the other hand, has the constitutional power to declare war.

>> **Granting reprieves and pardons:** The president has the power to pardon and grant reprieves to anyone for offenses against the U.S. (The only exception is impeachment. The president cannot pardon someone who has been impeached.)

>> **Making treaties:** The president has the authority to negotiate treaties with foreign countries. All treaties must be approved by the Senate with a two-thirds vote.

>> **Appointing Supreme Court justices and ambassadors:** The president has the power to select Supreme Court justices and ambassadors. In both instances, the Senate must approve of his choices.

>> **Giving an address:** The president must give a periodical report on the State of the Union. This was done early on in writing and today has become the State of the Union address, a major media spectacle on television.

>> **Filling vacancies:** The president can fill vacancies in executive departments while the Senate is not in session. The Senate must approve these appointments during its next session.

>> **Commissioning officers:** The president can appoint officers of the U.S. armed forces.

>> **Convening Congress to special sessions:** In emergency situations, the president has the power to call Congress into a special session.

>> **Receiving ambassadors:** The president has the right to receive foreign ambassadors and other foreign dignitaries to discuss policy with them.

>> **Ensuring that the laws are faithfully executed:** That's all the Constitution says about this power. Today, presidents interpret it as the power to make policy, as outlined in the annual budget the president submits to Congress.

REMEMBER *Expressed powers* are powers the Constitution explicitly gives to the president.

The president also enjoys *delegated powers*. These are powers Congress passes on to the president in case of emergencies.

TECHNICAL STUFF

Having veto powers

Additional powers of the president are found in Article I, Section 7. Even though Article I deals mainly with Congressional powers, it does discuss the veto power of the president. According to Section 7, the president possesses the power to veto legislation passed by Congress. He has ten days to veto a bill and must explain to Congress why he cast the veto. Congress then has the option to override a president's veto. This requires a two-thirds majority in both houses of Congress.

If Congress passes a bill within ten days of adjourning, the president can cast a pocket veto. All he must do is to let the bill sit on his desk until Congress adjourns and the bill has been vetoed. Pocket vetoes cannot be overridden, because Congress has no opportunity to vote on the veto.

Most presidential vetoes stand, or are not overridden by Congress. Only 4.3 percent of all vetoes in U.S. history have been overridden.

Giving executive orders

The power to issue executive orders is not directly mentioned in the Constitution. Article 2 of the Constitution only states: "The executive Power shall be vested in a President of the United States of America." Every president has interpreted this clause very broadly in order to make quick decisions unilaterally, without getting Congressional approval. With the exception of William Henry Harrison (1841), executive orders have been used by all presidents.

An executive order is a directive by the president ordering the federal government to carry out a certain task. A president can modify executive orders or even make exceptions to them. Only a president can cancel an executive order. Executive orders have the force of law and remain in law as long as the president allows or the courts permit.

Historically, some major policy choices have been executive orders, and the U.S. today would not be the same without them. Examples of the most prominent and famous executive orders include President Lincoln's Emancipation Proclamation, President Truman's desegregation of the U.S. armed forces, and President Obama's creation of the Deferred Action for Childhood Arrivals (DACA), which allowed children who entered the U.S. illegally to get work permits in the U.S and be protected from deportation.

President Roosevelt issued the most executive orders, 3,522. President Biden issued 162 executive orders, and President Trump has issued so far 89 executive orders in the first two months of his second term.

Enjoying executive privilege

The Constitution does not mention executive privilege. *Executive privilege* refers to the right of the president and other members of the executive cabinet to maintain communication confidentiality and refuse to have it subpoenaed by the other branches of government. Executive privilege is not mentioned in the Constitution, but it is supported by the doctrine of separation of powers. The courts ruled that one branch of government does not have the right to inquire about inner workings of another branch. In addition, the president has the right to expect his advisors to be candid and open. If they know that their communication with the president can be obtained by the other branches of government, they cannot express themselves openly. In U.S. v. Nixon (1974), the Supreme Court reaffirmed that there is a right to executive privilege but stated that there is no absolute right to executive privilege from the judicial process.

Having implied powers

Implied powers are powers of the president that are not listed or spelled out in the Constitution but can be implied from it. Implied powers have allowed the presidency to slowly accumulate power.

Interpreting presidential powers

The Constitution is not very specific on presidential powers. Many are vague and open to broad interpretation. For example, does to "faithfully execute the laws" mean that a president just observes Congress and then makes Congressional legislation law? Or can the president make laws himself? As commander in chief, is the president just some kind of super-general reacting to Congress, which has the power to declare war, or is he the supreme war maker in the United States? It is thus left up to the president to define his role.

Receiving Unofficial Powers

With many presidential powers being vague, the president must persuade three audiences to accomplish his goals. First, he must convince his fellow politicians in Washington, D.C. If he is well liked and respected, the president will have an easier time getting his agenda passed.

Second, a president must convince his supporters outside of Washington, D.C. This includes state and local politicians and partisans, namely supporters of him and his party. Third, he must convince the American public of the righteousness of his cause and policies.

The greatest power a U.S. president has is therefore not found in the Constitution. It is the power to persuade and convince the U.S. public. If the president can get the public to support his policies, he becomes unstoppable. Congress cannot and will not oppose him if he can show Congress that the public supports him on a certain issue. For this reason, the power to shape public opinion is a great one.

Convincing the public

Theodore Roosevelt was the first U.S. president to take advantage of the power of public opinion. He coined the term *bully pulpit*, which refers to using the presidency as a platform to convince others and gather public support for his policies. Whenever Congress began to oppose him, he toured the country and gave speeches to convince the public to support his programs. With the public behind him, Congress started to support his agenda.

Woodrow Wilson, a political scientist, recognized the power of shaping public opinion and continued in Roosevelt's tradition. In addition to touring the U.S. and giving speeches, Wilson established the tradition of holding regular press conferences. To be able to talk directly to Congress, Wilson rekindled the tradition of giving his State of the Union address in person to Congress. In 1801, President Jefferson had started to deliver it in writing which then became a precedent of delivering the address to Congress in writing. Wilson transformed the State of the Union address into the public spectacle it still is today.

Using the media

The invention of the radio, and later television and the Internet, made it easier to talk to and persuade the American public and shape public opinion. Radio, television, the Internet, and, more recently, social media, have made it possible to reach the U.S. public without ever leaving the White House.

The first president to take advantage of this was Franklin Delano Roosevelt in the 1930s. A week after presenting his first inaugural address in 1933, FDR began addressing the U.S. public directly over the radio with his famous fireside chats. In these addresses, Roosevelt attempted to explain his policies to the U.S. public and to calm a public spooked by the Great Depression. Roosevelt delivered a total of 27 fireside chats during his presidency.

It was John F. Kennedy who became our first television president. Kennedy and his advisors figured that the best way to reach the public was through television appearances heavily laden with political messages. Nothing was more successful in gaining the support of the U.S. public than a well-timed, well-written, and well-delivered speech.

TECHNICAL STUFF

Kennedy was the first president to allow his press conferences to be covered on live television. Eisenhower had his press conferences taped and reserved the right to edit them before they were broadcast. Kennedy delivered 64 live press conferences before he was assassinated.

Today, using television and social media to reach the public is common. Inaugural addresses, State of the Union addresses, and press conferences are all designed to reach out to the U.S. public and convince them that the president's policies merit their support. Clearly, a well-written and well-delivered speech can sway public opinion in a president's favor. This in turn facilitates his dealings with Congress.

More recently, President Obama organized large pep rallies to get support for his policies and had them livestreamed on the Internet. He successfully combined the use of live rallies with social media.

President Trump does the same, enjoying large-scale rallies, but he also uses social media, especially Twitter, now X, and his own social media platform, Truth Social. During his first term (2017-2021) President Trump sent 26,000 tweets to his followers.

President Obama (2009-2017) was the first president to use social media. He especially used Twitter to create support for his legislation and policy proposals.

The relationship between a president and the media is crucial. Some of the most successful presidents had a good relationship with the media and were able to manage the media. These include Ronald Reagan and Barack Obama. It is here where a good, well-liked press secretary comes in. The press secretary organizes news conferences, briefs the press, and prepares the president for news conferences. The more a press secretary is liked by the media, the better the president is treated by the press.

Growing the Presidency

The U.S. presidency has changed over the last 236 years. What started out as a basically ceremonial office led by prominent men has turned into the most powerful office on earth. For most of its history, the U.S. was led by Congress, with an occasional president assuming some power. However, today the president makes policy, and Congress often defers to him. What has happened and how?

Starting out weak

During the period from 1789 to 1824, most U.S. presidents were prominent men known to most U.S. citizens. They included many of our Founding Fathers and others who had served their country valiantly in the Revolutionary War. Except for John Adams, each of the first five presidents served two terms, bringing a measure of stability to the young country.

They legitimized the new government, or in other words, they created public support for the new form of government. Even if one disagreed with the new form of government created by the Constitution, how could one oppose George Washington as president? These presidents set the foundation for the United States. However, during this time period, Congress dominated and made most decisions for the United States. The president was considered to be a caretaker, and his job was to implement policies passed by Congress.

Challenging Congress: Andrew Jackson

When Andrew Jackson (see Figure 4-1) assumed office in 1829, he believed that he had a mandate from the people and that it was his job not only to implement policies passed by Congress but to make his own. He saw himself as a guardian of the people, with a mission to protect them from the excesses of Congress. He challenged Congress and vetoed major congressional legislation not just on constitutional grounds as was previously done, but also on political grounds. If he did not like a bill, he would veto it. None of his vetoes were overridden by Congress.

FIGURE 4-1:
Andrew Jackson.

Ritchie, Alexander Hay/Library of Congress/Public domain

Andrew Jackson cast 12 vetoes, more than all of his predecessors combined. His record stood until Andrew Johnson became president in 1865. He cast 29 vetoes. The record today is held by President Franklin Delano Roosevelt, who cast 635 vetoes from 1933 until 1945.

Jackson was the first president to show us what a popular president could do. With the public's backing, he successfully challenged Congress for eight years. However, his idea of a powerful president disappeared with him. His successors went back to their traditional role of not acting but reacting to Congress.

With the exception of Abraham Lincoln, Teddy Roosevelt, and Woodrow Wilson, all presidents for the next century subordinated themselves to Congress. Congress made policy for the United States, and the presidents passively endorsed it.

Creating the imperial presidency: Franklin Delano Roosevelt

Until the Great Depression, presidents reacted to Congress, rarely initiating any kind of policy. Even if they offered an initiative on occasion, Congress would regularly block or just ignore it. It was said that during this period the Speaker of the House was more powerful than the president and that he ran the country.

Congress directed policymaking and was responsible for the direction of the country. This all changed in the 1930s. With the Great Depression hitting the country hard in 1929, and World War II (WWII) starting in Europe in 1939, the U.S. public looked for strong leadership.

They found it in Franklin Delano Roosevelt (see Figure 4-2). Starting with his election in 1932, FDR single-handedly created the imperial presidency by implementing the New Deal programs, which greatly enhanced the powers of the presidency. The New Deal created a large federal bureaucracy over which the president presides. Roosevelt put a massive welfare state in place and had government take an active role in the economy.

When FDR took over in 1933, foreign policy came to the forefront with Japanese aggression in Mongolia and later China, the Spanish Civil War, and, later, Germany's attack on Poland and France. FDR moved the U.S. away from its traditional isolationism and the U.S. slowly became involved in world affairs. He moved the United States to support the Allies during WWII, even though Congress was at first skeptical, preferring to stay out of world affairs. During the war, he met with Allied leaders and hammered out major agreements. The subsequent Cold War further involved the United States in global affairs, enhancing the powers of the presidency. The American public looked not at Congress to protect them from communist aggression but to the president.

FIGURE 4-2:
Franklin Delano
Roosevelt.

Harris & Ewing/Library of Congress/Public domain

The trend of the president dominating foreign policy continued, and presidents today are the foreign policy leaders in the United States. By the time Lyndon Johnson assumed the presidency in 1963, Congress was reacting to the president, who now made both domestic and foreign policy for the country.

Weakening the imperial presidency: Richard M. Nixon

In 1974, Richard Nixon destroyed the imperial presidency with the Watergate scandal. Congress saw a weakened president and decided to restore some of its lost authority, especially in the realm of foreign policy.

To regain some say in war-making, Congress passed the War Powers Act in 1973 over President Nixon's veto.

The War Powers Act of 1973 placed the following restrictions on the president when using force:

» The president must report to Congress in writing 48 hours after committing troops into an area where hostilities have occurred or are likely to occur.

» Within sixty days after sending troops into a hostile situation, Congress must declare war or authorize a new commitment.

>> If Congress fails to provide such an authorization, the President must withdraw the troops.

>> If Congress passes a *concurrent resolution*, a resolution passed by both houses of Congress, to recall the troops, the president cannot veto this resolution.

Suddenly, Congress had reinserted itself into war-making powers. It now had the power to recall troops that a president committed into a hostile situation.

Ironically, every president affected by the act, beginning with Nixon and up to Presidents Biden and Trump, has claimed that the War Powers Act is unconstitutional and has refused to be bound by its terms. The Supreme Court has so far refused to rule on the constitutionality of the act.

The Budget Act of 1974 is the second example of how Congress reasserted itself. Presidents historically had given themselves the power to refuse to spend money appropriated by Congress for certain programs. Most presidents, beginning with Jefferson, used it frequently.

In 1974, Congress passed the Budget Reform Act, which stated that the president can refuse to spend or delay the spending of money, but he must tell Congress about it. Congress then can pass a resolution demanding the spending of the money. After the resolution passes, the president must spend the money. With the Budget Reform Act, Congress gave itself the power to force a president to spend money allocated for programs the president opposed.

Restoring the imperial presidency

The terrorist attacks on the United States on September 11, 2001, restored the imperial presidency. With the country in shock, President Bush had to act quickly and with bipartisan congressional support launched attacks on Afghanistan in 2001 and then Iraq in 2003. In the name of fighting terrorism, the Bush administration authorized warrantless wiretaps, the kidnappings of suspected terrorists, and interrogation techniques such as waterboarding. These measures were explained to the public as necessary to keep the country safe. Congress stayed quiet and Bush's successor, Barack Obama, would enjoy similar discretion in foreign policy when it came to the fight against terrorism.

Presidents Biden and Trump have continued the imperial presidency. As long as there are foreign threats and Congress is too divided to challenge the president, the imperial presidency will continue.

Presidential Resources

With the growth of the federal bureaucracy, the president has suddenly an enormous apparatus to control, supervise, and use in policymaking. This is facilitated with the help of certain offices and people who the president is close to and can express his wishes and frustrations to. In other words, he has many additional resources he can use to run the country. The most important are discussed below.

The vice president

Most vice presidents in U.S. history did not matter much. They were rarely asked for advice, and it was uncommon that they moved up the ladder to become president. It is rare that sitting vice presidents win the presidency. Only five vice presidents have ever managed to become president. They were John Adams, who won in 1796, Thomas Jefferson who won in 1800, Martin Van Buren who won in 1836, George Herbert Walker Bush who won in 1988, and Joe Biden who won in 2020. The public is aware of how little vice presidents really matter and tends to ignore them and their activities.

Besides succeeding the president, if he should die or resign, vice presidents have few official powers. They come mostly into play when there is a tie in a Senate vote, and they can cast a tiebreaker. That is usually their most visible function.

REMEMBER

It is rare that a vice president succeeds a president who dies in office or has to resign. The most famous instances in the 20th century were Harry Truman who succeeded President Franklin Delano Roosevelt after he died in office in 1945 and Gerald Ford who became president in 1974 after President Nixon resigned.

However, lately, there has been a subtle change in the role of vice president. Recent vice presidents have started to perform more important roles. They have become key advisors to the president and have helped him supervise the presidential apparatus. Vice President Al Gore was a close advisor to President Clinton, even heading the National Performance Review to increase government efficiency. Dick Cheney, vice president to George W. Bush was a close foreign policy advisor to the president, and many consider him to be the driving force behind the U.S. invasion of Iraq in 2003. Joe Biden, vice president to President Obama and later the 46th president of the United States, often interjected himself into controversial policies. For example, when he publicly announced his support for same-sex marriage, he also drove the Obama administration into supporting same-sex marriage.

Currently, Vice President J.D. Vance (see Figure 4-3), President Trump's vice president, has been very involved in President Trump's foreign policy. He has given speeches on the topic and even lectured European allies on their domestic policies and lack of military spending. It looks like vice presidents are becoming more active in American politics, and the public is starting to notice.

FIGURE 4-3:
Vice President
J.D. Vance.

Torok, Daniel/Library of Congress/Public domain

The cabinet of the United States

The Constitution envisioned for executive department heads to be major advisors to the president. There are 15 heads of executive departments, appointed by the president and confirmed by the Senate, who serve in the cabinet. In addition, the vice president is a cabinet member, as are eight other cabinet-level officials considered to have cabinet rank.

The positions that have currently cabinet-level status include the director of national intelligence, the director of the Central Intelligence Agency, the director of the Office of Management and Budget, the trade representative, the administrator of the Small Business Administration, the White House chief of staff, the ambassador to the United Nations, and the administrator of the Environmental Protection Agency.

A large cabinet meeting attended by all members of the cabinet is mostly for show; real policy is made in smaller meetings with only a few select cabinet members present. The members present depend on the topic discussed.

The current cabinet includes the vice president and the heads of 15 executive departments. They are the secretaries of Agriculture, Commerce, Defense, Education, Energy, Health and Human Services, Homeland Security, Housing and Urban Development, Interior, Labor, State, Transportation, Treasury, Justice, and Veterans Affairs.

The executive office of the president (EOP)

The executive office of the president (EOP) was created in 1939. It consists of numerous agencies and has about 2,000 employees. Some of its agencies, such as the Office of Management and Budget (OMB), the Council of Economic Advisors, and the Office of the U.S. Trade Representative, have near-permanent status. Other agencies come and go depending on their objectives.

For example, during the Cold War, agencies that focused on civil defense and atomic war preparedness existed. They have since been eliminated. The EOP further includes the White House staff, about 450 of them. Their major functions are speech-writing, scheduling, public relations, Congressional relations, and communications. They are managed and organized by the White House chief of staff, who is a member of the cabinet. The chief of staff controls access to the president and has become one of the most important people in Washington, DC.

The First Lady

The Constitution does not mention the position of First Lady, and her role in U.S. politics is not officially defined. There are no official powers listed for First Ladies. So, the powers First Ladies enjoy are informal and determined by the culture of the times. In the 19th century, a First Lady would not have been allowed to discuss politics publicly and campaign for her husband. This was considered improper. Women were supposed to run households and take care of families and guests. So, not surprisingly, in the early years of the republic, First Ladies mostly performed social functions, such as hosting state dinners. They were not publicly involved in policymaking and rarely expressed their opinions on controversial policy items in public. Privately, however, many were involved in politics. They had policy discussions with their husbands and used their social powers to influence U.S. policy.

By the 20th century this changed. The First Lady that set the tone for the role First Ladies play in politics today was Eleanor Roosevelt (see Figure 4-4). She held press conferences, wrote articles for newspapers and magazines, and lobbied her whole life for issues dear to her heart, such as equal pay for women. She even argued with her husband over some of his New Deal policies, which she considered unfair to women and minorities.

After her husband's passing, she started a second career with the United Nations and became instrumental in creating the Universal Declaration of Human Rights, as shown in Figure 5-4. By the time she stopped being First Lady, being involved in politics was not unladylike anymore.

FDR Presidential Library & Museum/Flickr

FIGURE 4-4:
First Lady Eleanor Roosevelt.

Today First Ladies have professional roles, express their opinions on policy, and are even involved in policymaking. They are educated, raise money for their husbands, hit the campaign trail, and actively pursue policy passions.

They have become close advisors to presidents and sometimes even pursue their political dreams after their husband's term ends. A good example is Hillary Clinton, who went on to become a U.S. senator from New York and secretary of state under President Obama. She even ran for president but narrowly lost to Donald. J. Trump in 2016.

Performing Many Roles: Today's President

Today the president performs many roles in U.S. society. The president has become the preeminent politician in the United States. Some of his roles include:

>> **Head of state:** The president symbolizes the United States. In this role, he fulfills certain ceremonial and symbolic roles. This can include meeting with foreign dignitaries or lighting the national Christmas tree. The president is the

symbol of our government, and the nation and other countries judge the United States by what kind of president is in office.

>> **Commander in chief:** This is the most important role presidents play. The president oversees the U.S. military and commits U.S. troops into battle. The public and Congress hold him accountable for the successes or failures of military operations.

>> **Chief diplomat:** The president makes foreign policy and negotiates treaties.

>> **Chief executive:** The Constitution gives the president the power to enforce the law. To accomplish this, he is given command of the federal bureaucracy, which includes the cabinet departments, the Office of Management and Budget, and the military, more than 3 million people altogether.

>> **Chief legislator:** Today, the president is responsible for most major legislation. He proposes the budget, works closely with Congress to get his agenda passed, and lobbies for his policy proposals. In addition, he can veto acts of Congress and shape policy with executive orders. The president acts, and Congress usually reacts to his policies.

>> **Crisis manager:** In times of emergencies and crises, the U.S. public looks to the president for action and comfort. After the terrorist attacks on the United States in September 2001, the public expected the president, not Congress, to react.

>> **Leader of his party:** Today, the president is widely considered to be the leader of his party. He sets party policy in the party platform, selects the party's national chairperson, and determines the party's legislative agenda. The public will judge the presidential party by its president and his policy successes.

Today, the president is the chief politician in the United States. However, he still has to share his powers with Congress on many occasions, and Congress can keep his power in check, if necessary.

IN THIS CHAPTER

» Analyzing different types of law

» Studying sources of law

» Looking at the federal court system

» Getting on the Supreme Court

» Serving on the Supreme Court

» Making decisions

» Being checked

Chapter **5**

Adjusting the Judiciary Framework

Of the three branches of government, the judiciary is the least known to the U.S. public and also the least understood. Why is this the case? First, judicial proceedings are rarely covered by the media, so the public is not aware of them. In addition, most Americans hardly ever have contact with the judiciary, except for the occasional traffic ticket. Finally, the judiciary and its proceedings seem complex and, unless you're a lawyer, its use of confusing, jargony language helps keep the public tuned out.

This is too bad, because the judicial system, the third branch of government, not only interprets law but often makes it. Although the judiciary is tasked with making sure that the executive and legislative branches are in compliance with the Constitution and other legal traditions, the power to check for compliance or interpret the law, gives the judiciary the power to make law. In the U.S., the third branch of government has the power to nullify law of the other two branches and even state governments. This is called the power of judicial review, where the federal courts look at laws and determine whether they are constitutional. If they believe they are not, they can declare them unconstitutional, thus nullifying them.

The judiciary is also the least democratic of the three branches of government. If U.S. citizens disagree with acts of the president or Congress, they can vote them out of office. Federal judges are isolated from popular will, being appointed for life and are never up for reappointment. This allows them to make unpopular decisions.

Studying Different Types of Law

When studying law, one notices that there is not just one type of law but many. *Law* is usually defined as authoritative rules made and enforced by government. Following are the most common types of law.

>> **Higher law:** Law made by God.

>> **Natural law:** Law that comes from nature and not rules of society or government. These are rights every person possesses. In other words, people are born with rights guaranteed by natural law. They are a part of human nature.

>> **Positive law:** Positive laws are laws written by people.

>> **Common law:** Common law is judge-made law handed down through legal opinions. Common law evolves over time by establishing precedents. New rulings are based upon precedent. The U.S. and Great Britain use common law today. Common law allows for judges to modify previous judicial decisions.

>> **Civil law:** derived from Roman law, civil law systems are based on a written collection of laws. They are arranged in codes and in books. In 1804, the Napoleonic code codified civil law in France, and the code later spread through western and southern Europe and into Latin America. When using coded law, judges do not have the power to make law, they can only apply already existing law as mentioned in codes and books.

>> **Criminal law:** A body of rules and regulations that declare what kind of acts and conduct is considered an offense against society and what type of punishments can be imposed. Criminal laws against murder can be found in just about any society. Noncriminal law includes crimes against a person's property or contract violations. It is referred to as civil law.

>> **Constitutional law:** Constitutional law is a body of rules, doctrines, and practices found in in the fundamental law of nation-states. Constitutional law governs the operation of the political community. It is usually found in constitutions. The Constitution of the U.S. contains constitutional law, which governs the U.S. It is the supreme law of the land.

- » **Administrative law:** Administrative law is a body of rules, laws, and regulations issued by administrative agencies of a government. Administrative law covers the structure, power, and duties of bureaucracies. A good example are rules set down by the Environmental Protection Agency, requiring industries not to pollute.

- » **International law:** International law is a body of rules and regulations binding upon civilized nations. It consists of works of great writers, such as Hugo Grotius, who created the concept of just and rightful war, without which treaties and customs cannot be enforced. Civilized nations abide by it. It creates order in a chaotic world and is designed to maintain peace in the international arena.

- » **Public law:** Laws, rules, and procedures that govern disputes and issues involving the government directly. It includes constitutional, administrative, and criminal law.

- » **Private law:** Part of the law that directly involves private citizens, such as in a divorce or a private individual suing the government for wrongdoing.

Looking at sources of law

U.S. law comes from a variety of sources: They include the Constitution, state constitutions, federal and state legislatures, and case law.

The U.S. Constitution is the supreme law of the land. Nobody and no institution can go against it. The Constitution establishes the structure of the federal government and all the guidelines the federal government and the states have to follow. The U.S. Supreme Court has the power to nullify any law that goes against the Constitution. This allows for the Supreme Court to also make law. Over the last 200 years, the Supreme Court on many occasions has made constitutional law. Supreme Court decisions have over time varied from court to court, and this is how constitutional law evolves over time.

State constitutions are similar, with one caveat. They have to abide by the U.S. Constitution, acts of Congress, and presidential decisions, and cannot contradict them.

Legislative acts are the most rapidly growing source of U.S. law. Every year, federal, state, and local legislative bodies make new laws and regulations for Americans to follow. These include speed limits, legalization of recreational cannabis, and criminal conduct.

Case law refers to decisions made by previous courts over the past two centuries. Case law is found in court opinions; therefore, it is made by judges. It also called judge-made law based on the U.S. common law tradition. It is very adaptable and can evolve over time.

TECHNICAL STUFF

Stare decisis is a Latin term meaning "let the decision stand." It states that courts are supposed to follow precedent, or, in other words, follow previous rulings on similar cases. This ensures an equal application of the law in cases and makes legal decision making more predictable. Similar outcomes are guaranteed for similar legal cases. It is rare that courts violate stare decisis even though the Supreme Court has done it a few times itself.

Most recently the U.S. Supreme Court decided to not abide by stare decisis in Dobbs v. Jackson Women's Health Organization when it overturned its 1973 decision in Roe v. Wade to legalize abortion. Instead, it gave the power to regulate abortion to the states. With this decision, the Supreme Court changed U.S. society for generations.

Explaining decisions

The U.S. Supreme Court is the highest law of the land. It has the power to strike down any laws by lower levels within the judiciary, all acts of Congress, and presidential actions. In recent years, it has impacted every American with decisions such as legalizing gay marriage and banning restrictions on campaign donations.

TECHNICAL STUFF

The Supreme Court can overturn any state Supreme Court ruling because of the Supremacy Clause contained in Article VI of the Constitution. The Supremacy Clause states that federal law is the supreme law of the land.

When making decisions, the U.S. Supreme Court employs two schools of thought:

>> **Judicial restraint:** This states that Supreme Court justices base their rulings on purely what is stated in the Constitution. If the Constitution does not mention an issue, such as abortion or gay marriage, the Supreme Court should not deal with it.

>> **Judicial activism:** This school of thought states that the Supreme Court has the power to go beyond what is mentioned in the Constitution. Judicial activists believe that times have changed since the Constitution went into effect in 1789, and even though an issue is not explicitly mentioned in the Constitution, decisions can be inferred from it. This allows the Supreme Court to infer law and individual rights from the Constitution even though they are not mentioned by it. The right to privacy or the right to have an abortion are examples.

Looking at the federal court system

Article III of the Constitution establishes a Supreme Court and inferior federal courts that Congress may wish to create. In the beginning, the court system was the weakest of the three branches, and even after the principle of judicial review was established it was rarely used. This would not change until the 20th century.

The Constitution does not specify the number of justices on the Supreme Court. Therefore, during the 18th and 19th century, Congress altered the size of the Court a few times. We had anywhere from five to ten justices serving on the Supreme Court until 1869 when Congress determined there should be eight associate justices and one chief justice on the Supreme Court. Since then, the U.S. has had nine justices on the court.

The most serious and well-known attempt to increase the size of the Court occurred in 1937. After the Supreme Court blocked President Roosevelt's New Deal programs, he proposed a 15-justice court. However, that never happened, because one justice changed his votes (see Chapter 4 on the presidency).

Court cases today begin in the federal court system and not the state court system only if they fit three categories. If they do not, they start in state courts. So, for a case to start in federal court, it has to fall into at least one of three categories:

>> The lawsuit must involve an interpretation of the Constitution, a federal law, or a treaty the U.S. government signed.

>> The federal government is suing someone or is being sued by someone.

>> The lawsuit is between citizens of two different states suing for an amount of over $75,000.

With Congress being active in creating new federal law, more cases are coming to the federal system. For example, federal crimes are heard by the federal system. Today, this includes carjacking, money laundering, and possession of certain illegal drugs.

In addition to the federal court system, there are also a few specialized courts included. There are tax courts, bankruptcy courts, and military courts located throughout the country. These are also a part of the federal court system.

Structuring the federal court system

The federal court system is structured in the following way. There are 94 federal district courts in the U.S., and these are where most cases start out. District court judges have original jurisdiction over both civil and criminal cases. All that means is that they have the power to rule in the first instance. In other words, they get to go first. Figure 5-1 shows the 94 federal district courts and the 13 federal appeals courts.

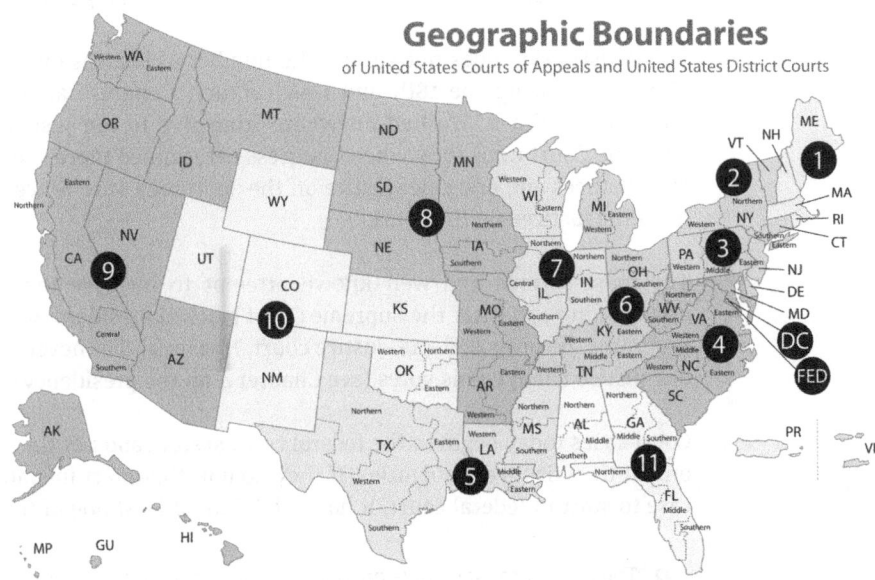

Geographic Boundaries
of United States Courts of Appeals and United States District Courts

ChristianGlaeser/Wikimedia Commons/CC BY-SA 3.0

FIGURE 5-1:
Geographic boundaries of U.S. federal courts.

Federal cases start out in the federal district courts. There are 94 district courts, located all over the U.S., with 674 judges on them. After they have ruled on a case, the losing side can appeal to a U.S. court of appeals. There are 13 federal appeals courts located in the U.S., with 179 judges on these courts. However, in a normal case, only three judges will be picked to decide cases. They are selected from a pool of judges available to each court of appeals. However, litigants can ask for *en banc*, which means that the whole court and not just three judges rule on the case.

If a litigant loses a case in a federal appeals court, they can then appeal to the U.S. Supreme Court. They can ask the Supreme Court to review a lower court decision; however, the Supreme Court does not have to accept the case. The Supreme Court has absolute discretion over which cases to review. They can reject any case. Overall, the Supreme Court only accepts about three percent of the cases they are asked to review.

TECHNICAL STUFF

Litigants who lose in a state supreme court can also petition the U.S. Supreme Court to hear their case. In a normal year, half the cases the Supreme Court hears come from the federal level and half come from the state level.

Looking at state and local courts

Local and state courts shoulder most of the cases heard in the U.S. They are responsible for cases that arise under state law. They have to deal with cases from murder to medical malpractice. Every state organizes its judicial structure differently. For this reason, there is a lot of variation around the U.S. when it comes to a state's judicial structure. Usually, cases start out in state trial courts, but decisions can be appealed to state appeal courts. The final appeal is to a state Supreme Court, the top court in every state. With the exceptions of Texas and Oklahoma, which have two top courts, one for civil and one for criminal cases, all states have only one top court. Many of the most important cases in U.S. history originated at the state level. An example is Roe v. Wade, which legalized abortion. It originated in Texas.

Getting Judicial Review

The power of judicial review is the greatest power the U.S. federal courts have. It is not mentioned in the Constitution. It refers to the ability of courts to overturn legislative laws and executive acts that violate the Constitution. This power allows for the courts to make policy. The federal judiciary having the power of judicial review has the power to overturn acts of Congress, initiated by a body representing the people. Keep in mind, justices are appointed for life and can act against the will of the majority if they choose to do so.

The power of judicial review was asserted to the court system in 1803 in the case of Marbury v. Madison.

Marbury v. Madison

In the 1800 election, incumbent President Adams was defeated by Thomas Jefferson. Adams's party, the Federalists, also lost control of Congress in the election. He was furious and worried that Jefferson would implement policies he opposed, such as eliminating tariffs and having better relations with France. So, he decided that one branch of government had to stay being controlled by his Federalist Party. This branch was the judiciary. So, he decided to make as many appointments to the court system as he could before leaving office. These so-called Midnight Appointments consisted of dozens of judicial appointments, all loyal Federalists. In addition, President Adams named his secretary of state, John Marshall, chief justice of the Supreme Court. The appointments were supposed to be delivered before Adams left office. However, not all appointments were sent out on time, and they were left for the incoming president to deliver.

Newly elected President Jefferson and his secretary of state, James Madison, were furious when they discovered what had happened and refused to deliver the remaining letters of notification of appointment. William Marbury, one of the men appointed to a federal court, was one of the appointments whose letter of notification had not been delivered in time. President Jefferson ordered Madison not to honor the appointment. Marbury was furious for not being appointed, so he sued the Jefferson administration. He based his lawsuit on the Judiciary Act of 1789, claiming that by not appointing him, Madison was violating the act. His lawsuit asked the Supreme Court to issue a *writ of mandamus*, which is a judicial order forcing a public official to engage in an official duty. The duty was to deliver the commission. The Judiciary Act of 1789 gave the Supreme Court the power to issue such writs.

REMEMBER

Ironically, the whole mess was Chief Justice John Marshall's fault. He was President Adams's secretary of state and was supposed to deliver all notifications of appointments. He failed to do so.

The case went all the way to the Supreme Court, where John Marshall, (see Figure 5-2), who had been appointed chief justice by President Adams, saw an opportunity to expand judicial power.

FIGURE 5-2:
John Marshall, chief justice of the U.S. Supreme Court (1801–1835).

Ambler, Pennsylvania/Library of Congress/Public domain

Marshall faced a dilemma. If the Supreme Court ruled in favor of William Marbury and ordered the Jefferson administration to appoint him, President Jefferson and Secretary of State Madison had already declared that they would not abide by the ruling. If he sided with the Jefferson administration, he would undermine Federalist strength in the judiciary. So, he set out to find a different solution.

Finding a solution

So, Marshall decided to declare that Section 13 of the Congressional Judiciary Act of 1789, which granted the Supreme Court the power to compel public officials to engage in an official act (writ of mandamus), was unconstitutional, because the Act allowed litigants to go straight to the Supreme Court for a writ of mandamus. Marshall said that was not in the Constitution. Litigants first had to go through the federal courts before they could appeal to the Supreme Court. For this reason, Section 13 was unconstitutional.

Marshall then stated that Madison was wrong to withhold the commission from Marbury and usually would have had to follow a writ of mandamus. However, Marbury based the whole lawsuit on Section 13 of the Judiciary Act and by declaring the act unconstitutional, Marshall nullified the lawsuit.

So, Marbury's lawsuit was now baseless and was dismissed. With one stroke, John Marshall resolved a politically sensitive situation and established the principle of judicial review. From then on, not just the Supreme Court but all federal and state courts received the power to declare acts of Congress unconstitutional, thus nullifying them.

During Marshall's long tenure as judge, serving 34 years on the bench, he wrote 519 opinions. He consistently sided with the federal government over state interests. In doing so, he was responsible for the strong role the federal government plays in U.S. politics today.

In the beginning, the Supreme Court used the new power of judicial review sparingly. However, beginning in the 1930s with FDR's New Deal programs, the power of judicial review was routinely used by the courts. Today, it has become a common occurrence in American politics.

Being on the Supreme Court

On the first Monday of each October, the U.S. Supreme Court begins a new session. Between October and July, the court hears close to 100 cases. In recent times, Supreme Court sessions have become politically charged and are now covered by the media. Lower federal courts, on the other hand, are rarely mentioned in stories unless they revolve around a famous person.

The U.S. Supreme Court, seen in Figure 5-3, has one chamber consisting of nine justices. They have the power to deal with any issues and are appointed for life. The only way to replace a Supreme Court justice is if they retire or die. Congress does have the power to impeach Supreme Court justices and remove them from office. Like a presidential impeachment, the House of Representatives has to investigate and convict and then impeach a justice. The Senate then will constitute the judge and jury and with a two-thirds vote can remove a justice (for a detailed discussion of impeachment, see Chapter 3 on Congress).

In the history of the U.S., only one Supreme Court justice was ever impeached. It was Samuel Chase, a signee of the Declaration of Independence, who was impeached in 1804 for publicly criticizing President Jefferson. The Senate, however, refused to remove him from office.

FIGURE 5-3:
Supreme Court building in Washington, D.C.

Highsmith, Carol M/Library of Congress/Public domain

Getting on a federal court

In the beginning of the republic, the average Supreme Court justice served about seven years on the court. Today, this has increased to about 16 years. The longest-serving judge was William O. Douglas, who served 36 years. Clearly, justices are staying longer than ever, and the process has also become more partisan. Most federal judges used to be confirmed by the Senate with large vote margins, but today, some are barely squeaking by in the Senate. At the lower federal court levels, it is even worse. Until 1970, it was rare for a federal judge nominee to be voted down by the Senate. By the mid-90s, however, only a little over half were easily confirmed, and by 2025, the number has dropped to less than 40 percent.

All federal judges are nominated by the president but have to be confirmed by the Senate.

REMEMBER

TECHNICAL STUFF

The Constitution only requires Supreme Court justices to be confirmed by the Senate. Congress added the requirement that all federal judges must be confirmed by the Senate.

The Constitution does not mention the qualifications federal judges should have. Qualifications for judges is left up to the president and Congress. Senatorial courtesy has been used for a long time when it comes to nominating and confirming judges in the Senate. Without the support of home state senators, a federal judge nominee's confirmation is unlikely. Presidents thus consider not only ideological reasons for selecting judges, but also Senatorial recommendations for potential nominees.

TECHNICAL STUFF

In 2013, the Senate banned the use of the filibuster (see Chapter 3) against lower court federal judicial nominees. This made it harder for the minority party in the Senate to block judicial nominees. It now only takes a simple majority vote of 51 to confirm. Previously it was 60 votes. In 2017, this was extended to the Supreme Court.

Characteristics of Supreme Court justices

Certain characteristics and qualifications are necessary to become a Supreme Court justice. Supreme Court nominees are typically reviewed and rated by the American Bar Association (ABA), an interest group composed of lawyers who rate candidates for every federal vacancy based on their legal backgrounds and accomplishments. However, this is not a formal requirement, and some presidents have ignored ABA ratings.

In addition, political loyalty matters. Presidents will choose a nominee who has previously served the president's party or the president himself. Since 1900, 90 percent of all Supreme Court nominees have belonged to the president's political party. Many have been cabinet members or members of Congress. Once, even a former president was chosen to serve on the Supreme Court. It was William Howard Taft (see Figure 5-4), who was president from 1909 until 1913 and then chosen to be the chief justice of the Supreme Court in 1921 by President Harding. He served until 1930 and told people he enjoyed being chief justice a lot more than being president.

Ideology and policy preferences also matter. A conservative president is likely to pick a judge that agrees with him on policy matters. However, Supreme Court justices have been known to change their minds after being appointed and confirmed. President Eisenhower nominated Chief Justice Earl Warren to the Supreme Court, believing he was a moderate conservative. He was not, and turned out to be one of the most liberal justices ever on the court. Eisenhower later confessed that appointing Earl Warren to the court was his greatest political mistake.

Recently, demographic factors have started to matter. Lyndon Johnson appointed the first African American to the Supreme Court, Thurgood Marshall, and President Reagan the first woman, Sandra Day O'Connor. Later, President Obama appointed the first latina, Sonia Sotomayor, and President Biden the first African-American woman, Ketanji Brown Jackson. Currently, in 2025, there are five men and four women on the Supreme Court.

The federal judiciary does not reflect the U.S. population. Currently 67 percent of all federal judges are men, and 33 percent are women (51 percent of the population is female). 74 percent of all federal judges are white, whereas only 58 percent of the population is. 11.8 percent are African American whereas 14 percent of the population is black. Hispanics comprise only 7.5 percent of justices while being about 20 percent of the U.S. population. Finally, 4.2 percent of federal judges are Asian American whereas 6 percent of the overall population is Asian American.

In addition, age matters. Presidents want to appoint judges who can serve for decades on the court. An older judge might be experienced but cannot serve for decades. The average age of Supreme Court justice nominees has dropped in the last decades. President Trump's third appointment, Justice Amy Coney Barrett, was only 48 years old when appointed.

Most Supreme Court justices are confirmed by the Senate. Between 1900 and 2022, 63 of 67 Supreme Court nominees were confirmed. That is a 94 percent confirmation rate.

REMEMBER

One of the traditions of the Supreme Court is to be nonpartisan. Officially, Supreme Court justices are not beholden to a political party and any ideology. They attempt to implement nonpartisan rulings, and all their discussions and votes are confidential.

Making decisions

To get a case to the Supreme Court, four justices have to agree to hear a case. This is called the Rule of Four, and the Supreme Court never gives reasons why it accepts or rejects a case. If the court refuses a case, it accepts the lower court decision.

After a case makes it onto the docket, the litigants must submit a legal brief, summarizing the legal issues to be resolved. The court then holds oral arguments. For a lawyer, that can be the defining moment of a career. Most lawyers never get a chance to argue a case before the Supreme Court. Each lawyer is given 30 minutes to make an argument, then the judges will ask questions. When the oral arguments are complete, the justices convene that same week to discuss and then vote on the case.

Besides arguments made by the lawyers representing the two sides, an *amicus curiae* can be filed. Translated as *a friend of the court*, this allows for interested parties to submit written briefs or even oral arguments in front of the court.

A *brief* is a written statement by an attorney that summarizes the case and the laws and rulings supporting it.

During the meeting, only the nine justices are allowed in the room. Nobody else is in the room and, of course, the discussions are not televised. The chief justice summarizes the case and then states how he will vote and why. Then the other eight justices will do the same. The justices get to speak in rank of seniority, and after they are done, there is a vote.

After the votes are counted, the chief justice, if in the majority, will assign a judge to write an opinion or do it himself. If the chief justice is not in the majority, the senior member of the majority gets to write the opinion.

This opinion of the court explains the decision. Some judges can issue a concurring opinion. In this case, the judges agree with the majority ruling but for a different reason then mentioned.

After the opinion is written, the justices can either sign it or dissent. If they dissent, they can write a separate opinion explaining why they dissented. This is called a *dissenting opinion*.

LIVING IN THE SHADOWS

Recently, the issue of the *shadow docket*, also called *non-merits docket*, has come to the forefront. A shadow docket involves court cases that receive brief, limited hearings by the Supreme Court and are decided in a week or less. The shadow docket is used if the Court believes that an applicant will suffer irreparable harm if the request for a hearing is not immediately granted. In other words, the Supreme Court agrees to hear a case quickly and then rules within a week on the case. The shadow docket was rarely used until 2017 (the term did not even exist until 2015) but has been used more frequently lately. For example, it can involve the Department of Justice asking for emergency stays of lower court rulings. Shadow Docket decisions are unsigned and unexplained by the Supreme Court, which results in a transparency and accountability problem.

Limitations on Judicial Power

Having read so far, one would believe that the court system in the U.S. is all-powerful and cannot be held accountable by politicians and the public. This is only partially true. There are limitations on judicial power.

First, courts themselves cannot initiate or maintain lawsuits. Unlike the legislative branch, which can initiate bills on their own, the judiciary has to wait until a case comes to them in the form of a lawsuit. As long as nobody sues over an issue or bill the courts cannot intervene and just have to sit and watch powerless.

Second, according to Article III of the Constitution, courts can only hear and resolve cases that are legitimate and cannot deal with hypothetical or theoretical cases. This means that cases that are moot, where it is too late to provide a remedy, are off-limits. For example, if a student sues a university for a poor education but by now has moved on and graduated from another university, the case would be considered moot. It has already been resolved.

In addition, courts cannot deal with cases that could happen in the future and refuse to hear cases where litigants have no *proper standing*, meaning that they are not uniquely affected by the case. To have standing a person must have suffered injury, clear causation of the injury must exist, and the court must be able to remedy the injury.

Not being able to enforce decisions

Courts are in the unenviable position of being unable to enforce their decisions. They have to rely on the legislative and executive to do so. Who puts court decisions into effect? It is usually the executive through bureaucrats, like police officers. The court does not have this option. Although court decisions are usually enforced, there are a few exceptions. In 1832, President Jackson ignored a Supreme Court order to free a white missionary who had been arrested and jailed for living on Cherokee land, which was illegal at the time, even though he had been invited by the Cherokee nation to live there (Worcester v. Georgia). After John Marshall issued a ruling to free the missionary, President Jackson said: "John Marshall has made his decision . . . now let him enforce it." The governor of Georgia resolved the situation in 1833 by freeing Worcester.

Changing jurisdiction

The Constitution gave Congress the power to change the jurisdiction of the Supreme Court. This allows Congress to remove the jurisdiction of the court system from certain issues. This means that Congress can tell the Supreme Court that this topic is not under your jurisdiction so you cannot rule on it.

Amending the Constitution

The most controversial way to check the Supreme Court is by amending the Constitution. This measure can be used to invalidate a Supreme Court decision both Congress and the States dislike (for a discussion on how to amend the Constitution, see Chapter 1). It has occurred only four times in U.S. history.

The best example is the 26th Amendment to the Constitution. In 1970, Congress wanted to give eighteen-year-olds the right to vote. This was challenged in court, and the Supreme Court ruled that the federal government giving eighteen-year-olds the right to vote was unconstitutional because it violated states' rights. The court argued that the federal government could not tell states what the voting age was. So, Congress passed the 26th Amendment to the Constitution, which made it legal for eighteen-year-olds to vote. This was now a part of the Constitution, and obviously the Supreme Court cannot declare a part of the Constitution unconstitutional.

IN THIS CHAPTER

» Studying the concept of bureaucracy

» Looking at the functions of bureaucracies

» Controlling bureaucracies

» Analyzing bureaucratic structures

» Evolving over time

» Stopping bureaucratic expansion

Chapter **6**

Building the Bureaucracy

What comes to mind when people hear the terms *bureaucracy* or *civil servant*? They usually cringe and think of rules and regulations and lots of red tape. So, what are bureaucracies? Are they necessary for a country and its government to be successful or are they a handicap to economic and political progress?

Bureaucracies are large organizations that implement rules made by government, both the legislative and the executive. Bureaucracies exist today at the federal, state, and even local level. A *bureaucrat* is a career civil servant that staffs a bureaucracy. Today the U.S. has local, state, and federal civil servants.

Although officeholders, executive and legislative, come and go, civil servants constitute a permanent government. They are appointed based on merit and basically have lifetime jobs. Keeping this in mind, it is imperative that a country has a bureaucracy that is professional and based on merit. The U.S. did not have this until 1883 when Congress passed the Pendleton Act. As a comparison, France developed its professional bureaucracy, the first in Europe, in the 1790s.

France is widely considered to have one of the best bureaucracies in the world. The French bureaucracy became professional after the French revolution had failed by 1794. It was the new leader Napoleon Bonaparte that decided that France needed a better, more professional bureaucracy to run the French empire. He centralized the country, creating 96 prefects to carry out government policy. He also established specialized universities to create a future well-educated French bureaucracy. Access to these universities was open to everybody, rich and poor; students just had to be bright. At these universities, students were trained to work for the good of France and not to enrich themselves.

Today, 90 percent of all federal bureaucrats are career civil servants. They are non-political appointees who maintain their position regardless of who wins the White House and Congress. Unlike 19th century federal bureaucrats, civil servants today are merit-based and not political appointments.

The major purpose of a bureaucracy is to implement rules and administer laws and policies passed by Congress and the president. Bureaucracies establish programs, implement rules, and put in place regulations. Often, they make policies as well.

Most civil servants (bureaucrats) in the U.S. work at the state or local level. Only about 15 percent work for the federal government. Local level bureaucrats can include police officers, teachers, and firefighters.

Going Bureaucratic

The study of bureaucracies can be traced back to Max Weber (see Figure 6-1), a German social scientist widely considered a central figure in the development of the social sciences. While studying the topic of why citizens obey orders from others, he discovered that all major societies had bureaucracies to implement rules. Based on his discovery, Weber developed the concept of an ideal bureaucracy, which had the following six characteristics:

>> **An ideal bureaucracy is hierarchical in nature, structured with a leader on top and a chain of command from top to bottom.** Like a diagram of a pyramid, hierarchies see command and control flowing downward and feedback or response flowing back upwards. Every civil servant works for someone above him/her and wants to move up the ladder to acquire more power and monetary rewards.

>> **Bureaucracies are structured based on the specialization and expertise among the civil servants or bureaucrats.** A well-developed division of labor exists where people become experts in their areas and leave other areas to other experts. Specialized bureaucracies exist not just at the federal level but also in hospitals, universities and large corporations.

>> **Bureaucracies have a common set of goals and rules for carrying out functions.** The goals of the organization determine the structure of the organization and how authority is spread throughout.

>> **To qualify as a good capable bureaucracy, bureaucracies must maintain good records of actions taken such as policy implementation, periodic reviews, and efficiency of operation reports.**

>> **Bureaucracies are expected to follow fixed routines, with every civil servant following standard operating procedures established by the bureaucracy.**

>> **Finally, effective bureaucracies must hire and promote based on merit-based criteria and not patronage.** In other words, civil servants need to be hired based on their qualifications, and the rules within the bureaucracy must apply to everybody equally.

Exploring the functions of a bureaucracy

A federal bureaucracy is not mentioned in the Constitution. It started out small with the founding of the republic; however, over time, it has developed and evolved, and today it is referred to as the fourth branch of government. Most of the federal bureaucracy is a part of the executive branch. The reason is Article II of the Constitution, which states: "the executive power shall be vested in a President of the United States of America." To be able to successfully fulfil this function the president must rely on a federal bureaucracy that carries out and administers specific laws. The federal bureaucracy serves both elected officeholders and average citizens alike.

Implementing policies

The major function of bureaucracies is policy implementation. *Policy implementation* is the process of carrying out laws. Most of the laws Congress passes involve the creation or modification of federal programs, and this is where the bureaucracy comes in. Bureaucrats interpret and implement these programs. A good example is the creation of the social security program. In 1935 Congress passed the Social Security Act. It created the current social security system, which is overseen by the Social Security Administration. The act created the Social Security Administration, a bureaucratic agency, to set up and administer the social security program. In other words, bureaucrats take a law of Congress and turn it into reality.

REMEMBER

After Congress passes laws, bureaucracies take these laws and turn them into reality. They come up with a set of rules and regulations that guide the new programs. On occasion, there is a difference between the original Congressional intent of the law and the bureaucracy's enactment of the law. This is called a *bureaucratic drift.*

Often, laws passed by Congress are very vague. Civil servants have the power of administrative discretion, which gives them a lot of freedom to decide how to implement the law. This allows civil servants to shape federal laws.

However, occasionally Congress passes a very specific law, which tells the bureaucracy exactly how to implement a new program or policy, and the bureaucracy has no freedom to modify it while implementing it. These laws must be implemented as-is.

Making regulations

Bureaucracies have the power to make formal rules to implement new policies or change existing policies. These rules have to be published in the Federal Register. On average, about 60,000 pages of new rules are published by bureaucrats in the Federal Register annually.

The Federal Register has been published daily by the U.S. government since 1994. It contains government agency rules, proposed rules, regulations, and public notices. It is accessible online at FederalRegister.gov.

To be able to make new rules and regulations, a series of steps have to be taken. First, bureaucrats announce the new rules, and then they hold hearings attended by interested parties such as interest groups (see Chapter 15) or the public. Next, civil servants must conduct research on the ways the new rules and regulations impact U.S. society. Finally, the public is allowed to comment on the new rules and regulations. After all of this is concluded, the new rules and regulations can be published in the Federal Register. They now carry the force of law and can be changed only by the bureaucracy or Congress by passing a new law signed by the president.

Interpreting rules and regulations

Federal agencies not only write and implement new rules and regulations, but they also interpret and adjudicate them. They decide when public or private actors, such as corporations, have abided by the rules and hold hearings to determine whether some actors have disobeyed their rules. Administrative law judges and attorneys are involved in these hearings and the judges can force compliance. If found guilty, judges can impose fines or other corrective actions to force compliance.

Creating alliances

Once in a while, bureaucrats align themselves with interest groups and members of Congress, forming what are called *iron triangles* (see Figure 6-2). Iron triangles refer to an alliance between bureaucrats, Congress, and interest groups. The three come together to make public policy that benefits all three. Around for decades, iron triangles allow for bureaucrats to continue to be funded while interest groups get the policies they prefer and members of Congress receive interest group support when running for reelection.

Issue networks are more common today than iron triangles. These are composed of a wide variety of actors who get together to lobby Congress on a specific issue. Members of issue networks can include interest groups, bureaucrats, legislators, and even scholars, activists and members of the media. Issue networks are therefore broader and often ad hoc, meaning that if the issue they lobby for is resolved, the issue networks go away.

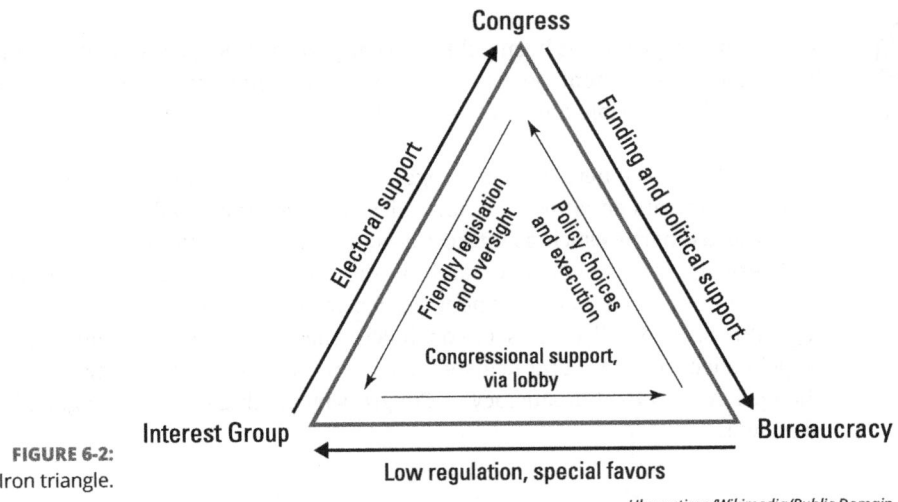

Congress

Electoral support

Funding and political support

Friendly legislation and oversight

Policy choices and execution

Congressional support, via lobby

Interest Group

Low regulation, special favors

Bureaucracy

FIGURE 6-2:
Iron triangle.

Ubernetizen/Wikimedia/Public Domain

Studying Different Types of Bureaucracy

Today, the federal bureaucracy consists of four different structures: the cabinets discussed in Chapter 4 on the presidency, and the following three:

>> **Independent executive agencies:** Executive agencies are independent bureaucracies located outside of cabinet departments. They report directly to the president, who appoints their chief officials. There are about 70 independent executive agencies, and they can vary in size. Some are very large, such as NASA (National Aeronautics and Space Administration), and some are smaller, such as the Peace Corps.

>> **Independent regulatory commissions:** These commissions are created to regulate certain parts of the U.S. economy. They are totally independent from the presidency and were created by Congress to have oversight and regulatory responsibilities. They are usually run by boards of commissioners appointed by the president and confirmed by the Senate. The appointments are bipartisan, and the president cannot remove commissioners for political reasons.

Most commissioners are experts in their fields, academics, or former elected officeholders. The commissions were first created in 1887 when Congress established the Interstate Commerce Commission (ICC) to regulate industry in the U.S. Other examples of independent regulatory commissions include the Federal Reserve of Governors and the Equal Employment Opportunity Commission, created in 1964. These commissions have usually less than 2,000 employees.

>> **Government corporations:** Government corporations or quasi-governmental agencies are created by the government to conduct commercial business. They are similar to private corporations and generate revenue through buying and selling of federal property, lending money, and conducting other business in the American economy.

They are structured like a private company, headed by an executive officer and supervised by a board of directors. The president selects the board of directors, and there are no public shareholders. The government corporation also does not pay taxes and with no shareholders to pay, the government keeps all profits. Examples of government corporations are the U.S. Postal Service and Amtrak.

Controlling the Bureaucracy

Bureaucratic agencies are established by Congress with help from the presidency. However, in the end, oversight lies with Congress. Congress makes sure that each agency performs its functions properly. But what if a bureaucratic agency does not perform its job well or refuses to implement a program passed by Congress?

REMEMBER

Often, bureaucrats disagree with a policy passed by Congress and the executive. They cannot challenge Congress or the president publicly by criticizing the policy or openly refusing to implement it. That would cost them their job. However, bureaucrats can stall a policy, move slowly to implement it, or just ignore it, hoping the next presidential administration or Congress will change the policy.

Having the power of the purse

How can Congress force a bureaucracy in line? The most effective way is the power of the purse. Congress controls the money. It appropriates money for agencies, and if it cuts or eliminates appropriated money, those agencies will decline. That being said, the appropriation of money is automatic in rare instances, such as for the Social Security Administration. This is called a *permanent authorization*. More often, authorization for monies is periodic, and Congress can use it to force agencies in line. By being able to increase, decrease, or even eliminate funding, Congress controls bureaucratic agencies.

Having other powers

Besides the power of the purse, Congress has other nonmonetary powers to control the bureaucracy, such as

>> **Having hearings and investigating:** If Congress suspects any bureaucratic wrongdoing or an agency not implementing required policies, it can summon heads of agencies and have them testify in front of a congressional committee or subcommittee. It can even ask the Congressional Budget Office to investigate, and report on an agency's conduct.

>> **Having a legislative veto:** Congress has what is a called a legislative veto. It allows Congress to reject an agency's policy proposal or action. The U.S. Supreme Court found the legislative veto unconstitutional in 1983 but Congress continues to use it occasionally and bureaucratic agencies continue to abide by it, even though the legislative veto has no legal standing.

>> **Having mandatory reports:** Congress has the power to ask bureaucratic agencies, including executive departments, to assess programs and report the results to Congress. Congress through these reports can evaluate agencies and decide whether they are performing up to their capacity and whether the laws Congress has passed are actually working. If agencies are not doing well in reports and policies are nor working as intended Congress can cut funding.

TECHNICAL STUFF

In 1976, Congress passed the Sunshine Act. It requires federal agencies, unless they are involved in court proceedings, to meet and discuss policies in public. Today, many states have started to use *sunset laws*, which require bureaucratic agencies to terminate after a certain period of time has passed. For them to continue, they must be reauthorized by a state government.

Being restricted politically

Federal employees face restrictions when it comes to political activities.

In 1939, Congress passed the Hatch Act. It is a federal law that makes it illegal for federal employees, except for the president and vice president, to participate in some forms of political activity. The law prohibits federal employees from running for office in partisan elections, to solicit or receive any political contributions, and to engage in any official political activity while on duty or on federal property. As a side note, federal employees can run for office freely if the election is a nonpartisan election.

Under the law, federal employees cannot use public funds for political activities, and federal employees cannot promise federal contracts or jobs to people who make campaign contributions. Further, federal employees cannot join any organization that advocates the overthrow of the U.S. government, such as the Communist Party of the United States.

Today, the Hatch Act is also applicable to local and state employees, whose positions are paid for by federal monies.

Evolving Focus and Function Over Time

The federal bureaucracy started out small. In 1787, it consisted of three departments, the Department of Treasury, the Department of War, (from 1949 until 2025 the Department of Defense), and the Department of State. During Washington's first term, the positions of attorney general and postmaster general were added. Overall, the number of bureaucrats during Washington's first year in office numbered about 50 people.

With the role of government in the economy increasing and U.S. territorial expansion, the bureaucracy grew rapidly. Wars such as the War of 1812 and subsequent Indian wars led to a larger military and larger military bureaucracy. A growing economy resulted in a national bank. Suddenly the U.S. government was involved in the economic and monetary system in the U.S. as well as foreign policy.

When the U.S. began to develop economically after 1840, more areas of the economy needed regulating. Not surprisingly, this resulted in an increase in the size of the bureaucracy. The Department of the Interior was created to manage the expansion of the country to the west and the Department of Agriculture was created in 1862 to promote farming and increase agricultural output during the Civil War. Finally, the Department of Justice was set up in 1870.

With the country industrializing rapidly after the Civil War and more large-scale industry being created, a large working class was suddenly created in the U.S. This resulted in the Bureau of Labor being set up in 1884 to address concerns of the labor force.

Loving patronage — The spoils system

The *spoils system* refers to handing out government jobs as political favors to supporters and political allies. It is also known as a *patronage system*. *Patronage* refers to handing out government jobs based on party ties. In the 19th century, people assumed that all federal jobs belonged to the party that won the presidential election, and so the party had the right to hand out these jobs to its followers. Many

U.S. citizens joined political parties for this reason. They expected that after years of loyal party service they would be rewarded with a cushy government job. In the late 19th century, this expectation was quite realistic because the party in power controlled over 130,000 federal jobs.

The system was put in place by President Andrew Jackson, and he set the tone for presidents to come. After the Jackson presidency (1829-1837) almost all government jobs were handed out to party followers, even though they were often utterly incompetent. Both major parties participated in the spoils system until the Pendleton Act of 1883 began to make the practice illegal.

Enacting the Pendleton Act in 1883

In 1883, Congress, under pressure from new President Chester Arthur (1881-1885) (see Figure 6-3), passed the first civil service reform bill in U.S. history.

FIGURE 6-3: President Chester Arthur.

Charles Milton Bell/Library of Congress/ Public domain

The Pendleton Act of 1883 established the following reforms:

» Hiring based on political loyalty or party affiliation was curtailed.

» Appointments were to be based on qualifications, excluding those unable to perform duties effectively due to substance abuse such as alcoholism.

» Competitive tests for some civil service positions became mandatory. However, only 14,000 out of 131,000 civil service positions available were affected by this.

» The act allowed for later presidents to add positions to the competitive test category.

Although the Pendleton Act was a necessary first step in civil service reform, it only affected a small part of the federal workforce. However, both parties agreed that civil service reform was necessary, and the U.S. public supported reform wholeheartedly. For this reason, by 1900 the Pendleton Act had been applied to most civil service positions, and the U.S. now had a civil service where hiring was based on merit.

The Pendleton Act of 1883 over time ended the spoils system in the U.S. The Act mandated a merit-based system of hiring and promoting federal employees and allowed for a Civil Service Commission to oversee the implementation of the Act itself.

Overall, the idea was to create a more professional and more effective federal bureaucracy.

The Pendleton Act applied only to the federal government, so localities and states continued with the spoils system, which survived into the 20th century. New York City did not reform its civil service until the 1950s, and Chicago used patronage into the early 1980s. Today, the spoils system has mostly disappeared.

Some federal positions are still excluded from the Pendleton Act. A great example are ambassadors who are picked by the president of the U.S. and confirmed by the Senate. Many of them are big party donors and even friends of the president.

REMEMBER

The merit system is a system for hiring that looks at a person's qualifications, including educational background, related job experience, and performance on civil service tests.

Undertaking Civil Service Reform in 1978

In 1978, Congress passed the Civil Service Reform Act of 1978. It established the Office of Personnel Management (OPM) and the Merit Systems Protection Board (MSPB). The Office of Personnel Management manages civil servants today. It recruits, interviews, and evaluates civil servants for job openings and recommends hiring decisions to the various agencies in the federal bureaucracy.

Today, the OPM is responsible for administering the system for hiring civil servants, protecting the rights of federal employees, and conducting hearings on wrongdoing in federal jobs. The OPM even decides cases on the hiring and firing of federal employees. Finally, the OPM regulates how federal employees can participate in U.S. politics.

Under current law, federal employees cannot run for office in partisan elections or raise money and influence votes for candidates.

Growing Rapidly

It was the Great Depression in 1929 and the subsequent creation of a welfare state by Franklin Delano Roosevelt that started the largest expansion in U.S. bureaucratic history. FDR's New Deal created an activist government and needed thousands of bureaucrats to administer his new programs. From the Social Security Administration to the Civilian Conservation Corps, programs were established that needed to be administered. By 1940, about 700,000 U.S. citizens worked for the federal bureaucracy with $9.5 billion now spent on federal programs.

Between 1940 and 1975, the federal bureaucracy grew even more. The Great Society implemented by President Johnson in the 1960s was a major reason for this. However, it was not just federal programs like Medicare and Medicaid that increased the New Deal bureaucracy but also WWII and the Cold War with the Soviet Union. The number of federal bureaucrats increased to 2.2 million and the federal budget increased to $332 billion.

By 2000, the number of federal bureaucrats had declined by 500,000. Then the terrorist attacks of September 11, 2001, happened. As a result, the Bush administration created the Department of Homeland Security in 2002, which employs almost 240,000 people. It is responsible for public security, including border patrol, cybersecurity, and anti-terrorism measures.

With the ongoing war on terror and the wars in Afghanistan and Iraq, the federal workforce increased again. The recession of 2007/2008 and Obamacare further increased the size of the federal bureaucracy, as did the first Trump administration when it increased defense spending. Finally, federal spending to offset the negative economic effects of the pandemic by both the Trump and Biden administrations brought the federal bureaucracy back to a little over 3 million civil servants.

The Bureaucracy Today

There are many common misperceptions about the bureaucracy. Most people believe that most bureaucrats live in Washington, D.C. This could not be further from the truth. About 90 percent of all bureaucrats live outside of the capital. Another misperception is that most bureaucrats work to administer large welfare programs such as Medicare, Medicaid, and Social Security. Again, that is not the case. Only five percent of all bureaucrats work for welfare agencies. Most federal bureaucrats work for the Department of War, the Postal Service, the Department of Homeland Security, and the Department of Veterans Affairs.

Today, about 3 million people work for the federal bureaucracy, which is close to its height in 1990 when it had 3.4 million people working for it.

Stopping the expansion of the bureaucracy

Beginning in the late 1970s, the expansion of the U.S. economy came to an abrupt halt. The American economy was in a slump, and budget deficits began to increase. No money was left for new, expensive programs for bureaucrats to administer. In the 1980s, for the first time, President Reagan attempted to cut back the size of the federal bureaucracy and every president since has followed his tradition.

Deregulation

By the 1980s, deregulation became suddenly the goal of the new Reagan administration. *Deregulation* refers to eliminating government oversight and regulation of certain activities resulting in less government and more private involvement, ideally increasing efficiency. For example, back in the 1970s, the Civil Aeronautics Board, a government agency, protected the airlines industry. It was abolished in 1985. Since then, results have been mixed. On one hand, consumers receive frequent-flyer programs and have more flight choices; on the other, prices for tickets vary more and airline customer service has been cut back.

Privatization

Today, privatization has occasionally replaced government-provided services, meaning that those services are now provided by the private sector. It is often cheaper for the federal government to hire out than to create a specialized agency and staff it with civil servants. For example, job training for the unemployed is often undertaken by private companies and not the federal government. Another example is security provided to U.S. citizens working or travelling abroad, an example being diplomats and their families, which is provided by private companies at a cheaper cost than the federal government could do.

Devolution

In the 1980s, the Reagan administration began to push for *devolution* of federal services. This means that those services would be provided by state governments, not the federal government. A good example is the Clinton administration's welfare reform in 1996, which shifted the administration of many welfare programs back to the states.

Chapter **7**

Addressing Civil Liberties

F reedom is an integral part of U.S. culture. The early colonists fled England to escape persecution, hoping for political and religious freedom in the Americas. The colonies enacted declarations protecting individual freedoms, and Thomas Jefferson made freedom an integral part of the Declaration of Independence. In it, he proclaimed that King George had trampled on the colonists' freedoms and that the colonists had therefore the right to replace the current government.

The Bill of Rights has become the most visible document in the Constitution. Most Americans can recite a least a few of the rights guaranteed in the Bill of Rights, even if they aren't able to discuss congressional or presidential powers outlined in the Constitution. For many foreign citizens, the idea of a Bill of Rights, which guarantees personal freedom such as the right to freedom of speech or the right to practice any religion, makes the U.S. an attractive destination to visit and even move to, if possible. Most countries in the world do not have a Bill of Rights in their constitutions, and even if they do, they rarely follow it. In most societies, citizens cannot freely express themselves, or assemble publicly, and they definitely can't practice the religion of their choice.

Ironically, this beloved document, the Bill of Rights, was not even in the original version of the Constitution, which already had been ratified by the states; it had to be added later in the form of the first ten amendments to the Constitution (refer to Chapter 1 for a discussion of the Constitution and the amendment process).

REMEMBER

Civil liberties are defined as rights and freedoms given to U.S. citizens by the Constitution, namely the Bill of Rights, a part of the U.S. Constitution. They cannot be infringed upon by government.

The discussion of personal liberties began in the colonies in the 17th century. Many colonies had already enshrined some personal liberties into their colonial constitutions. Massachusetts had adopted the Body of Liberties in 1641, which guaranteed the right to free assembly, the right to a jury trial in civil cases, equal protection in front of the law, and even the right to get compensated if the government took your property for a public purpose. Maryland then passed the Toleration Act guaranteeing religious liberty in 1649. Therefore, a long history of government guaranteeing civil liberties existed in the U.S.

REMEMBER

Rights are privileges that individuals are entitled to. *Natural rights* are rights a person is entitled to because they are a human being. These rights exist even if there is no government. Now, *positive rights* are rights a government has given to people. This includes civil liberties and civil rights and can be modified at any time by government.

After the acceptance of the Declaration of Independence, the colonies wrote new state constitutions enshrining civil liberties. In Virginia's state constitution was a sixteen-point Declaration of Rights that restrained all three branches of government. Pennsylvania was the first to introduce the separation of church and state, the right to bear arms, the right to legal counsel in criminal cases, and even the right to travel. Delaware made it illegal to house troops in private people's homes and Maryland outlawed finding a person guilty of a crime without a trial.

Coming up with a Bill of Rights

When the Constitution was signed in Philadelphia in September 1787, it contained no Bill of Rights. The matter of a Bill of Rights was not really discussed by the delegates; they considered it unimportant and did not think people would mind much. Boy, were they wrong. As the signed document was publicized — keep in mind the meetings were held in secret, so nobody really knew what was in the Constitution — all hell broke loose. It was not just the Anti-Federalists (see Chapter 1) but state legislators and members of the public who were outraged.

The signees of the Constitution realized that they had committed a political blunder that could sink ratification of the Constitution. James Madison right away promised to add a Bill of Rights to the Constitution as soon as the first Congress met, after the Constitution was ratified. This promise satisfied many opponents of the Constitution, and the Constitution was ratified by 1788.

James Madison, seen in Figure 7-1, looked at the civil liberties contained in state constitutions and researched the topic in writings going back to the Magna Carta. In the summer of 1789, he proposed nine amendments to the Constitution to the House of Representatives. After lengthy discussion in committee and on the floor of the House, the House approved 17 amendments to the Constitution and sent the bill to the Senate. The Senate in turn cut the number of amendments to 12, which were later approved by the House. Now Congress had approved 12 amendments to the Constitution, and these were sent to the states for ratification.

Ten of those amendments would be approved by the states and became the Bill of Rights after Virgina became the eleventh state to approve it, fulfilling the requirement that 75 percent of all states had to approve amendments to the Constitution.

The two amendments rejected by the states were in regard to Congressional salaries and reapportionment of seats to the House of Representatives.

Pendleton's Lithography.Stuart, Gilbert/
Library of Congress/Public domain

The Bill of Rights was not a hot political topic in the 19th century because it was understood to apply only to the federal government. Thus, the states, which guaranteed their citizens' rights in state constitutions, were not bound by the Bill of Rights. The Supreme Court even ruled on this issue in 1833 in Barron v. Baltimore, stating that the Bill of Rights was not applicable to the states.

Not much changed until the 20th century, when the Supreme Court, after passage of the 14th Amendment in 1868, suddenly had a tool to apply the Bill of Rights to the states. The 14th Amendment could be used to extend civil liberty protections to the states. The 14th Amendment states: "no state . . . shall abridge the privileges and immunities of citizens of the United States; nor shall any State deprive any person of life, liberty, or property without due process of the law; nor deny any person within its jurisdiction the equal protection of the laws."

From now on, if a civil liberty such as freedom of speech was deemed fundamental by the Supreme Court, a state could not legitimately refuse to guarantee it without depriving a person of the equal protection of the laws. This of course would be a violation of the 14th Amendment. The process of applying the Bill of Rights to the states is known as *incorporation*.

REMEMBER

Selective incorporation refers to the application of the Bill of Rights to the states one right at a time.

Using the 14th Amendment, the Supreme Court now slowly applied the Bill of Rights to the states, saying that states had to respect due process and guarantee equal protection under the law.

TECHNICAL
STUFF

Not all civil liberties guaranteed in the Bill of Rights have been incorporated and applied to states. Several only restrict the federal government but not state governments today. These include the Third Amendment protections of citizens against the involuntary quartering of troops, the Fifth Amendment requirements that defendants be indicted by a grand jury, the Seventh Amendment guaranteeing a jury trial in civil cases and the Eighth Amendment provision against excessive bail.

Incorporating the Bill of Rights

Not surprisingly, the First Amendment contains the most important rights guaranteed in the Bill of Rights. The Founders believed that democracy could not function without freedom of speech, assembly, press, and religion. Liberty without these rights was not possible. The Supreme Court took over 200 years to incorporate many of these rights. The rest of this part of the chapter discusses the process of incorporation of the Bill of Rights to the states.

Guaranteeing freedom

The First Amendment states: "Congress shall make no law respecting an establishment of religion or prohibiting the free exercise thereof, or abridging the freedom of speech, or of the press; or the right of the people peaceably to assemble, and to petition the government for a redress of grievances."

Believing in freedom of religion

The Constitution addresses two issues in this passage in regard to freedom of religion. The establishment of a state religion and the free practice of religion in the U.S.

During colonial times, several colonies established the equivalent to a state religion. Official churches were put in place, and citizens had to attend their religious services. In Virginia, for example, from 1616 to 1618, colonists who missed the Sunday services were punished with prison terms and forced labor. In addition, religious minorities were not tolerated and often mistreated. For this reason, James Madison, seen in Figure 7-1, decided that freedom of religion was an absolute necessity. He put the guarantee to this freedom in the First Amendment, which provides U.S. citizens the freedom of religion. The First Amendment prohibits the establishment of a state religion with the Establishment Clause and also makes it illegal for the U.S. government to outlaw any religion. This is called the *Free Exercise Clause*. The U.S. government and later state governments cannot set up a church or give preference to one religion over another.

REMEMBER

The Establishment Clause in the First Amendment states that the government cannot establish an official religion.

Second, the U.S. and state governments cannot ban religious practices or interfere with people's beliefs. In 1993, Congress passed the Religious Freedom Restoration Act, which required the national, state, and local government to accommodate religious conduct in the least restrictive manner possible.

REMEMBER

The Free Exercise Clause, contained in the First Amendment, states that government cannot interfere with religious practice.

Freedom of religion did not become an issue in U.S. politics until the 20th century. In the 19th century, most people in the U.S. were protestant, and often churches openly collaborated with the federal or state governments. It was not until later in the 19th century and the early 20th century that the U.S. became more religiously diverse. Most immigrants from Eastern and Southern Europe were Catholic, and suddenly the U.S. saw more migration from Asia. The country experienced more religious diversity.

In the 20th century, the U.S. Supreme Court became active and in 1940 incorporated the Free Exercise Clause in Cantwell v. Connecticut and in 1947 the Establishment Clause in in the case of Everson v. Board of Education.

In Everson v. Board of Education, the Supreme Court ruled that there was a wall of separation between government and religion, and that government could not provide any aid to religion. No public monies could be used to support any religious activities or institutions as long as they teach or practice religion.

The Supreme Court therefore ruled that the Constitution has erected a wall of separation between church and state. Government at all levels cannot be involved with religion. The government cannot require a person to profess a certain belief and cannot support religion or spend any tax money on religion. Today, it is even illegal for a public school to ask a minister, priest, or rabbi to perform a benediction at a graduation ceremony.

In 2000, the Supreme Court ruled in Santa Fe Independent School District v. Doe that a person cannot lead a football team in a student initiated prayer before a game in a public school. However, if the players want to pray privately before a game, that is perfectly fine; the prayer just cannot be organized by a coach or the school administrators or broadcast over the school public address system.

In 2022, in Kennedy v. Bremerton, the Supreme Court changed its ruling and allowed for prayer after a game by a coach as long as it was voluntary for players to attend and it was not broadcast over the public address system.

After freedom of religion had been incorporated, the Supreme Court ruled consistently on behalf of freedom of religion. For example, the court ruled that members of the Amish religion were not required to continue to attend school after 8th grade because the Amish religion believes in learning through doing, and the state of Wisconsin could not force them to do so.

A continuing question involves the separation of church and state. Often this involves public displays, such as a nativity scene or the display of menorahs. The U.S. Supreme Court been very lenient when it comes to religious practices that are steeped in history. For example, Congress and many state legislatures open their session with a prayer. The Supreme Court has ruled this as acceptable. The U.S. currency displays the phrase *In God We Trust*. Again, the Supreme Court said that was OK. The Court actually went so far as to allow the display of the Ten Commandments outside of the state capital in Texas (but not inside the state capital in Kentucky).

Today, freedom of religion is being treated by the U.S. Supreme Court like freedom of speech. You can pretty much do or say whatever you want as long as you do not cause harm to the public.

3

Safeguarding the People

IN THIS PART . . .

Study the Bill of Rights and the protections provided by it to the American people.

See how these fundamental rights were slowly applied to the states in a process called incorporation. Then, observe how the Supreme Court can overrule itself and change previous judicial outcomes.

Discover the concept of civil rights. See how African Americans were denied basic civil rights and observe how it took a civil war to slowly provide civil rights to former slaves.

Observe the slow process of desegregation and look at the civil rights movement.

Discover the process of emancipation for women in the U.S. and see how far women's rights have advanced today.

Believing in freedom of speech

Freedom of speech is another cornerstone of a free society in which people enjoy civil liberties. However, is freedom of speech absolute or can the government curtail it if necessary?

In 1919, the U.S. Supreme Court set down the rules for freedom of speech. The case was Schenck v. U.S. Schenck was a member of the executive committee of the Socialist Party of the U.S. opposing U.S. entrance into WWI. He mailed out 15,000 flyers to men who could get conscripted for war, telling them not to submit for the draft. He was subsequently arrested and charged with treason under the Espionage Act of 1917. After being convicted he appealed to the U.S. Supreme Court. Justic Oliver Wendell Holmes, depicted in Figure 7-2, came up with the clear and present danger test in regard to free speech. The test was simple. If someone's speech presented a clear and present danger to the U.S. public, the government had the right to curtail it. If not, the person could say whatever they wanted. Urging men not to fight in WWI was a clear and present danger to the U.S. public in times of war.

Holmes made this famous analogy. If someone yells fire in a crowded public theatre that person could panic people which in turn could hurt the public. So, this type of free speech was not protected. Schenck was deemed to present a clear and present danger to the war effort and stayed in jail.

TECHNICAL STUFF

The "clear and present danger" test states that speech was protected unless it presented a clear and present danger of producing harmful actions.

FIGURE 7-2: Oliver Wendell Holmes, Jr.: associate justice of the U.S. Supreme Court.

Harris & Ewing Collection/Library of Congress/ Public domain.

A similar case arose in 1925 in Gitlow v. New York. Benjamin Gitlow was a socialist and former member of the New York State Assembly, writing a manifesto advocating the overthrow of the present U.S. government. He was convicted by the state of New York for sedition. His conviction was upheld by the Supreme Court, but the court at the same time ruled that freedom of speech and freedom of the press are among the fundamental rights protected by the Due Process Clause in the 14th Amendment. From then on, freedom of speech, assembly, and the press were protected from any state infringement. In other words, freedom of speech, the press, and assembly had been incorporated and were now applicable to the states.

Still dealing with free speech

In 1940, the U.S. Congress passed the Smith Act, which made it a crime to advocate the overthrow of the U.S. government. WWII had started in Europe and Stalin was in control of the Soviet Union. The U.S. government was afraid that either communist or fascist groups would attempt to overthrow the U.S. government. Thus, the U.S. wanted to make sure that it was possible to crack down on the extremes, right or left.

Under the Smith Act, the Supreme Court upheld the conviction of 11 leaders of the American Communist Party in 1949, stating that the U.S. government did not have to wait until the Communist Party implemented a violent class revolution to destroy the government but that it could act preemptively against people advocating the overthrow of the government.

Beginning in the 1960s, the courts moved to the liberal or progressive side and started to make free speech more absolute. In 1969, the Supreme Court used the Brandenburg v. Ohio case to get rid of the "clear and present danger" doctrine. The case arose when Clarence Brandenburg, a Ku Klux Klan leader in Ohio, made a speech talking about taking revenge against blacks and Jews and called for a march on the capital of Washington, D.C. He was arrested and convicted for advocating violence.

The Supreme Court took his appeal and reversed the conviction. It ruled that his speech did not incite imminent unlawful action, and the First Amendment protects speech that abstractly advocates violence unless the speech incites imminent lawless action. In other words, the Supreme Court replaced the "clear and present danger" doctrine with an "imminent danger" doctrine.

The courts have stuck with this definition of protection for speech. Today, no matter how offensive or provocative speech is, it is constitutionally protected unless your speech ends up presenting imminent danger to someone.

Dealing with the media

Another right contained within the First Amendment is the freedom of the press. There are four forms of speech and writing that are not automatically protected:

>> Libel

>> Obscenity

>> Symbolic speech

>> Commercial and youthful speech

Being libelous

Libel is defined as writing something that falsely injures or defames another person. (If such a statement is spoken, it is called *slander.*) Now, to be able to sue someone for libel or slander, the statements must be proven to be false and must actually hurt the person. So, it is upon the person who was slandered or libeled to prove actual harm. In addition, it is tougher to win a libel suit if you are a public official. Any public figure, such as an elected official or a candidate or even a well-known celebrity or sports star must prove first that the defamation was false and damaging. Next, the libeled person must prove that the words were published or spoken with "actual malice," meaning that the person who published or spoke the statements had knowledge that the statements were false.

In other words, one must prove that the published facts were published with malice, or bad intent, or reckless disregard for the truth, and that the media is ignoring clear evidence.

Being obscene

According to the courts, obscenity is not protected by the First Amendment. It has no redeeming value and thus is not protected. The question is, what is obscene? Some judges believe that all so-called obscene materials should be protected by the First Amendment whereas others believe that no obscene materials should be protected at all. Over time, the judges have ruled that nudity and sex are not by definition obscene. They can have First Amendment protection if they have political, artistic, or literary merit.

Further, the Supreme Court has ruled that it is up to the locality to decide what is obscene, or acceptable, or not. So, hardcore pornography is legal in some localities but not in others in the U.S. In 1973, the Supreme Court created the Miller test, in Miller v. California, trying to clarify the issue. The Miller test consists of three questions and if all are answered affirmatively, no constitutional protection exists.

TECHNICAL STUFF

The questions ask whether the work is sexually stimulating, patently offensive, and finally whether the work lacks literary, artistic, political, or scientific value. If all three questions are answered affirmatively, then the material is obscene and no constitutional protection exists.

The Internet has changed everything. Pornography is readily available, and the Internet is really not controlled by anyone. This is about to change. Recently, the Supreme Court has upheld a Texas law where Internet users have to prove that they are 18 years old before entering a pornographic website. This is done by providing a government-issued identification such as a driver's license. With the Supreme Court approving the new law, more states are likely to follow the Texas example.

REMEMBER

In 2008, the Supreme Court ruled that child pornography is illegal.

Being symbolic

Symbolic speech is defined as an act that conveys a political message. For example, a person who is burning an American flag is, according to the court, engaged in a free-speech activity. Even as despicable as the act is, the person is making a political statement and has the right to do so. Laws making flag burning illegal have been struck down by the courts for this reason. The only way to make flag burning illegal would be to add a constitutional amendment, making it illegal to burn the American flag.

TECHNICAL STUFF

In 1989, in Texas v. Johnson, the Supreme Court ruled that there cannot be a law to ban flag-burning.

Being commercial and youthful

The courts have ruled that government can place more regulations on speech for commercial organizations, such as businesses, than for private citizens. For example, the government can regulate cigarette advertising, which is now illegal on television and in magazines. So, government can regulate harmful products. Similarly, when it comes to statements made by minors, the government has the right to censor free speech if it is, for example, a part of a school-sponsored activity. For example, if a student newspaper publishes an article on a very divisive topic, the school can step in and censor or eliminate the article.

Bearing Arms and Guaranteeing Due Process

Civil liberties do not just apply to freedom of speech, press, assembly, and religion but also contain restrictions on the activities of the government in regard to its citizens. Although people agree that government must maintain order and punish criminal offenders, these offenders also have rights. These rights are contained in the Fourth, Fifth, Sixth and Eighth Amendments. They are discussed below. First, however, let's discuss the right to bear arms.

The right to bear arms is contained in the Second Amendment to the Constitution. It simply states:

"A well regulated Militia, being necessary to the security of a free State, the right of the people to keep and bear Arms, shall not be infringed."

The question for the last 200 years has been over the meaning of the amendment. Does it mean that the states have the right to create a militia to defend themselves and/or does it mean that every U.S. citizen has the right to arms themselves? So, on one side, supporters of the right to bear arms are arguing that Americans have the right to arm themselves, whereas on the other side, some state governments and the federal government have passed gun control laws.

The Second Amendment was not incorporated until 2010 and so all federal rulings on gun control did not apply to the states until then. For example, in 2008, the Supreme Court ruled in District of Columbia v. Heller that the Second Amendment confers the right to possess a firearm for personal protection. The ruling was a response to the District of Columbia banning the private ownership of handguns. At the same time, the Court stated that that the federal government can still regulate the commercial sale of handguns and can prohibit the possession of handguns by felons and the mentally ill and in sensitive places such as schools.

However, the ruling applied only to the District of Columbia, because it is a federal enclave under federal jurisdiction and not to the states, so a city like Chicago could make it illegal for its citizens to own handguns.

Then in 2010, the Supreme Court incorporated the right to bear arms. So today, the Second Amendment is applicable to the states, and they must abide by it. The case was McDonald v. Chicago. Otis McDonald was a 76-year-old resident of Chicago who wanted to purchase a handgun to protect himself. Chicago, however, had banned handguns in homes for nearly 30 years. McDonald argued that all the criminals in Chicago had handguns so why couldn't he to protect himself? So, he asked the U.S. Supreme Court to incorporate the Second Amendment. In a 5:4 decision the Second Amendment was incorporated in 2010 and now the states must abide by it.

However, restrictions exist. In 2022, Congress passed a law making it illegal for people accused and convicted of domestic abuse to own guns, giving the states incentives to remove guns from people deemed a threat to themselves and others.

Being protected at home

One of the most divisive decisions by the Supreme Court is in regard to the *exclusionary rule*. The exclusionary rule states that evidence inappropriately gathered cannot be used in a criminal trial. The rule comes from Supreme Court decisions in regard to the Fourth Amendment, which states:

"The right of the people to be secure in their persons, houses, papers, and effects, against unreasonable searches and seizures shall not be violated, and no Warrants shall issue, but upon probable cause, supported by Oath or affirmation, and particularly describing the place to be searched, and the persons or things to be seized."

In other words, the amendment protects the U.S. public against unreasonable searches of people's property and arrests by government agents. To be able to search a home or arrest a person, a warrant is now needed. In the beginning, the Fourth Amendment applied only to the federal government, but this changed in 1961.

The case that gave the country the exclusionary rule occurred in 1961. The case was Mapp v. Ohio. Dollree Mapp was a resident of Cleveland, Ohio. In 1961, the police broke into her home, looking for a bombing suspect. They did not find him in her house, but while searching they found some obscene pictures, which violated a law prohibiting the possession of obscene literature. She was arrested, but the Supreme Court held that police should have gotten a search warrant, and without it had conducted an unreasonable search. The evidence, the pictures, were therefore illegally obtained and could not be used against her. With this case, the Supreme Court incorporated the Fourth Amendment.

Since then, police need a search warrant to go into people's homes, and a judge needs probable cause to issue such a warrant. A warrantless search actually can be legal in a few circumstances, however:

>> If a defendant gives consent to have his home searched.

>> If police legally inside a home see evidence in plain view. An example would be police questioning a person and noticing their drug paraphernalia on the kitchen table.

>> If the police are in hot pursuit of a suspect.

>> If the search accompanies a lawful arrest.

REMEMBER

A *search warrant* is an order from a judge to search a place; the warrant must list what is to be searched and seized and the judge can only order it if he believes there is probable cause to find evidence.

In 1984, the Supreme Court relaxed the exclusionary rule, by creating the "Good Faith Exception." It states that if police officers act in good faith in obtaining evidence, the evidence can still be used at trial even if it was obtained illegally. For example, if a judge puts the wrong date on a warrant, it can still be used.

Preventing unjust prosecutions

The Fifth Amendment assures protection against double jeopardy, which means a person cannot be tried twice for the same crime, and guarantees the right not to be compelled to give evidence against oneself.

DEALING WITH TERRORISM

After the terrorist attacks of September 11, 2001, Congress passed the USA Patriot Act, which limited some rights in the U.S. For example, it became a crime to aid terrorist organizations, an example being raising money for them. A person can verbally express support for a terrorist organization — that is protected free speech — but the person cannot engage in any activity to aid the organization. The Act further increased penalties for helping terrorist activities.

In addition, the National Security Agency, which is a part of the Department of Defense and is tasked with monitoring, collecting, and analyzing global data for intelligence, received the power to conduct international surveillance on suspected terrorists and terrorist organizations without a warrant being necessary.

The Fifth Amendment lists an assortment of rights the accused can use for their defense. The Fifth Amendment states:

"No person shall be held to answer for a capital, or otherwise infamous crime, unless on a presentment or indictment of a Grand Jury, except in cases arising in the land or naval forces, or in the Militia, when in actual service in time of War or public danger; nor shall any person be subject for the same offense to be twice put in jeopardy of life or limb; nor shall be compelled in any criminal case to be a witness against himself, nor be deprived of life, liberty, or property without due process of law; nor shall private property be taken for public use, without just compensation."

According to the Fifth Amendment, it is unconstitutional to be forced to give evidence against yourself. This is called the self-incrimination clause. Therefore, involuntary confessions are illegal and cannot be used in federal trials but still could be used in state trials. Then, in 1966, the Supreme Court changed its mind.

The case of Miranda v. Arizona incorporated the Fifth Amendment to the Constitution and made it applicable to the states. Ernesto Miranda was accused of kidnapping and raping a young girl. He was caught and after being questioned for two hours, he admitted his guilt and signed a written confession. However, he was never informed that he had the right to remain silent until a lawyer was present. He was sentenced to 20-30 years for kidnapping and rape, and the Arizona Supreme Court upheld this sentence. An appeal to the Supreme Court followed, where Miranda was represented by the American Civil Liberties Union, which emphasized that Miranda had no lawyer present and had not been informed of his rights to remain silent. For this reason, the U.S. Supreme Court overturned his sentence, stating that because Miranda was not informed of his rights his sentence was vacated.

TECHNICAL STUFF

The American Civil Liberties Union (ACLU), a nonprofit organization that protects civil liberties in the U.S. was founded in 1920. It is active in all 50 states and provides direct legal representation, such as in the Miranda case, or presents *amicus curiae* (friend of the court) briefs, providing assistance to the court with information, facts, or other insights. The ACLU participated in major civil liberties cases such as Mapp v. Ohio and Gideon v. Wainright.

From then on, accused criminals must be read their rights (see Figure 7-3) before they can be interrogated by police. We refer to this as the Miranda rules.

TECHNICAL STUFF

Miranda was retried in 1967 and was sentenced again even without his confession being admissible in court. His former girlfriend identified him at the trial. He was paroled in 1972 but got into a bar fight in 1976 and was stabbed to death.

> **A commonly used version of the**
> # MIRANDA WARNING
>
> 1. You have the right to remain silent.
>
> 2. Anything you say can and will be used against you in a court of law.
>
> 3. You have the right to an attorney.
>
> 4. If you cannot afford an attorney, one will be provided for you.
>
> 5. If you decide to answer questions now without an attorney present, you will still have the right to stop answering at any time until you talk to an attorney.
>
> ## WAIVER
>
> Do you understand the rights I have just read to you?
> With these rights in mind, do you wish to speak to me?

FIGURE 7-3: Example of a Miranda warning.

REMEMBER

The public safety exception allows the police to question a non–Mirandized subject if there is urgent concern for public safety.

In 2010, the Supreme Court ruled that the testimony of criminal suspects who know about their right to be silent and to have an attorney present but have chosen specifically to not invoke these rights can have their testimony used against them.

Having a right to a lawyer

The Sixth Amendment guarantees defendants the right to have a lawyer in criminal cases. It states:

"In all criminal prosecutions, the accused shall enjoy the right to a speedy and public trial, by an impartial jury of the State and district wherein the crime shall have been committed, which district shall have been previously ascertained by law, and to be informed of the nature and cause of the accusation; to be confronted with the witnesses against him; to have compulsory process for obtaining witnesses in his favor; and to have the Assistance of Counsel for his defense."

In the beginning, the Supreme Court decided that a right to have a lawyer represent you was only for capital cases, where the possibility of the death penalty existed. Later, the court argued that the right to have a lawyer present should be present in any felony case where imprisonment exceeded one year. Today, the right to an attorney exists for all felony cases and if the defendant cannot afford one, the court must appoint them an attorney.

The Sixth Amendment was incorporated in 1963 in the case Gideon v. Wainwright. Clarence Gideon, seen in Figure 7-4, was accused of breaking into a pool hall and stealing money and alcohol. He was convicted by a judge without a counsel even though he asked for one. In prison, he studied law books and came across the Sixth Amendment. He believed he had the right to counsel and so an appeal began. The Supreme Court agreed with him and ruled that the right to counsel in felony cases was a necessity and that in any felony case from then on, states had to provide a lawyer to defendants. Gideon was retried with a court-appointed lawyer defending him and was found innocent and set free.

In subsequent decades, the Supreme Court decided the right to counsel was so fundamental that whenever a defendant faced prison time or probation, even for a misdemeanor, counsel had to be provided.

FIGURE 7-4:
Clarence Gideon.

State Archives of Florida/Wikimedia Common/Public Domain/https://commons.wikimedia.org/wiki/File:Clarence_Earl_Gideon.jpg/ Last accessed on October 06, 2025

Prohibiting cruel and unusual punishments

The Eighth Amendment states: "Excessive bail shall not be required, nor excessive fines imposed, nor cruel and unusual punishments inflicted."

A continuing debate is over whether the death penalty is cruel and unusual punishment. The Supreme Court has consistently rejected the notion that the death penalty in inherently cruel and unusual, but some methods of execution could be. This includes public hanging, beheading, or torture. Torture also cannot be used to extract confessions from suspected criminals.

So today, lawyers defending prisoners on death row focus not on the legality of the death penalty but on the manner of execution. In addition, after a defendant is found guilty, a second phase of the trial is started where the jury discusses whether the death penalty should be given or whether mitigating circumstances should result in a different sentence, such as life in prison. Finally, certain groups of people cannot receive the death penalty in the U.S.: defendants who committed crimes while under the age of 18 and defendants who have intellectual disabilities.

Having a right to privacy

No U.S. Supreme Court decision has been as controversial as the right to have an abortion. Roe v. Wade, which legalized abortion in the U.S. until 2022, was based on the right to privacy. The right to privacy itself is not mentioned in the Constitution but the judges claimed that they could infer it from the Nineth Amendment, which states:

"The enumeration in the Constitution, of certain rights, shall not be construed to deny or disparage others retained by the people."

The right to privacy is often called an unwritten right, because it is not in the Constitution, but the judges believed that it can be inferred from it. When analyzing the Nineth Amendment, one can see that it states that the written rights in the Constitution do not mean that other rights do not exist and can be recognized.

The right to privacy can be traced back to the 1965 case Griswold v. Connecticut. Miss Griswold was selling contraceptives and handing out information on them. This was a violation of an 1879 Connecticut law. She was arrested and tried and sentenced to pay a fine. Her conviction was upheld by the Connecticut Supreme Court. She appealed her conviction, and the Supreme Court heard her appeal. It decided that even though birth control is not mentioned in the Constitution, several provisions in the Bill of Rights together suggest that every citizen has a right to privacy.

According to Supreme Court Justice Douglas: "The rights that are specifically mentioned in the Bill of Rights have penumbras, . . . that give them life and substance." These penumbras, or shadows, create a zone of privacy. The right to privacy thus comes from a penumbra, a group of rights, derived from other rights in the Constitution, specifically the Bill of Rights. This includes decisions as to whether a person wants to use birth control. The decision was not controversial at the time but would become so when the right to privacy was used to legalize abortion in the U.S. in 1973.

Legalizing abortion

By the early 1970s, fifteen states had legalized abortion. The rest had not. Norma McCorvey, who used the pseudonym Jane Roe, lived in Texas, where abortion was illegal. She had become pregnant and wanted an abortion. So, she sued, claiming that all 50 states had to legalize abortion because the right to have an abortion was a constitutional right. The Supreme Court agreed to take her case.

By the time the Supreme Court agreed to hear her case, Norma McCorvey had given birth to the child and had given it up for adoption.

The Supreme Court decided that there was a right to abortion, even though abortion was not mentioned in the Constitution. The right to an abortion was a part of the right to privacy, but certain medical restrictions existed. During the first trimester of the pregnancy, the right to have an abortion was absolute. During the second trimester, the right was nearly absolute, states could not forbid abortions, but they could enact regulations to protect a pregnant person's health.

Finally, in the third trimester, the states could restrict abortion unless the life or health of the mother was threatened. Thus, Roe v. Wade legalized abortion in all 50 states in 1973.

Roe v. Wade changed American life and politics. Two sides emerged. The pro-choice side believed a woman could choose to have an abortion because it was a woman's right to make this choice. It protected women's health and was a part of gender equality. On the other hand, the pro-life group believed that life begins at conception and that abortion was murder.

Although the pro-choice group overwhelmingly favored the Democratic Party, the pro-life group joined the Republican Party, which had committed itself to overturning Roe.

Soon, challenges occurred, and abortion was slowly curtailed. In 1980, Congress voted to make federal funding for abortions illegal. Then, in 1992, the Supreme Court in the Casey decision allowed the states to implement measures such as a 24-hour waiting period and counselling, and minors had to seek permission from a parent or court to get an abortion.

Finally, in 2022, the U.S. Supreme Court in Dobbs v. Jackson Women's Health overturned Roe v. Wade. The Court ruled that abortion was not a constitutionally protected right, and that state legislatures had the right to pass laws on abortion. As of 2025, 12 states have banned abortion, and 28 states have limited abortion bans based on gestational duration.

Closing it out

The final amendment of the Bill of Rights, the Tenth Amendment, is one that does not need to be incorporated. It already applies to the states by giving them all the rights not given to the federal government by the Constitution or prohibited by it.

The Tenth Amendment states: "The powers not delegated to the United States by the Constitution, nor prohibited by it to the States, are reserved to the States respectively, or to the people."

In addition to the Bill of Rights, the first ten amendments to the constitution, there have been 17 additional amendments. They are discussed in various chapters throughout the book.

IN THIS CHAPTER

» Starting with slavery

» Slowly getting civil rights

» Starting a movement

» Judging affirmative action

» Tackling gender discrimination

» Dealing with sexual discrimination

» Being disabled and getting rights

Chapter **8**

Continuing the March for Civil Rights

C ivil rights are rights individuals living in the U.S. possess that shield them against unfair treatment based on personal characteristics such as race, ethnicity, gender, age or disability.

This includes the right to be treated equally in front of the law. Other political scientists define civil rights as the freedom to participate in the community; this includes the right to vote, the right to have equal access to public facilities, and the right to have equal economic opportunities. Citizens who are excluded from any of these rights face discrimination.

This chapter deals with the long battle African Americans had to fight for civil rights, beginning with slavery and ending with the civil rights movement and the subsequent Civil Rights Act of 1964. Besides looking at the quest for civil rights by African Americans, the chapter will analyze the quest for civil rights for women, Latinos, Native Americans, gay people, and people with disabilities.

Two types of discrimination exist:

>> *De jure discrimination*, which is discrimination established by law. Examples include laws such as the grandfather clause, literacy tests, or laws restricting access to public facilities. By the 1970s, de jure segregation had been successfully ended in the U.S.

>> *De facto discrimination,* which is discrimination not supported by laws but ingrained in a society. It is discrimination that just exists and often is not noticed. In other words, it is the result of patterns of history. This can include residential segregation or educational segregation.

Dealing with Slavery

The Declaration of Independence and the Constitution do not explicitly deal with the issue of slavery. Slavery was predominantly found in the Southern United States, whereas most Northern states opposed it. As soon as the country grew after the Louisiana Purchase and then the Mexican American War, slavery became the predominant issue in the U.S. Northerners opposed slavery not just for moral reasons but also economic reasons. Westward expansion opened up new land for settlers, many from the North, and they did not want to see slavery spread to these areas. This would provide unfair economic competition. Southern states, on the other hand, wanted slavery to spread so that the institution could survive in the long run. So, every time a territory applied to become a state, the question arose whether the new state should be a slave state or a free state.

The Missouri Compromise, seen in Figure 8-1, and reached in 1820, was the first settlement on slavery reached between the Northern and Southern states. The Missouri Compromise admitted Missouri as a slave state and Maine as a free state to restore the traditional balance between slave states and free states in the U.S. It further drew a line through the newly acquired Louisiana Territory and basically said that all states north of the 36°30' parallel in the remaining lands of the Louisiana purchase would be free states, not tolerating slavery, and all states south of the line would be slave states.

The Missouri Compromise was updated in 1850 when California wanted to enter the union. The state was so big that it would have been split by the line drawn by the Missouri Compromise. So, Congress decided that from then on, the population living in the territories applying for statehood should have the power to decide whether to be a free or a slave state. California in turn was allowed to enter as a free state. At the same time, the law also stated that Northern states had to return escaped slaves back to their owners in the Southern states.

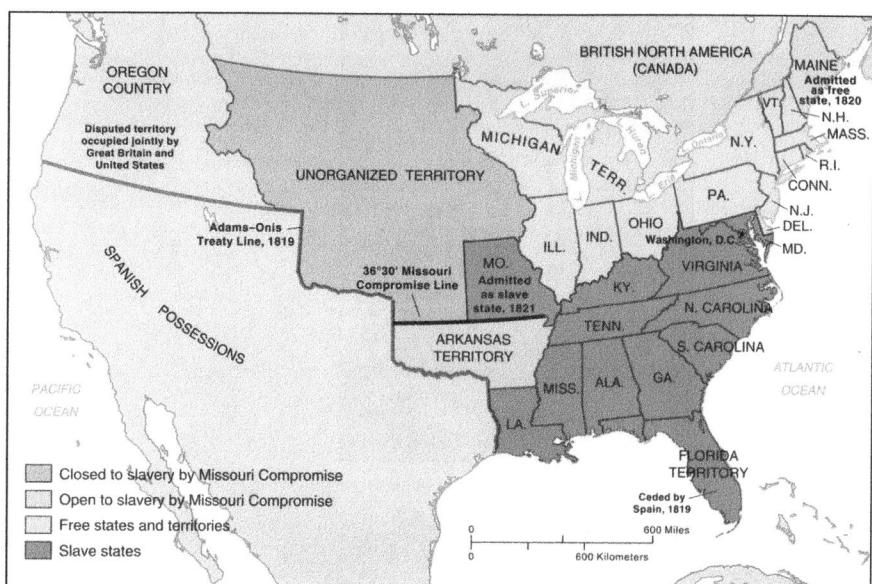

FIGURE 8-1:
The Missouri
Compromise.

Then in 1857, came the Dred Scott Decision, which propelled the country closer to Civil War.

Making a mistake

Dred Scott, seen in Figure 8-2, was a slave who had been taken from a slave state, Missouri, by his owner, to a free state, Illinois. When his owner returned home to Missouri, Scott argued that because he had lived in a free state, Illinois, he was now a free man and a U.S. citizen enjoying all the rights citizenship confers. After the Missouri courts had ruled against him, he appealed to the Supreme Court.

The Chief Justice of the Supreme Court, Roger Taney, came from a slaveholding Southern family. Under his direction, the Supreme Court ruled in a 7-2 decision against Scott. The ruling stated that people of African descent were not citizens of the U.S. and could never be so. Therefore, they could not claim any of the protections and privileges of the Constitution. Taney further added that the federal government does not have the power to make slaves citizens.

Finally, Taney ruled that Congress did not have the constitutional power to outlaw slavery in any state. With this decision, he overturned the Missouri Compromise (discussed above), which had restricted slavery to certain territories.

The Dred Scott decision was later overturned with the 13th, 14th and 15th Amendments to the Constitution. The Dred Scott decision is widely considered to be the worst decision in the history of the U.S. Supreme Court.

Achieving freedom

The question over slavery was finally settled by a bloody Civil War lasting from 1861 to 1865. After the North proved to be victorious, Congress added three amendments to the Constitution: the 13th, 14th, and 15th Amendments.

The 13th Amendment abolished slavery in the U.S. and its territories, whereas the 14th Amendment made anyone born or naturalized in the U.S. citizens of the country and contained both the Equal Protection Clause and the Due Process Clause (see Chapter 7 for a discussion of the 14th Amendment). Finally, the 15th Amendment gave former slaves the right to vote, stating that voting rights "shall not be denied . . . on account of race, color, or previous condition of servitude." Ironically, gender was not mentioned, and women continued to be disenfranchised.

Reconstructing a country

Reconstruction of the South began right after the Civil War had ended. The idea was to rebuild the South in the image of the North. Union troops were sent to the former Confederate states to enforce the new laws, especially those pertaining to former slaves. Former slaves got the right to own property and the right to vote, and ex-slaves were elected to Congress. At the same time, many Southerners were stripped of the right to vote, because they had collaborated with the Confederacy. Twenty-two black Americans were elected to the House of Representatives and two to the U.S. Senate. Congress passed several laws such as the 1875 Civil Rights Act, which made it illegal to discriminate in public accommodations. The Supreme Court overturned the law in 1883, stating that the federal government does not have the right to protect the invasion of civil rights by private individuals. So, restaurants, hotels, and theatres could freely discriminate if they wanted to do so.

When reconstruction ended in 1877 and the Northern troops left the South, many Southern states passed restrictions on voting for former slaves. These included the poll tax, literacy tests, the grandfather clause and later the white primary (discussed in Chapter 12). Further, the South started to resegregate and passed restrictions that did not allow former slaves to own land or guns and restricted their movements. By the late 1890s, voting restrictions were in place and segregation was back and even legalized in 1896 by the Supreme Court in the case of Plessy v. Ferguson.

Soon, blacks could not go to white schools, stay in white hotels, or eat in white sections of restaurants. They had their separate water fountains and even separate hospitals and doctors.

TECHNICAL STUFF

Homer Plessy, a man of mixed race, actually 7/8 white, boarded a whites-only first-class train cabin deliberately in 1892, in New Orleans, Louisiana. He wanted to challenge the Louisiana Separate Car Act, passed in 1890, which required separate accommodations on trains for blacks and whites in Louisiana. He was charged under the Act and after the Louisiana Supreme Court upheld his conviction, he appealed to the U.S. Supreme Court.

He argued that the Louisiana law was a violation of the 14th Amendment to the Constitution. In Plessy v. Feguson (1896), the U.S. Supreme Court, in a 7:1 decision, with one abstention, sided against him, stating that it was not unconstitutional to segregate if the facilities for both white and black citizens were equal. The U.S. Supreme Court, with this decision, established the "separate but equal doctrine" which legitimized segregation in the U.S. and allowed for the Southern states to legally reestablish segregation. Homer Plessy ended up paying a $25.00 fine.

One year later in 1898, in Williams v. Mississippi, the U.S. Supreme Court even ruled that both literacy tests and poll taxes were constitutional. This virtually disenfranchised blacks in the Southern states.

In addition, the black population faced constant threats by the Ku Klux Klan and white vigilante groups, which tried to keep them under control and denied them basic rights. Through constant intimidation, the Klan made sure that the black population remained intimidated and politically powerless.

REMEMBER

The Ku Klux Klan was founded in 1865 by former Confederate veterans who opposed reconstruction. They assaulted and murdered politically active black people, white Southerners who were sympathetic to black causes, and Northerners coming to the former Confederacy. The Klan was violently anti-black, anti-Semitic, and anti-Catholic. By the 1920s, it had several million members and several members of Congress proudly proclaimed membership in the Klan. After WWII, its membership and political power declined, and today its membership is down to about 6,000 people, according to the Southern Poverty Law Center, a nonprofit advocacy organization specializing in civil rights.

REMEMBER

African Americans were not the only ethnic group in the U.S. that was discriminated against. In California, in 1885, the state segregated Latin students from white students, a practice that continued into the 1950s. In addition, Congress passed laws limiting immigration from China and denied U.S. citizenship to Chinese already living in the U.S. In 1924, Congress even passed the National Origins Act, which stopped all immigration from Asia.

Moving up North

After WWI, many African Americans moved up North for open factory jobs. This is called the *great migration*. By the 1950s, forty percent of all African Americans in the U.S. were living in Northern states.

TECHNICAL STUFF

The National Association for the Advancement of Colored People (NAACP) was founded in 1909 to begin fighting segregation. The organization's activities included lobbying in Washington, D.C., and publicizing black grievances in the media. Most importantly, it battled segregation, mainly in the courtroom. Their first successes were in 1941 when President Roosevelt signed an executive order banning discrimination by defense contractors, and in 1948, when President Truman desegregated the U.S. military, making it the first integrated federal institution in the U.S.

A result of the New Deal era was the remaking of the Supreme Court by FDR. Serving for 12 years, he was able to put eight justices on the Supreme Court, creating a Supreme Court that was very sympathetic to civil rights. In 1944, the court struck down white primaries (see Chapter 12) and then slowly eliminated segregation in the U.S.

By 1954, segregation was over in law schools and graduate schools and interstate buses. Then, in 1954 the court ruled in Brown v. The Board of Education of Topeka that segregation in public schools was unconstitutional, ruling that separate educational facilities were inherently unequal and thus a violation of the equal protection clause of the 14th Amendment.

Oliver Brown lived in Topeka, Kansas, and tried to enroll his daughter into an all-white school in 1951. His daughter was refused admission. So, Mr. Brown sued, stating that segregation was unconstitutional. The Supreme Court ruled unanimously that racial segregation in public schools is unconstitutional because it violates the equal protection clause of the 14th Amendment, even if segregated facilities are comparable. According to the Court, segregation instilled a sense of inferiority in black children and is thus a violation of the 14th Amendment.

With this ruling, the U.S. Supreme Court desegregated public schools in the U.S. by striking down all state laws allowing for racial segregation in public education. The decision proved to be the first step towards racial integration in the country and spurred on the civil rights movement.

Integrating education

In 1954, the Supreme Court ruled that segregated schools violated the equal protection clause of the 14th Amendment and that the doctrine of separate but equal had no place in public education. The court, however, set no timetable to desegregate public schools, and by the mid-1960s, less than one percent of public schools in the former Confederacy had been integrated.

White Southerners vehemently objected to the court decision and attempted to block black students from attending public schools. The governor of Arkansas, Orval Faubus, even called out the National Guard to turn away the nine black students at Little Rock's central high school. He became a local hero.

President Eisenhower finally had to send the 101st Airborne to enforce the court order to integrate the school.

Starting The Civil Rights Movement

The civil rights movement began in December of 1955. Rosa Parks, seen in Figure 8-3, an African-American woman, was riding her bus home in Montgomery, Alabama, sitting in the colored section of the bus. The bus was packed, and when an additional white bus rider came on the bus, the bus driver called out that he needed another white row of seats. The black people sitting there were supposed to get up so that the white person could sit down. Rosa Parks did not and refused to give up her seat. She was arrested. The local NAACP chapter called for a boycott of the bus system and put a young pastor by the name of Martin Luther King in charge of the boycott. Martin Luther King soon became famous for his eloquent speeches and his pacifist philosophy of nonviolent civil disobedience.

FIGURE 8-3:
Rosa Parks.

John Mathew Smith/Flickr/CC BY-SA 2.0

Civil disobedience refers to opposing a law one considers unjust by peacefully disobeying the law and accepting the resulting punishment.

Martin Luther King had studied at the Crozer Theological Seminary in Chester, Pennsylvania and was there introduced to the pacifism of Mohandas Gandhi in India. Gandhi had used pacifist philosophy and actions to free his country from British rule.

King, seen in Figure 8-4, organized a new form of resistance, Christian non-violence. Using nonviolent civil disobedience, black and white students organized *sit-ins*. In February, 1960, four black students sat at a white lunch counter, and this form of protest spread soon to other segregated facilities throughout the country. In 1961, the *freedom rider movements* started, where black and white activists sat together on buses to protest segregation on bus lines.

Nonviolent disobedience reached new heights between 1963 and 1965. In 1963, in Birmingham, Alabama, police overreacted and violently attacked young peaceful marchers, many coming from churches. Some of the protesters were school-children, and police used firehoses and attack dogs against them. The whole affair was later viewed on television not just in the U.S. but around the world. The Democratic Party decided it had to act, even if that meant losing the Southern wing of the party, which supported continuing segregation. Finally, the Kennedy administration submitted civil rights legislation.

FIGURE 8-4:
Martin
Luther King.

Dick DeMarsico/Library of Congress/Public domain

Challenging the system

The following tactics have been used by civil rights groups to achieve their objectives:

>> **Legal Action.** The NAACP focused on legal challenges to segregation and discrimination. When legislative activities were not working, civil rights legislation usually stalled in committee in Congress, the courts proved to be receptive to challenges. The greatest success of the NAACP was the case of Brown v. Board of Education (1954), which desegrated public schools.

>> **Legal boycotts.** A good example is the boycott of the bus lines in Montgomery, Alabama, after the arrest of Rosa Parks. Black residents refused to ride public buses for over a year, almost bankrupting the bus system. Legal boycotts, especially economic boycotts, can work well.

>> **Civil disobedience.** Here you just do not obey the law. This method may result in fines and even arrests. A good example is Rosa Parks, who got arrested for not giving up a seat to a white passenger on a Montgomery bus.

>> **Legal Protests.** The idea behind protests is to bring a group's issues to public attention. Protests are usually covered by the media, and when the public becomes aware of an issue, it usually demands action. Recent examples include protests organized by the Black Lives Matter movement to call attention to social justice issues.

Passing a Civil and Voting Rights Act

After the bloody civil rights protest in Birmingham, Alabama, a march on Washington was organized in 1963. At this rally, Martin Luther King proclaimed his famous words in his "I Have a Dream" speech.

It was the assassination of President Kennedy in November of 1963 that sped up the process of the passage of the Civil Rights Act. After his death, there was a lot of goodwill towards Kennedy's legislative agenda, and President Lyndon Johnson pushed quickly to get the legislation passed. The Civil Rights Act of 1964 was landmark legislation that forbade discrimination on the basis of race, sex, religion, or national origin.

The Civil Rights Act made it illegal for local and state governments to discriminate in access to public facilities. The law further prohibited employers from discriminating in hiring on the basis of race, sex, religion, or national origin, and barred discrimination on the basis of race, sex, religion, or national origin in all public places, including privately owned ones such as private hotels, motels, theatres, restaurants, lunch counters, gas stations, stadiums, arenas, and lodging houses with more than five rooms. Further, the legislation withheld public funds from segregated schools. Within a decade, most public Southern schools were integrated.

Additions to the Civil Rights Act in 1968 banned discrimination in the sale and renting of housing.

The Johnson administration, after winning reelection in a massive landslide victory in 1964, which gave the Democratic Party full control of Congress, was now able to move forward. The administration knew that even without Southern support it could pass just about any legislation. The Voting Rights Act was thus passed in 1965. It protected the right to vote, struck down literacy tests, and allowed for federal observers in states where discrimination had been practiced in the past. The Voting Rights Act demanded that any kind of changes to voting laws or voting procedures needed to be approved in advance by the U.S. Department of Justice in states where discrimination had been practiced in the past. This was called a *preclearance*.

In 2013, in Shelby County v. Holder, the Supreme Court practically struck down the Voting Rights Act preclearance formula, which stated that a Southern state or locality must have any major changes to their voting laws or procedures approved in advance, by eliminating the coverage formula. This included voter-identification requirements, online voter registration, restrictions on early voting, and the number of polling stations. The court ruled that "Things have changed dramatically in the South since 1965" and preclearance was not necessary anymore.

The process of desegregation was slow and tedious. Why was this the case? First, Southern Democrats controlled many key Congressional positions and aligned themselves with conservative Republicans to block many proposed civil rights bills.

What changed? Public opinion was changing, and the white population, even in the Southern states, was becoming receptive to civil rights and desegregation. Second, violence against peaceful civil rights demonstrators changed public opinion, especially in the Northern part of the U.S. The 1963 Birmingham attacks on demonstrators shocked the public and were condemned by many. The March on Washington attended by 250,000 people and Martin Luther King's "I Have a Dream Speech" were positively seen by not just Americans but people all over the world.

Finally, there was President Kennedy's assassination, which resulted in the 1964 landslide election that sent huge Democratic majorities to Congress, mostly liberal Northern Democrats. Even though 88 percent of all Congressional Southern Democrats opposed the Civil Rights Act, it passed easily.

REMEMBER

Martin Luther King Jr. was assassinated on April 4, 1968, in Memphis, Tennessee. King was posthumously awarded the Presidential Medal of Freedom by President Carter, and his birthday became a national holiday in 1986 during the Reagan administration.

Dealing with affirmative action

Affirmative action refers to programs and laws designed to remedy past discriminatory hiring practices, government contracting, and school admissions. Between the 1970s and 1990s, government agencies and businesses actively used affirmative action to increase the number of minorities and women in the workforce and in college. For example, the number of women physicians doubled in the U.S. and the number of women lawyers and judges quadrupled. Affirmative action became one of the most controversial topics in the 1970s.

TECHNICAL
STUFF

Affirmative action is defined as laws or regulations that require a business, government agency, labor union, college, or university to take steps to increase the number of African Americans and other minorities or women in the organization.

REMEMBER

Reverse discrimination refers to using race to give preferential treatment to some people.

Many places put a quota system in place by which ethnic minorities and women receive a certain number of open seats or jobs from the start. This was labelled *reverse discrimination* and soon legal action challenged the practice.

A great example is the case of medical student Allan Bakke. He applied for medical school at the University of California, Davis. In total, there were 2664 applicants and 100 open slots. Bakke received an in-person interview and was told that he was a very desirable applicant. To his great surprise, he was not chosen for one of the open seats in 1973. He applied again in 1974 and was denied admission one more time. When he found out that in both instances, 16 applicants were admitted with a lower GPA and lower MCAT score because of a minority admission quota, he sued. He believed that it was a violation of the equal protection clause in the 14th Amendment to deny admission based on a racial quota.

The Supreme Court took the case and, in 1978, in Regents of the University of California v. Bakke, ruled that race can be taken into account for admission but that an official quota, in this case setting aside 16 out of 100 open seats for minorities, was unconstitutional. Bakke was finally admitted to medical school in 1978. The university was forced to pay his tuition, and he graduated as an anesthesiologist in 1982. He was 42 years old. He had a distinguished career at the Mayo Clinic in Minnesota and passed away in 2024.

Affirmative action continued to be a hot topic. In 1996, an initiative preventing state authorities from using affirmative action for a criterion in hiring or school admissions or granting preferential treatment based on race sex, color, or national origin was passed by the California public. Similar initiatives were subsequently passed in Michigan, Washington, and Nebraska.

In 2003, the Supreme Court ruled that the admission requirement for the University of Michigan was unconstitutional. The university had given a bonus of 20 points to each applicant if they were African-American, Hispanic, or Native American. 100 points were needed to get admitted. The Supreme Court ruled that giving points was too close to a quota. However, using race as a factor among many factors in school admission was upheld as late as 2016 in Fisher v. University of Texas at Austin et al.

Then in two cases in 2023, the U.S. Supreme Court ruled that taking race into consideration when determining admission to a university was a violation of the 14th Amendment to the Constitution and officially banned race as an admission requirement. The cases were Students for Fair Admissions v. Harvard and Students for Fair Admissions v. University of North Carolina.

Becoming More Powerful

Latinos have become the second largest ethnic group in the U.S. and have achieved majority status in states like New Mexico and Texas, where they have become the largest ethnic group, making up 40 percent of the population. They make up 19.5 percent of the population in the U.S. Back in 1980, they were 6.4 percent of the population. Latinos have also faced discrimination and segregation like African Americans, and still today they are likely to be poorer and less educated than their white counterparts, even though that is rapidly changing.

Especially in the political system, Latinos are underrepresented in state legislatures, Congress, and the federal court system. This will change over time. In Texas, for example, Latino voter turnout is currently low, but this is not because of legal restrictions. Latinos are the youngest ethnic group in Texas, and many are just too young to participate in politics. Studies have also shown that political participation increases with age and income. In addition, Latinos are the least-educated group in Texas, with almost a quarter not having a high school degree. Being educated is one of the major determinants of political participation. For these reasons, Latino political participation will increase in the foreseeable future.

In 1929, Hispanics established their counterpart to the NAACP, the League of United Latin American Citizens (LULAC). Similar to the NAACP, LULAC uses the legal system to battle segregation and discrimination. For example, in Mendez v. Westminster in 1947, the U.S. Court of Appeals for the 9th circuit in California struck down Latino racial segregation in schools in Orange County, California.

Having Special Status

Native Americans are in a special category of their own. They have faced extermination and then discrimination over the last four centuries. When the European colonists arrived, there were about 10 million Native Americans living in the U.S. Today, that is down to 2.93 million, but the numbers are growing.

After having been decimated by disease and war and having been pushed out of their ancestral lands to make space for white settlers, the Supreme Court in 1831 gave Indian tribes domestic dependent status, which means that they enjoy full sovereignty on their tribal lands but have to remain a part of the U.S. It was not until 1924 that Congress passed the Indian Citizenship Act, which made Native Americans citizens of the U.S., giving them civil rights. Today, about half of all Native Americans still live on reservations. These reservations are not controlled by the states they are in, but are subject to federal law. The Bureau of Indian Affairs, a part of the Department of the Interior, is responsible for Native American issues.

Today, Native American poverty rates are twice as high as the rest of the population. They suffer from low educational levels, high infant mortality rates, and low life expectancy.

However, many Indian tribes have been able to take advantage of their lack of regulation by state laws when it comes to gaming. The Supreme Court even ruled in 1987 that reservations are exempt from state prohibitions on gaming. For this reason, about half of all the 565 tribes in the U.S. run casinos. These casinos generated $41.9 billion in 2023, which was used for social programs and economic expansion. Forty-five percent of all gaming revenue in the U.S. is generated by Indian casinos today.

Finally Getting Rights

Until the early 20th century, women had no rights in the U.S. They could not vote, serve on juries, or enter into any kind of legal contract after marriage. A woman's husband controlled her property. By the mid-1840s, women had enough. In 1848, the Seneca Fall Convention, the first convention dedicated to women's rights, was held. By the 1870s, the women's rights movement grew in momentum. The Women's Christian Temperance Union, which wanted to outlaw alcohol because it resulted in domestic violence, also asked for the right to vote and for higher wages for working women. At the same time, the American Woman Suffrage Association focused on winning the right to vote at the state level.

Women often face what is called *compounded* or *intersectional discrimination,* which occurs when a person experiences discrimination based on two different characteristics. For example, a black female can face discrimination on the basis of race and gender.

REMEMBER

In 1869, Wyoming was the first state to give women the right to vote, and Utah followed suit in 1870.

WWI changed women's roles in U.S. society. With the U.S. entering the war in 1917, suddenly more women were brought into the workforce to take the place of men who had gone off to war. This increased the pressure for women's rights, and President Wilson (1913-1921) supported women's suffrage as a war-time measure. The 19th Amendment to the Constitution was introduced, and women received the right to vote after the states ratified it by 1920. It took women over 60 years to catch up with men in voting, and today they are more likely to vote than men. (See Figure 8-5.)

National Photo Company Collection/Library of Congress/Public domain

FIGURE 8-5: Women demonstrating for the Bristow-Mondell Federal Suffrage amendment, which would have given women the right to vote in 1914.

The Civil Rights Act of 1964 proved beneficial for women, too. It was now illegal to discriminate on the basis of race, ethnicity, gender, and national origin, not just in public areas but also employment.

The Equal Employment Opportunity Commission, which monitors compliance with the Civil Rights Act, was established in 1964, and women organized into NOW, the National Organization for Women in 1966, to push for equality. In 1972, Congress passed the Equal Rights Amendment stating "Equality of Rights . . . shall not be denied or abridged . . . on the account of sex." By 1977, the ERA was short only three states to be ratified, but conservative opposition, stating that many women want to be mothers and housewives, stopped the amendment. By 1982, when the ratification period ended, only 35 states had ratified the amendment; 38 were needed to pass the amendment.

TECHNICAL STUFF

After the deadline for ratification for the Equal Rights Amendment had expired in 1982, three more states ratified it. In 2020, Virginia became the 38th state to ratify it. With the ERA being expired, the courts have decided that it needs to be reintroduced by Congress to be reconsidered.

There has been much progress on women's rights in the U.S. since the 19th Amendment was ratified in 1920. Four out of nine justices on the Supreme Court are women. Women are more likely to receive bachelor's degrees than men today. In addition, two women representing one of the major parties have run for the presidency, Hillary Clinton and Kamala Harris, and women have held the position of Speaker of the House and vice-president. By 2025, 125 women were in the House of Representatives and 26 (16 Democrats and 10 Republicans) in the Senate. Back in 1970, fifty years after women gained the right to vote, only 2 percent of all members of the House of Representatives were women.

Achieving equality

It was not until the 1960s that gay Americans openly asked for political equality. Suddenly, there were protests to draw attention to their cause. However, no anti-discrimination legislation followed, and many states continued to criminalize homosexual behavior. The Supreme Court left it up to the states to regulate gay rights, and many states, especially in the South, made certain intimate behaviors illegal. It was not until 2003, in Lawrence v. Texas, that the Supreme Court legalized same-sex partners engaging in certain types of intimate relations. In 2015, in Obergefell v. Hodges, the U.S. Supreme Court then found same-sex marriage constitutional, ruling that a fundamental right to marry was guaranteed by the 14th Amendment.

Today, the Supreme Court seems to have settled on the following policy: Sexual-orientation cases are treated differently depending on whether they involve private or public areas. For example, the court ruled in the case of 303 Creative LLC v. Elenis in 2023 that private business can discriminate against gay people but public institutions, such as governmental organizations, public universities, or agencies providing public welfare benefits, must ensure gay Americans enjoy the same rights as heterosexual U.S. citizens do.

In 2004, Massachusetts became the first state to legalize same-sex marriage.

REMEMBER

Getting more rights

In 1990, the U.S. Congress passed the Americans with Disabilities Act. The Act extended many of the protections given to racial minorities and women to disabled persons. For example, disabled Americans cannot be denied employment or promotion if reasonable accommodation is needed. *Reasonable accommodation* refers to employers providing only accommodations that would not cause undue hardship on the employer. Disabled people cannot be denied access to government programs and new public accommodations. New buildings or modes of transportation such as buses, trains, and taxis must be accessible to those in wheelchairs.

Disabled people must have full and equal access to hotels, restaurants, stores, school museums, and so on. To achieve equal access, existing facilities must be altered where possible and new facilities must be made accessible.

Most of these rights are, however, dependent on undue hardship or excessive cost. For example, making a 200-year-old building accessible for disabled people in wheelchairs would not be required but a brand-new building must be wheelchair-accessible.

4

Making Policy: What a Government Must Do

Discover various economic theories and see how they have influenced policymaking. Then observe the complex process of making a budget and be surprised how many agencies are involved.

Learn about the history of social security and observe President Johnson's Great Society programs, which gave the U.S. Medicare and Medicaid.

Investigate U.S. foreign trade relations and become familiar with the concept of globalization.

See who makes American foreign policy and observe the kind of powers the president has in foreign policymaking.

Study presidential doctrines and observe how they have impacted American foreign policy.

Chapter **9**

Making Public Policy

Public policy comes in various forms. It includes fiscal policy, monetary policy, social policy, and foreign policy (discussed in Chapter 10).

Policymaking includes the making of laws, passing of regulations, and even conducting military actions. Making policy is a long process involving many actors. Actors involved in making of public policy in the U.S. include Congress, the president, and the bureaucracy that implements policy (see Chapter 6). Being able to implement policy also gives the bureaucracy the power to shape policy. If there is a conflict involving policymaking actors or the actual policy implemented, the judiciary gets involved. However, it does not stop here.

Interest groups (see Chapter 15) and think tanks are involved in the early stages of policymaking and so is the media. The media highlights certain policy issues, and responds to public concern . . . As soon as the public is involved, political parties and politicians begin to take note.

Studying Economic Theories

The role of the government in the economy has been an ongoing discussion in U.S. politics. As early as the founding of the republic in 1789, politicians clashed on what the proper role of government in the U.S. economy should be.

The majority of our Founding Fathers followed the ideas of Adam Smith (see Figure 9-1) set out in his seminal work "The Wealth of Nations." In his work, Smith argues for a small government with a limited role in the economy. Smith believes that it is up to the free market to run the economy and not the government. Government's role needs to be restricted to making sure that the free market can work undisturbed. In his work, Smith argues that the government has only three major roles to perform in the economy:

>> **The government has to provide for the defense of the country.** With the world full of enemies, a nation must be able to protect itself to survive in the long term. The free market cannot perform this function, so the government needs to step in and set up a military to provide protection for a country.

>> **The government has to set up laws to allow the free market to function freely.** Economic transactions cannot freely occur in a society with no laws and lots of violence. If an economic transaction occurs, the person selling a good must be assured that this is a protected action. No stealing or forcibly obtaining a good can be allowed. If this is not the case, who would buy a good when they could just steal it?

>> **The government must provide an infrastructure so that economic transactions can take place.** A working economy has to have roads, canals, and other parts of an infrastructure. Goods must be able to be shipped to markets to be sold, and people have to be able to travel to places to sell and purchase goods.

FIGURE 9-1:
Adam Smith.

Library of Congress/Public Domain

So, there has to be a government, but it must be quite limited, according to Smith. Government has no right to interfere with the market or restrict it. This is called *laissez-faire liberalism, or classical liberalism.*

When applying Smith's ideas to international economics, economists argue that free trade between nations will lead to an increase in wealth for those nations. It should be the free market that determines international trade and not governments. So, a government should not implement barriers to free trade such as tariffs or other trade barriers.

Believing in mercantilism

Mercantilism is one of the oldest economic theories in the world. It was the dominant theory from the 15th until the 18th century. Unlike economic liberalism, it believes that politics and economics are related and indeed dependent on each other. Economics is a tool to serve the government. It can help countries to get wealthier and more powerful. All economic actions are designed to enhance the power of a country, which in turn guarantees security in the world today.

For a mercantilist, international trade and economic relations are designed to increase a country's wealth and power. Therefore, economic dependence on another country is unacceptable because it undermines a country's power. A great country cannot be dependent on another country for an important commodity such as steel, which is necessary for the defense industry.

Tariffs are needed to protect vital industries, and the domestic market needs to be protected to shelter some of these vital industries. Government intervention to protect the economy is necessary for the survival of the country. Currently, many of President Trump's economic policies are quite mercantilist in nature.

Bringing about state capitalism

This brings us to *state capitalism*, a variant of mercantilism. Also referred to as *etatism*, which means *statism* in French, the economic theory has staged quite a comeback in recent years. Countries such a Hungary, France, and even the U.S. under President Trump have started to apply parts of it.

This economic theory believes that the government has the right to intervene in the domestic economy for the good of the country. As the term implies, it is the state, the country, that matters most, and private industry should do what is best for the country. Profit should not be the ultimate decision-maker; industry should do what is good for a people. For example, producing automobile parts in Mexico might be more profitable for the U.S. auto industry but it needs to be done in the

U.S. to allow for American workers to benefit. If domestic industries are threatened by foreign competition, often unfair, the U.S. government cannot just sit by; it has to protect native industries. This can be accomplished using tariffs and other voluntary trade restrictions. It needs to be pointed out, however, that the government does not outright own property, except for a few select industries, and that making a profit is legal in state capitalism, even though on occasion country trumps profits.

Implementing Keynesianism

Keynesianism is an economic theory named for British economist Lord Maynard Keynes, seen in Figure 9-2. It is also called *demand-side economics* because it focuses on the demand side in an economy. For Keynes, demand determines whether an economy is growing or declining and whether government intervention is needed.

FIGURE 9-2:
Lord Maynard
Keynes.

Bettmann/Bettmann/Getty Images

During the Great Depression, demand for goods had collapsed in the U.S. So Keynes advocated that the government focus on stimulating demand. This was done through the implementation of the welfare state and public works programs. Suddenly, with social security and unemployment benefits, the elderly and the unemployed had money to spend. So did workers employed by public works programs. People spending money increased demand for goods and services, and industry began to produce more goods as a result. Producing more required hiring more workers, so unemployment went down. In addition, Keynes advocated for tax cuts and low interest rates to provide the public with more spending money. All of these policies stimulated demand.

However, over time, the public suddenly made too much money and businesses producing goods could not keep up with demand anymore. Too much demand results in inflation and so the price of goods went up. People could afford less, and production of goods declined. As a result, people got laid off and unemployment rose. This in turn resulted in even less demand and it was time for the government to come in one more time and stimulate demand.

Now, Keynes never advocated continuous government spending to prop up demand. He knew that would result in increasing government deficits. For this reason, he advocated that during good times, with an economy booming and the danger of inflation rearing its ugly head, government had to step in to take money from the people. So taxes and interest rates were raised to take money from the public. This allowed for government to accrue more in revenue, which it could use to pay off its debt.

Taking a look at supply-side economics

Supply-side economics is an alternative to Keynesianism that became popular in the 1980s during the Reagan administration. It argues that instead of increasing government spending to combat economic problems, government should stop spending to increase demand for goods. Instead, it needs to focus on supply in the economy. Supply-side economics advocates for cutting taxes so that more money is in the economy. Because high taxes take money out of the economy, cutting taxes, puts more money into the economy. That will spur investment and increase production, creating new jobs, lowering unemployment, and stimulating the economy even more. Thus, a government needs to cut taxes and reduce spending, which will also allow it to balance the budget in the long run. Both Presidents Reagan and Trump ran on cutting taxes and actually implemented tax cuts while in office.

Coming Up with a Budget

In 1789, Congress passed its first revenue-generating bill. Back then, income taxes did not exist; the whole federal government's revenue came from tariffs. *Tariffs* are taxes on foreign goods. Up until the Civil War, tariffs financed most of the federal government. This would slowly change after the Civil War when the federal government started charging payroll taxes and corporate taxes, and then, with the passage of the 16th Amendment in 1913, everything changed in the U.S. Federal income taxes were legalized.

The 16th Amendment authorized Congress to tax a person's increase in wealth whether it comes from wages, benefits, bonuses, or any other form of income. Today, the federal income tax is the major source of income for the federal government. The U.S. uses *progressive income taxation*, where the tax rate increases as a person's income increases. A *regressive tax* charges everybody the same rate regardless of income. So, the poorest and the richest pay the same tax rate. A sales tax is considered a regressive tax.

In 2024, the federal government spent 6.74 trillion on thousands of programs. These programs included well-known programs such as social security, Medicare, and Medicaid, as well as lesser-known programs such as the space program. These programs also include the defense budget, spending on infrastructure such as bridges and highways, and even monies for the endowment for the arts and humanities. The federal budget is huge and determines how the government spends its money. Not surprisingly, the debate over the budget is often bitter and partisan.

Analyzing the history of the federal budget

Scholars divide the history of budgeting in the U.S. into three different eras. Since 1789, there have been three distinct periods:

>> **A period of legislative dominance.** It lasts from 1789 until 1921, and it saw Congress being in control over the budget.

>> **A period of presidential control of the budget.** This lasted from 1921 until 1974.

>> **A period of Congress challenging the president one more time,** resulting in constant infighting between the executive and legislative branches over the budget.

The fiscal year for the federal government runs from October 1 until the following September 30.

Seeing legislative dominance

The Constitution of the U.S. gives Congress the power to raise funds through taxation and the power to appropriate, or spend, money. Congress took full advantage of this until 1921. The Constitution is very vague about how the budgeting process should work. It states that all money Congress intends to spend must come from appropriations bills and that Congress must account for the money it spends. Further, the Constitution mentions that all expenditures must be made for the general welfare of the U.S. and that military appropriations expire in two years. That is about it.

Why is the Constitution so vague on budgeting? The reason is actually quite simple: the practice of budgeting had not been invented yet. The current budget process was conceived in Europe in the 19th century and was not imported into the U.S. until the 20th century.

The Constitution does require that all spending bills originate in the House of Representatives and are then sent to the Senate. Also, all spending was to be put into one bill with the objective being a balanced budget, which is, however, not required. Following the Civil War, Congress established appropriations committees in both houses and the president stayed out of financial affairs.

Taking over

After WWI, Congressional spending skyrocketed, and the annual budget went from $725 million annually to $19 billion by 1920. Suddenly, Congress had accrued a debt of over $26 billion. In response, Congress decided to bring the president into the budgeting fold. In 1921, it passed the Budget and Accounting Act, which created a presidential budgeting process. Now it is the president who has to submit an annual budget to Congress. Congress now reacts to the presidential budget instead of creating its own, as before.

With this newfound power, presidents began to slowly set the agenda for the country. It was FDR who used it to shape policy and set budget priorities. He used his newfound budgetary powers to spend enormously on programs such as his New Deal agenda items, including social security, and later WWII. By the time he died in office in 1945, the country was in massive debt. Then, in the 1960s, Lyndon Johnson started his Great Society programs, including Medicare and Medicaid, and the country went even further in debt.

Creating the Office of Management and Budget (OMB)

The Office of Management and Budget (OMB) was originally created as the Bureau of the Budget in 1921 and renamed in 1970. It is responsible for putting together the president's budget but also monitors Congressional spending and spending proposals. The OMB consists of about 500 employees and is housed in the executive office of the president. Interestingly, the employees are a mix of political appointees, mostly at the top-executive level, and career nonpartisan civil servants. The OMB serves many functions, including providing an estimate of revenue and spending, reviewing budget requests by other executive agencies, and assessing the effectiveness of federal programs.

Having conflict

By the 1960s, conflict between Congress and the president broke out over the budget. President Johnson's Great Society programs, such as Medicare and Medicaid, and the Vietnam War put the country into increasing debt. So, Congress passed the Congressional Budget and Impoundment Act of 1974, which brought Congress back into the budgetary process. Congress now gave itself the power to come up with its own budget resolutions and could set spending and revenue goals. It also established the Congressional Budget Office (CBO), which provides Congress with both an economic analysis and budget recommendations. Finally, Congress no longer had to rely on the president's office for budget estimates. Now both legislative and executive branches have a say in budgeting. This has resulted in infighting, bargaining, and extreme partisanship. The budgeting process has become slow and acrimonious.

Making a budget

The budgetary process starts in early February when the President hands Congress a budget for the upcoming fiscal year beginning October 1. The presidential budget contains spending proposals for thousands of programs. It is the OMB that puts the proposal together, receiving financial requests from all federal agencies. Of course, the proposal is just a proposal. Congress can reject it, ignore it, build upon it, or pass it.

While the White House is busy preparing its budget, Congress is doing the same. Both houses of Congress come up with a budget resolution, which then must be passed by both houses. This usually involves bargaining and compromising on both sides, House and Senate. If they agree on a resolution, it must be passed by both the House of Representatives and the Senate. This joint resolution, which outlines Congressional targets for spending and revenue creation, is not binding but shows Congressional budgetary expectations. The joint resolution is supposed to be passed by April 15, which rarely happens.

Congress then has until September 1 to pass all 12 spending (appropriation) bills, which also rarely happens. If they are not passed on time, they are combined into one giant spending bill. If this bill is also not passed, Congress can pass a continuing resolution. This only happens when no national budget has been approved before the start of the new fiscal year on October 1. The resolution extends spending at the current level for a prescribed period of time. The last time all 12 spending bills were passed on time was in 1995.

A government shutdown occurs when Congress does not pass funding legislation before a fiscal year begins. The government now has to stop activities and services not deemed essential. The first government shutdown happened in 1980, and by 2024, nine more had occurred. The longest government shutdown occurred in 2018/2019 during the first Trump administration when the Congress and the president could not agree on building more barriers on the U.S.-Mexico border. The government was shut down for 35 days.

Government shutdowns can be temporarily avoided by Congress passing a continuing resolution, which extends current funding for a set period.

TECHNICAL STUFF

Budget reconciliation is a parliamentary procedure that can be used to expedite the passage of federal budget legislation in the Senate. It was created in 1974 in the Congressional Budget Act, and the procedure overrides the filibuster in the Senate. Instead of 60 votes, reconciliation bills can be passed with a simple majority of 51 votes. Although the reconciliation procedure also applies to the House of Representatives, it has less meaning there because the House does not use the filibuster. Because of more partisan fighting in Congress, budget reconciliation has assumed a greater meaning today. Famous recent bills using budget reconciliation include President Biden's American Rescue Plan Act of 2021 and President Trump's One Big Beautiful Bill Act of 2025.

Studying Public Policy

The student of public policy focuses on fiscal policy, monetary policy, social policy, and foreign policy. Government policy regarding spending and taxing is referred to as *fiscal policy*. Policy in regard to unemployment and inflation is termed *monetary policy*, and policy helping the public is referred to as *social policy*.

Today, citizens of a country tend to judge their government by economic performance. The better the economy, the more likely the government gets reelected. If the economy takes a nosedive, voters are angry and vote a government out of office. Bill Clinton and Barack Obama's presidencies are considered successful because the economy did well, while Joe Biden saw his economy hit with high inflation, which doomed the presidential run of his successor, Vice-President Kamala Harris. For this reason, public policy can make or break a presidency.

Dabbling with fiscal policy

As previously mentioned, the U.S. government started out small. Presidents and especially Congress believed in a small, limited government with a laisse-faire attitude. Government had only a few functions and mostly left the economy alone.

All of this changed in the 1930s with the Great Depression and, later on, WWII and the Cold War. A larger military and economic disaster required more revenue, so tax collections went up. Very expensive New Deal programs such as social security and unemployment benefits as well as public works projects cost billions. Government began to spend and even borrow money. Fiscal policy became a policy tool. After WWII, U.S. policy leaders became used to employing tax-and-spend policies to guide the economy. Both parties did practice it, with one major difference. Whereas Democratic politicians advocated for spending to stimulate the economy, usually on social programs, Republican politicians advocated for lowering taxes to stimulate the economy.

REMEMBER

Fiscal policy refers to tax-and-spend policies undertaken by the government to affect a country's national economic development.

Using monetary policy

Monetary policy differs from fiscal policy. It refers to the government manipulating the national money supply. Being able to control the supply and price of money allows the government to deal with both inflation and unemployment.

The government can control the money supply through the Federal Reserve System, established in 1913, which consists of 12 banks around the country and is headed by the Federal Reserve Board.

This independent agency acts as the central bank of the U.S. The Federal Reserve sets the discount rate at which all other banks can borrow short-term funds. With a high discount rate, banks can borrow more cheaply, which means that they can lend money to customers at a lower rate. This allows for the Federal Reserve to control interest rates in the U.S. In addition, the Federal Reserve sets the rate of how much money banks have to retain. In other words, the Federal Reserve determines how much in liquid assets each bank must keep in hand to back customers' loans. This determines how much banks can lend to customers.

By using the national money supply, it is possible to impact interest rates, which can stimulate or deflate an economy. By releasing more money into an economy, the government can stimulate the economy, but in the end, this can cause inflation. To combat inflation, the government takes money out of circulation. This can be done through higher interest rates. Lower interest rates allow people to have more money, and they can buy more. Higher interest rates, on the other hand, can reduce purchasing power, and people end up buying less, resulting in low inflation. Look at mortgage rates. When mortgage rates are low, people can afford to buy houses and the housing market is booming. When interest rates are high, fewer people can afford houses, and demand for houses goes down.

Monetary policy refers to the government's central bank, the Federal Reserve, manipulating the money supply, in turn stimulating or cooling down an economy.

Making Social Policy

Public policy comes in various forms. There is fiscal and monetary policy, which deals with issues such as monetary supply and the budget. Then there is foreign policy, which is covered in Chapter 10. Finally, there is social policy, which refers to public policies designed to help with individual and societal well-being.

In the early years of the republic, no social safety net was in place in the U.S. If a person was sick, there were no doctors or hospitals available unless you could pay for them. If you were old and could not take care of yourself and had no family, you had to go to a poor house where you lived in miserable conditions waiting to die. The unemployed were forced to work or went to jail. The term *poor relief* was a common phrase in the U.S. into the 20th century.

A *welfare state* is a social system in which government assumes responsibility for its citizens in the areas of healthcare, education, and retirement. The welfare state guarantees its citizens a safety net and subsistence survival. All modern democracies and even some non-democratic systems have welfare states in place. Some are better than others.

The U.S. did not have a welfare state in place until the 1930s. It was FDR's New Deal programs, such as social security and unemployment benefits, that gave the U.S. its first welfare state. However, unlike the democracies in Europe, the U.S. has never implemented public health insurance. In the U.S., people get private health insurance and then pick doctors without government interference. This changed a bit in 2010 when the U.S. received Obamacare, discussed later in the chapter.

The Patient Protection and Affordable Care Act of 2010 (Obamacare) mandated that all uninsured Americans bought health insurance or pay a fine. They could just buy insurance from private companies, or they could buy it from an insurance marketplace provided by the federal government. This individual mandate was later dropped.

Getting social security

In 1929, the Great Depression struck. Millions of Americans were suddenly unemployed, families were starving, and the elderly could not take care of themselves anymore. They were the first to be laid off, to use up their sparse savings, and their families were too poor to take care of them. The incoming administration of President Franklin Delano Roosevelt (FDR) decided it had to act to help the U.S. public. For this reason, it implemented extensive federal social welfare policies as a part of the administration's New Deal agenda. The most important policy was social security, as seen in Figure 9-3. It was designed for the elderly to receive monthly pay checks so that they would not starve after retirement.

FIGURE 9-3:
President Roosevelt signing the Social Security Act.

Library of Congress/Public domain

The program was implemented in 1935 and provided Americans sixty-five and older who had lived in the U.S. for at least five years a monthly living stipend. A reduced social security stipend could be had if a person retired at sixty-two, and a larger stipend was available if the person worked until seventy.

TECHNICAL STUFF

Social security benefits vary with income. If a worker has a higher income throughout their lives they will receive more in benefits than someone who made less. Currently, a person retiring at 67 and making $100,000 a year receives $2,163 in monthly social security income.

Social security is financed through a payroll tax on both employees and employers. If a person makes $100,000, they will pay 6.2 percent of their income into the social security fund. So will their employer. In other words, your employer matches your contribution. Overall, social security receives $12,400 from both employer and employee combined annually if a worker makes $100,000 a year. If workers are self-employed, they will have to pay the full $12,400 themselves.

The maximum taxable social security income was $176,100 annually in 2025 and if a person's income tops this level, no additional social security tax is collected by the government.

The Social Security Act further provided for unemployment insurance, paid benefits to disabled workers and their families, and provided assistance to low-income families with children.

REMEMBER

In 2024, social security paid out $1.6 trillion to about 69 million Americans. For close to forty percent of retired people, social security is their only source of income.

Social security has become the largest federal program today. Social security is rapidly approaching a level where the program cannot function as-is. Too many people are retiring, and not enough young workers are contributing funds anymore. In addition, people are living longer so they take out more money than they contributed into the social security fund, resulting in deficits.

Back in the 1930s when social security was created, life expectancy was about 63, so social security made huge surpluses because most people would pass before they could take advantage of the program. Today, life expectancy is 78 years. Most people retire at full retirement age at 67 or even earlier at 62, so they end up getting more money back than they put into social security. Over time, this results in a deficit in the social security fund. To make up for this deficit, some members of Congress have therefore recommended that the retirement age be increased to either 69 or 70.

Unemployment benefits were a part of the original Social Security Act. Unemployment had topped 25 percent in the U.S. in the 1930s; in many industrial cities, it was as high as 80 percent. For this reason, the Social Security Act included a provision for joint federal-state unemployment benefits funded similarly to social security. The program was funded through a payroll tax on employers, and the states administer the programs with funding assistance by the federal government, if required.

Creating Medicare

In the early 1960s, an interesting discrepancy existed in the U.S. The country was considered to be the wealthiest country in the world, but half of all senior citizens had no health insurance. Many could not afford treatment and medicines and lived in poverty because of medical expenses. To remedy this situation, the Democratic-controlled Congress passed the Medicare Act of 1965 as an amendment to the Social Security Act of 1935. As with social security and unemployment benefits, Medicare is financed through payroll deductions. Implemented in 1966, the program grew rapidly. Almost 67.3 million people receive Medicare benefits today, and the costs have risen to almost 1.2 trillion annually.

Adding Medicaid

Medicaid is a companion program to Medicare. It was also created by the Social Security Amendments of 1965 and was designed for low income and disabled citizens who cannot afford to pay into Medicare. Every state was asked to participate in it; Arizona was the last one to sign on in 1982.

Medicaid helps about 78.1 million Americans. Obamacare extended Medicaid to people below 138 percent of the poverty line. However, after being challenged in court, the Supreme Court ruled that it was up to the states to decide whether to expand the program. 39 out of 50 states have accepted the expansion of Medicaid so far. 78.1 million people relied on Medicaid in 2025, and it cost the government $914 billion. 64 percent of Medicaid costs are paid by the federal government and 36 percent by the states.

Recently, nursing home coverage and dental care have been added to Medicaid.

Passing the Patient Protection and Affordable Care Act of 2010

In 2010, under the leadership of President Obama, seen in Figure 9-4, Congress passed the Patient Protection and Affordable Care Act. It is more commonly referred to as Obamacare, a term President Obama himself used for the Act. The bill was passed in Congress without one Republican vote, setting up a bitter partisan debate for over a decade.

Obamacare made several important changes to the U.S. healthcare system. It mandated for Americans to have health insurance or pay a penalty to the government. This was called the *individual mandate*. At the same time, Obamacare expanded Medicaid and created health insurance exchanges from which people could buy insurance at a discount while receiving subsidies from the government to offset some of the insurance expenses. It further stipulated that children could remain on their parents' insurance until they turned 26 and required insurance to offer preventative screenings and procedures for free. Finally, not one person could be denied health insurance coverage for preexisting conditions.

Obamacare was successful in reducing the rate of the uninsured, seeing it drop from 18.5 percent to 10.5 percent. At the same time, premiums increased for many of the Obamacare health insurance plans, making them unaffordable for many people. Although the public is split on Obamacare, it supports many of its parts. Being able to keep your children on your insurance until they are 26 has proven to be very popular, as has the elimination of preexisting conditions as a factor when buying health insurance.

FIGURE 9-4: President Obama signing the Patient Protection and Affordable Care Act in 2010.

Nancy Pelosi/Flickr/CC BY 2.0/https://www.flickr.com/photos/speakerpelosi/4458512106/Last accessed on Last accessed on October 06, 2025

In 2017, newly elected President Trump tried to repeal Obamacare but the vote to eliminate it failed in the Senate when three Republican Senators voted to keep it. However, the individual mandate, penalizing people for not having health insurance, was repealed, and since 2019 no more penalties exist.

Spending the Taxpayers' Money

In 2024, government spending equaled $6.75 trillion whereas GDP sat at 28.83 trillion. *Gross domestic product*, or *GDP*, is an estimate of the total monetary value of all goods and service produced in the U.S. in a one-year period. In March 2025, the GDP of the U.S. was estimated to hit $30.5 trillion. It is the largest GDP in the world. China ranks second with a GDP of about 19.2 trillion and Germany ranks third with a GDP of about 5 trillion.

On the negative side, the current national debt in September of 2025, is $37.45 trillion. In 2025, government has spent about 4.85 trillion so far and is expected to top $7 trillion in annual spending. With this kind of spending the debt ceiling imposed by Congress will soon be reached.

The *debt ceiling* is a law established by the Public Debt Acts of 1939 and 1941, which limit how much the federal government can borrow. The laws have been amended multiple times to increase the debt ceiling. Since 2002, the federal government has been running budget deficits and had to consistently borrow more money. When the debt ceiling is reached, the government must stop borrowing, possibly defaulting on financial obligations. This could put the country into an economic recession.

In June of 2023, President Biden suspended the debt ceiling temporarily until December 31, 2024. Currently, President Trump is asking to eliminate the debt ceiling permanently. The debt ceiling stood 36.1 trillion in January 2025 and was raised to 41.1 trillion by President Trump's One Big Beautiful Bill Act.

It is the U.S. Constitution that gives Congress the ability to create a federal budget, by which it determines how much money the government can spend over the course of the upcoming fiscal year. In the budget, Congress decides how much discretionary spending and how much mandatory spending occurs.

Federal money comes from tax collections and borrowing. The federal government spends money on programs and goods that support both the U.S. economy and the U.S. public, as seen in Figure 9-5. In addition, money must be spent on interest on borrowed monies and the more debt the government gets into, the more it has to spend paying interest on it. To make matters worse, the federal government spends more annually than it collects in revenue, and so the debt increases over time.

REMEMBER

A budget deficit is the amount of money spent annually over what the government collects in revenue every year. In 2024, the budget deficit was $1.8 trillion, and the deficit forecast for 2025 is $1.9 trillion.

What does the federal government spend its money on? There are entitlement programs such as social security and Medicare as well as infrastructure such as highways and bridges, the military, and both military and civilian research. There are three types of spending: mandatory, discretionary, and supplemental.

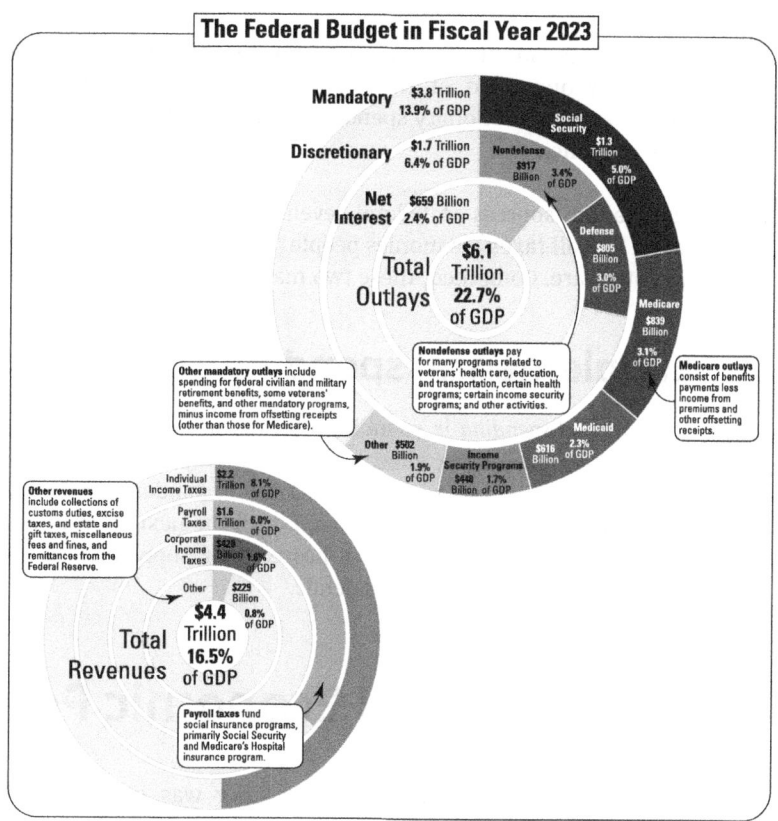

FIGURE 9-5: The federal budget in fiscal year 2023.

Mandatory spending

Mandatory spending represents about two-thirds of federal government spending. This type of spending does not need an annual vote by Congress on the money being spent. It already has been previously allocated. Mandatory spending is also known as *direct spending*, and as the term implies it is mandated by existing law. This spending includes entitlement programs such as social security and Medicare and payments to state and local governments. These payments were previously authorized, and Congress will pay them until it changes the law. For example, social security was authorized back in 1935 with the Social Security Act and was amended last in 2019.

Discretionary spending

Discretionary spending, on the other hand, is money formally approved by Congress and the president during the annual appropriations process. This money must be approved annually. Congress has the power to modify or even eliminate this type of spending. So, the battles over the budget one watches on television are only over one-third of the budget. The other two-thirds are untouchable. Examples of discretionary spending include defense spending and the funding of federal agencies.

REMEMBER

The leading sources of federal revenue are personal income taxes and payroll taxes. Payroll taxes are monies people pay out of their paycheck for social security and Medicare. Combined, these two make up 85 percent of federal revenue.

Supplemental spending

Supplemental spending is spending that occurs after the budget has been passed and monies have been allocated. Occasionally, programs suddenly run out of money or emergencies such as the COVID-19 pandemic arise and government has to spend money fast and cannot wait until the next appropriations bill is passed. In 2020, for example, Congress passed four supplemental appropriations bills dealing with the COVID-19 pandemic.

Making International Economic Policy

The current international economic order was established by the U.S. after World War II. It was based on the concept of *economic liberalism*, referring to free trade between nations, increasing the wealth of those nations. *Free trade* in turn is defined as unrestricted commerce between nations. There can be no trade restriction, such as tariffs or import taxes.

To implement this new liberal international economic order, the U.S. put in place three international organizations to guide the system and facilitate international free trade:

>> **The International Bank for Reconstruction and Development (IRBD), more commonly referred to as the World Bank.** It was designed to rebuild the war-torn economies after WWII and to help third-world countries to develop. Today, the World Bank has become the major source of low-interest loans for third-world countries to develop. Over 12,000 projects are funded by the World Bank. These include supplying safe drinking water, building schools, and increasing agricultural productivity in third-world countries.

>> **The International Monetary fund (IMF),** created in 1945. It had a dual purpose. First, it acted like a savings account. Richer countries could put money into it during times of economic booms. Then, when economic

downturns hit, these countries could take the money back to spend and stimulate their ailing home economies. In addition, it is a bank. Members can borrow from the IMF. In other words, they can take out loans with an interest rate attached to them. So, during tough economic times countries can get loans from the IMF but they have to repay them and pay interest on them.

» **The General Agreement on Tariffs and Trade (GATT),** which was set up in 1948. It was designed to lower trade barriers such as tariffs and other import taxes between member countries. GATT, however, did approve exceptions, so certain tariffs such as agricultural subsidies were considered acceptable. GATT was replaced in 1995 by the World Trade Organization (WTO) which is based on the same principle and is designed to stimulate free trade.

The World Trade Organization (WTO), unlike GATT, has an institutional structure headquartered in Geneva, Switzerland. The WTO negotiates trade agreements and resolves trade disputes between its members. It has the power to fine and impose sanctions on member states that violate trade agreements. Currently, the WTO has 166 members.

Trading with foreign countries

Congress and the president are responsible for making foreign trade policy. The balance of trade for a country measures the amount of goods a country exports and subtracts the amount of goods a country imports. When a country imports more than it exports, there is a negative trade balance. On the other hand, if the country exports more goods than it imports, there is a trade surplus. The U.S. has run trade deficits since the 1970s. The trade deficit in 2024 was $1.2 trillion. The last time the U.S. had a trade surplus was in 1975.

Businesses that can easily sell their products abroad want free trade with no trade barriers in existence. At the same time, businesses that face stiff foreign competition want those trade barriers to protect them from foreign companies. This often leads to conflicting demands by business groups and political decisions that go against accepted policy.

For example, George W. Bush, a free trade president, had no problems imposing tariffs that had to be paid on imported steel. The reason was that U.S. Steel was located in Ohio and Pennsylvania, two states important for his 2004 reelection. He did not want to alienate voters in these states, so tariffs were imposed. After being reelected, the tariffs were later removed.

Then there is the U.S. consumer. The consumer wants cheap foreign goods to keep up their lifestyles. This means no or low tariffs on foreign goods. At the same time, many consumers worry about their jobs and foreign competition, and thus they support tariffs. A good politician has to find the middle ground between the two. This is not easy.

Going global

The concept of globalization has become widely popular and does affect U.S. economic policy. *Globalization* refers to the integration of countries through increasing trade and contact. In other words, it is a form of global interconnectedness in all aspects of contemporary life. Globalization includes not just economics but also the social, religious, and even criminal aspects of life. Although a form of globalization existed in Europe in the 19th century, it now has become a worldwide phenomenon. With the new liberal economic order the U.S. put into place after WWII, global contact and trade began to increase, and today it is rare to find a country that is not closely tied to other countries. This is called *interdependence*.

To measure globalization, social scientists look at a country's sum of exports and imports and then divide the total by the country's GDP. The higher the score, the more interconnected the country is with the world economy. The U.S. has a score of 81. The highest possible score is a 100, which is a perfect interconnectedness score. The highest score of any country belongs to Switzerland with a score of 91. American allies Great Britain and France have scores of 88 and 87, respectively.

Chapter **10**

Conducting Foreign Policy

F*oreign policy* refers to a country's relations with external nations, groups, and organizations. U.S. foreign policy has three main objectives:

» **Security for the country:** *Security* refers to a country's ability to protect and defend itself. This requires a strong military. The U.S. currently spends more than any other country globally on its military. It spends six times as much on its military as the other top six military spenders combined. President Trump's budget for 2025/2026 actually increases this amount and the new defense budget will for first time hit $1 trillion.

» **Economic prosperity:** The U.S. is not just a military but also an economic superpower. Back in the 1960s, the U.S. economy accounted for 40 percent of the world's economy, but this has shrunk to 26 percent today. Although the U.S. still has the world's largest economy, economies in Asia and Europe are catching up.

Despite this decline, the U.S. still has an economy that is 40 percent larger than China's,and the U.S. dollar is still the world's largest reserve currency. (For a discussion of economic policies such as free trade and tariffs please see Chapter 9). The American government has used foreign policy for decades to achieve economic prosperity. A good example is the creation of the international economic order after WWII which enshrined the concepts of economic liberalism and capitalism into the international order.

TECHNICAL STUFF

Although the U.S. remains the world's largest economy by nominal GDP, which measures the total market value of a country's goods and services produced in a given period, China has narrowed the gap significantly. Currently, the U.S. Gross Domestic Product (GDP) is $30.5 trillion, whereas China sits at $19.2 trillion. However, in purchasing power parity terms, which adjust for cost of living, China's economy is already larger than the United States'. This reflects the increasing challenge China poses to U.S. global economic leadership.

>> **Spreading democracy and American values:** Often, foreign policy decisions in the U.S. are justified as promoting democracy and American values such as liberty and individual freedoms throughout the world. The invasion and subsequent occupation of Afghanistan was promoted as freeing a people, especially Afghani women, from a brutal regime.

At times, these three objectives can be complimentary, and at other times, they conflict.

Studying Foreign U.S. Policy

The U.S. has based its foreign policy on two worldviews: realism and idealism.

Realism

Realism is the first one. It can be traced back to the ancient Greeks but became the dominant foreign-policy school in the U.S. after WWII. The core assumption of realism is that world politics is all about struggle and survival in the international system. Only power, mainly military power, can guarantee the survival of the nation in the long run. The more powerful a country is, the more secure it is in the international system. Conflict among nations is common, because there is no global authority to prevent conflict in the international system. Security necessitates a strong, powerful military and a good economic foundation.

TECHNICAL STUFF

The term *international system* refers to a network of states, international organizations, and individuals that interact globally.

Political power is the ability to get others to do what you want. Power is not just based upon a country's resources, such as size of military or the status of the economy, but includes geography, political culture, and a willingness to use the power a country has. Power must be converted into actuality for it to make a difference in the international arena.

Power is the ability to prevail in conflict or to prevent a certain outcome. Power is actually more effective if it is used as a veto measure. A truly powerful country does not use its power to force other countries to engage in certain activities but instead uses it to prevent other nation-states from engaging in certain acts.

Idealism

The second worldview on which U.S. foreign policy is based is idealism. Similar to realism, idealism is also not a new school of thought. It goes back to the writings of great philosophers and economists such as John Locke and Adam Smith. Idealism believes that conflict does not have to arise in the international system. People by nature are good, can be educated, and convinced to do what is best for their nations.

Idealists believe that democracy is the best form of government. It is peaceful by nature, because good people elect good leaders, and in a world of democracies, fewer wars occur. Thus, democracy must be spread throughout the world. Human rights, especially individual rights should be the cornerstone of a foreign policy. These rights are guaranteed by the U.S. Constitution and should be disseminated throughout the world.

Although a military is necessary for any nation to survive, a country should use peaceful measures to settle conflicts with other countries before going to war. These include using international organizations such as the United Nations to mediate conflict and non-military measures such as economic sanctions. War is only a last measure.

Since the end of WWII, both schools have impacted American foreign policy. All presidents have relied on both worldviews when making their foreign policy. One of the two schools might dominate at times, but this does not mean that it continuously dominates. During the Carter administration, idealism often prevailed, such as in the area of human rights. However, after the invasion of Afghanistan by the Soviet Union in 1979, a shift occurred, and realism began to ascend. Similarly, Ronald Reagan's foreign policy was based mostly on realism. At the same time, Reagan's foreign policy was quite idealistic when it came to spreading democracy and individual rights globally.

Making Foreign Policy

Foreign policy is an area where Congress and the president share power. The Constitution gives Congress the power to declare war, raise armies, punish maritime crimes, and regulate foreign commerce. In addition, the Senate has to ratify every treaty negotiated with a foreign power and every ambassador nominated by the president. So, on paper, Congress should make U.S. foreign policy. Based upon the Constitution, the president has only one power, being the commander in chief of the U.S. armed forces.

However, if the American public is asked who makes foreign policy, the answer is clear: the president, and the public is right. Since the creation of the U.S., presidents have committed American troops 125 times into a conflict without Congressional support. Congress has declared war only five times since the founding of the republic. What has happened?

Since the founding of the U.S., power shifted from Congress to the president in the area of foreign policy. Although Congress dominated early, the president took over by the 20th century. With the U.S. becoming involved in international affairs, two world wars, and a cold war, the American public looked to the president to lead them. With Congress being a deliberate body, not being able to respond quickly to international challenges, the president, who is able to do so, came to the forefront of foreign policymaking. Today, the American public looks up to him and expects him to act swiftly and decisively in foreign affairs.

Many political scientists claim that the U.S. actually has two presidencies — a foreign policy one, where the president dominates, and a domestic one, where he is on an equal footing with Congress.

When looking at foreign policymaking, one notices that almost all agencies involved are under executive control. These include the State Department, the Central Intelligence Agency (CIA), the Department of Defense, and the National Security Agency.

TECHNICAL STUFF

Although the Senate is actively engaged in confirming U.S. ambassadors, and has confirmed over a 1,000 since 1789, and approving treaties, the president is able to make foreign policy through executive agreements, which have the force of law. These executive agreements do not have to be ratified by the Senate. Presidents have issued around 7,000 of these executive agreements since 1789.

REMEMBER

An *executive agreement* is an international agreement by the U.S. president that does not require Senate consent like a treaty. Executive agreements are binding under international law. The president has to inform the Senate within 60 days after ratification of an executive agreement, and Congress, if it disapproves, can vote to cancel or refuse to fund the agreement. Future Presidents can also cancel executive agreements.

Foreign policy is made in the U.S. by not just the president and Congress but by several other structures. Sources of foreign policy include:

» **The Congress:** The U.S. Constitution creates a system of checks and balances when it comes to foreign policymaking. Although Congress has the power to declare war and finance the U.S. military, the president is the commander in chief of the armed forces. Over time, however, the responsibility of Congress to declare war and fund the military has shifted toward the president. Congress has not declared war since 1941, even though major conflicts were fought in Korea and Vietnam. The major reason is that Congress is slow to react, internally divided, and focused on constant reelection.

Only once since WWII has Congress tried to reassert itself and that was in 1973 with the War Powers Act, which required the president to get Congressional approval for military action. However, the Act has been ignored or declared unconstitutional by every president since, Republican or Democrat alike.

(For a more detailed discussion of the War Powers Act, refer to Chapter 4 on the presidency).

» **The president:** The president commands the U.S. military, negotiates treaties and appoints ambassadors. The president also oversees relations with the rest of the world. Recent presidents have had enormous powers making foreign policy while they have not had a lot of experience with foreign policy issues. The last president with extensive foreign policy experience was George Herbert Walker Bush, who was president from 1989 until 1993 and used to oversee the CIA. To be successful in foreign policy, the president must rely on an extensive bureaucracy.

» **The Department of State:** The Department of State is headed by the secretary of state, who is nominated by the president and then confirmed in a simple majority vote in the Senate. The State Department manages diplomatic relations with almost 200 nations and many international organizations, such as the United Nations. The State Department oversees many foreign policy programs, such as foreign aid, and oversees the many foreign embassies and consulates the U.S. has all over the world.

The secretary of state today has become the major spokesperson for American foreign policy.

TIP

In the beginning of the republic, the position of secretary of state was the major steppingstone towards the presidency. Being secretary of state would usually give you the presidential nomination for your party.

>> **Department of War (Defense):** The Department of War is in charge of the U.S. military. In other words, it manages the country's armed forces. It is also the largest organization in the U.S. government and the biggest employer within the government. The DOD employs over two million military personnel and seven hundred thousand civilian employees. It is responsible for U.S. soldiers currently deployed in 177 nations.

The secretary of war, a civilian, oversees the department. The secretary is also a primary advisor to the president. For military advice, however, the president turns to the Joint Chiefs of Staff, which consists of six generals representing the military's six branches (Air Force, Navy, Marines, Space Force, National Guard, and Army).

Whereas the State Department deals with diplomacy, the Department of War deals with military matters. It comes up with military strategy, makes risk calculations, and plans future wars.

>> **The National Security Council:** The National Security Council was established in 1947 to advise the president on foreign, military, and economic matters that affect national security. It consists of the most important foreign policy officials in an administration. This includes the president, the vice-president, the secretaries of state, homeland security and defense, the director of national intelligence, the head of the Joint Chiefs of Staff, and the national security advisor. The president can also invite others to the meetings at his discretion.

>> **Department of Homeland Security:** The Department of Homeland Security (DHS) was established in the aftermath of the terror attacks on September 11, 2001. The DHS includes various security organizations to combat terrorism and protect the American public with a unified security structure. Today, the Secret Service, the Coast Guard, The Federal Emergency Management Agency, and the Bureau of Citizenship and Immigration Services are under the control of the DHS.

>> **Other intelligence organizations:** The U.S. has more than one intelligence organization. There are actually fifteen of them. The best known is the Central Intelligence Agency, or CIA. The CIA was created in 1947 as a part of the National Security Act and only deals with foreign intelligence. All branches of the military and the Departments of State, Treasury, and Defense also have their own intelligence officers. The Federal Bureau of Investigation (FBI) in turn deals only with domestic intelligence. All these agencies are slow to coordinate with each other and have overlapping jurisdictions. This can result in intelligence failures and drawn-out reactions.

- >> **Interest groups:** One would not suspect that interest groups could impact foreign policymaking, but they do. A good example is the war between Greece and Turkey over the island of Cyprus in 1974. The U.S. has millions of Greek- and Turkish-Americans. Both ethic groups are organized into interest groups. However, Greek Americans are among the best organized groups in the U.S. Turkish Americans are not so well organized. So, Greek Americans pushed for Congress to cut off aid to Turkey while increasing aid to Greece. Congress responded to organized interest group pressure and agreed to do so. Ironically, the U.S. cut off aid to a democracy, Turkey, and gave aid to a military dictatorship, Greece, because of interest group pressure. President Ford later on restored the balance and gave aid to both countries. The war was settled, and today, Greece dominates two-thirds of Cyprus and Turkey one-third.

- >> **Public opinion and the media:** Foreign policy is not something the American public is concerned about often. The media is most responsible for bringing foreign policy issues to the forefront of the American public's mind. The media sets the agenda, playing up certain foreign policy issues, while ignoring others. Suddenly, the American public becomes aware of an issue, gets concerned about it, and wants action on it. Now, with the public demanding action, the Congress and the president begin to react. This is the reason why some foreign events get dealt with by our officeholders, whereas others do not.

  For example, everybody knows about the current conflict in Gaza covered by the media in detail. Not too many people know about the conflict in South Sudan, so the public demands no action and our politicians in turn do not react.

Tracking U.S. Presidential Doctrines

Beginning with the Monroe Doctrine of 1823 and lasting up to the Trump Doctrine of 2025, presidential doctrines impact American foreign policy. Some of the U.S. major foreign policy successes or disasters can be explained by studying the doctrines of sitting or previous presidents. After a presidential doctrine has been established, it achieves a life of its own and future presidents feel compelled to abide by it.

For this reason, presidential doctrines outlive their creators, and some affect American foreign policy for centuries to come. A good example is the Monroe Doctrine, which still impacts American foreign policy towards Latin America today.

This section examines all the presidential doctrines in U.S. history and analyzes their impact on American foreign policy.

Presidential doctrines in American foreign policy

To start, a quick explanation of the term *doctrine* is in order. A doctrine is defined as a body of teachings or instructions; although the term is most common in the study of religion or the law, it has also found a place in foreign policy. In this area, a doctrine becomes the foundation upon which a country builds its foreign policy. The doctrine defines the actions the country takes when certain events occur. For this reason, foreign policy doctrines can lead to a consistency in foreign policy, allowing us and our enemies to predict what will happen if certain political circumstances arise. One could argue that foreign policy doctrines are beneficial, because they provide the international environment with some predictability, overcoming the anarchy that still dominates the international system today.

Doctrines are usually named after the political leaders who promulgated them, be they American presidents or Soviet premiers.

The Monroe Doctrine

Presidential foreign policy doctrines began in the United States in 1823. The sitting president was James Monroe, see Figure 10-1, and his secretary of state was future president John Quincy Adams. The period of 1815 to 1825 was a tumultuous decade in the Americas, especially South America. Former colonies of the Spanish empire were rebelling against their colonial master, Spain, and were striving for independence. Between 1815 and 1822 alone, Argentina, Chile, Venezuela, Peru, and Mexico became independent. Although the United States was supportive of these colonies gaining independence, it did fear that other European powers would attempt to take control over them.

In the beginning, Monroe and Adams feared that Great Britain, which had become Latin America's biggest trading partner, would intervene and take control of the new countries. By 1823, this changed. France became an absolute monarchy one more time after the fall of the Napoleonic Empire and expressed interest in acquiring colonies. The United States government was now more afraid that France would help Spain to regain control of Latin America and establish a colonial foothold in the Americas. The last thing Monroe and Adams wanted to see was the French empire moving into the Americas.

FIGURE 10-1:
James Monroe.

*Detroit Publishing Company photograph
collection/Library of Congress/Public domain*

**TECHNICAL
STUFF**

Monroe and Adams were rightfully afraid of the French attempting to acquire a colonial Empire. By 1830, the French had conquered Algeria in North Africa and Indochina in Asia.

For this reason, John Quincy Adams came up with what would be called the Monroe Doctrine. President Monroe presented the new policy to Congress on December 2, 1823. In his address, Monroe stated:

". . . as a principle in which the rights and interests of the United States are involved, that the American continents, by the free and independent condition which they have assumed and maintain, are henceforth not to be considered as subjects for future colonization by any European powers . . ."

". . . With the existing colonies or dependencies of any European power we have not interfered and shall not interfere. But with the Governments who have declared their independence and maintain it, and whose independence we have, on great consideration and on just principles, acknowledged, we could not view any inter-position for the purpose of oppressing them, or controlling in any other manner their destiny, by any European power in any other light than as the manifestation of an unfriendly disposition toward the United States . . ."

**TECHNICAL
STUFF**

In plain English, the Monroe Doctrine stated the following: "the Americas were from now on closed to further European colonization and free from European interference. In turn, the United States would remain neutral in future European wars and wars of European powers with their colonies outside of Latin America. Any interference with the new independent countries in Latin America would be seen as a hostile act towards the United States.

The Monroe Doctrine was not used forcefully for decades until James Polk became president in 1845. During the Polk presidency, the Monroe Doctrine became important in American foreign policy. On December 2, 1845, President Polk announced that he would enforce the Monroe Doctrine against European encroachment in the Americas. He especially targeted British interests in the Oregon territory and French attempts to prevent Texas from joining the union. Polk further argued that the United States as a part of the doctrine should expand to reach its manifest destiny to stretch from sea to sea.

This in turn was accomplished in part through escalating tensions with Mexico, especially over the disputed Texas border. Although many historians believe President Polk deliberately maneuvered events to provoke a conflict, others point to Mexico's refusal to negotiate and its attack on U.S. troops as key causes of the war. The result was a conflict that led to the U.S. acquisition of over 500,000 square miles of land, including the future states of California, Nevada, Utah, New Mexico, and Arizona. However, Polk's attempt to buy Cuba from Spain in 1848 failed.

From that day forward, the Monroe Doctrine became the cornerstone of American foreign policy towards Latin America and its effects are still felt today.

Roosevelt Corollary

In 1904, President Theodore Roosevelt, see Figure 10-2, decided to add to the Monroe Doctrine. In an address to Congress on December 6, 1904, Roosevelt proclaimed the Roosevelt Corollary as an extension to the Monroe Doctrine. According to Roosevelt:

"Chronic wrongdoing, or an impotence which results in a general loosening of the ties of civilized society, may in America, as elsewhere, ultimately require intervention by some civilized nation, and in the Western Hemisphere the adherence of the United States to the Monroe Doctrine may force the United States, however reluctantly, in flagrant cases of such wrongdoing or impotence, to the exercise of an international police power."

TECHNICAL STUFF

In plain English, Roosevelt stated that from now on, the United States gave itself the right to interfere in the affairs of the Americas to protect not just American investments, but to also ensure that European powers stay out of Latin America.

Even if a Latin American country wronged a European power, it had no right to interfere in Latin America. However, in this case, the United States would take up the European power's complaint and resolve the problem. Finally, any European power that interfered in Latin America, despite the United States' warning, would have to expect action against it.

FIGURE 10-2:
Theodore
Roosevelt.

Baker's Art Gallery/Library of Congress/
Public domain

The purpose of the corollary was to not just to keep European powers out of Latin America, but to ensure American hegemony over the continent. For the next three decades the United States would now enforce the Roosevelt Corollary religiously. This period of gunboat diplomacy saw the United States intervening militarily in Cuba, Nicaragua, Haiti, and the Dominican Republic.

After renouncing the Roosevelt Corollary in the 1930s, the United States did not become active again in Latin America until the end of World War II. With the beginning of the Cold War around 1946, the Monroe Doctrine assumed an even greater importance than ever before in American foreign policy. How could the United States justify the establishment of communist regimes closely tied to a European power, the Soviet Union, in its backyard? Wasn't this a clear violation of the Monroe Doctrine stipulating European powers to stay outside the Americas?

For this reason, the United States intervened in Guatemala in 1954, overthrowing a socialist government, and more importantly initiated the Bay of Pigs invasion of communist Cuba in 1961. In addition, non-communist regimes in Latin America, even if they were fascist or military dictatorships, received military and economic aid.

TIP

The Bay of Pigs was an attempt to aid Cuban exiles after the country fell to communism in 1959. The U.S. provided training, weapons, and logistical support to Cubans to defeat communism. The invasion failed in 1961, and Cuba now asked the Soviet Union for help against the U.S.

The impact of the Monroe Doctrine can still be felt in Latin America today. In 1965 President Johnson ordered the invasion of the Dominican Republic to prevent a pro-Soviet government coming to power. Johnson further stated that domestic revolution in Latin America with the objective of establishing a communist government was not a local matter. In other words, the United States would continue to prevent communism from spreading in Latin America by enforcing the Monroe Doctrine.

In the 1980s President Reagan supported the Contras trying to overthrow the communist government in Nicaragua, and, more recently, both President Clinton and President Bush intervened in the Caribbean Island nation of Haiti.

In 2025, President Trump pressured the nation of Panama, even threatening to take the Panama Canal back by force, unless Panama curbed Chinese influence in the country. It did, and Trump walked back his threats.

The Truman Doctrine

The end of WWII in 1945 created a power vacuum in Europe. The former great powers on the continent, Germany, France, and Great Britain were in shambles. An opportunity for domination of the European continent arose, and the Soviet Union under the leadership of Joseph Stalin decided to take it. The Soviet Union quickly expanded aggressively, and by 1946, it controlled most of Eastern Europe. Stalin decided to break the Yalta and Potsdam agreements, which called for the holding of free elections and the establishment of democracy in Eastern Europe; instead, he imposed communist dictatorships onto Eastern Europe.

This wasn't good enough for Stalin. He now sought to expand into Southern Europe. The Soviet Union began to actively support communist uprisings in Turkey and Greece. President Truman, see Figure 10-3, decided that he had to act and oppose Soviet expansionism. This resulted in the beginnings of the Cold War and the wartime friendship between the U.S. and the Soviet Union stopped.

On March 22, 1947, President Truman addressed Congress. In his speech he outlined what was to become the Truman Doctrine. According to Truman:

". . . I believe that it must be the policy of the United States to support free peoples who are resisting attempted subjugation by armed minorities or by outside pressures . . ."

". . . The free peoples of the world look to us for support in maintaining their freedoms. If we falter in our leadership, we may endanger the peace of the world. And we shall surely endanger the welfare of this nation . . ."

The Truman Doctrine called for military and economic aid for Greece and Turkey to save the countries from communism. Congress agreed and approved $400 million to help the two countries. In addition, U.S. military advisors were sent to both countries to help train the native forces against communist rebels. By 1950, $600 million in aid had been sent to Greece and Turkey, saving the two countries from communism. From this point onwards, official U.S. foreign policy called for a containment of communism by providing non-communist governments with U.S. aid in their fight against communism. Any government threatened by communism could now rely upon aid from the United States. Existing communist governments were, however, not targeted.

Chase-Statler, Washington/Library of Congress/Public domain

The Eisenhower Doctrine

The Eisenhower Doctrine is a direct extension of the Truman Doctrine. When President Eisenhower (see Figure 10-4) came to power in 1953, his major foreign policy goals were not only to contain the spread of communism but also to roll back communism by liberating communist countries. Although this new doctrine of rolling back communism was mostly rhetorical in nature, the United States, for example, refusing to help Hungary in its uprising against Soviet domination in 1956, the containment of communism was put to test with the Suez Canal crisis.

Great Britain and France had jointly owned the Suez Canal, located in Egypt, since 1875. In 1956, a new nationalist government headed by President Nasser nationalized the canal. Great Britain and France reacted by invading Egypt and taking back the canal. Nasser was closely aligned with the Soviet Union, which now threatened Britain and France. Both close NATO allies turned to Eisenhower for help. He, however, refused, fearing that Great Britain and France would attempt to recolonize the Middle East. At the same time, to make sure that he did not encourage Soviet expansionism in the Middle East, Eisenhower proclaimed the Eisenhower Doctrine to prevent Soviet aggression in the Middle East.

FIGURE 10-4:
Dwight
D. Eisenhower.

Bachrach, Fabian/Library of Congress/
Public domain

On January 5, 1957, President Eisenhower in an address to Congress said the following, establishing the Eisenhower Doctrine:

". . . It would, first of all, authorize the United States to cooperate with and assist any nation or group of nations in the general area of the Middle East in the development of economic strength dedicated to the maintenance of national independence."

"It would, in the second place, authorize the Executive to undertake in the same region programs of military assistance and cooperation with any nation or group of nations, which desires such aid."

"It would, in the third place, authorize such assistance and cooperation to include the employment of the armed forces of the United States to secure and protect the territorial integrity and political independence of such nations, requesting such aid, against overt armed aggression from any nation controlled by International Communism."

In his speech, Eisenhower further pledged to assist militarily any nation, or even groups of nations, in the Middle East, requesting assistance against communist aggression. Furthermore, any nation with an anti-communist government could from now on expect U.S. economic aid.

The Eisenhower Doctrine was soon put to test. In April of 1957, militant left-wing groups threatened King Hussein of Jordan, a close American ally. Eisenhower immediately provided military and economic aid. In 1958, President Chamoun of Lebanon faced an uprising by Muslim extremists. He asked President Eisenhower for help. Eisenhower decided to show the world that the Eisenhower Doctrine was not just rhetoric and sent 10,000 marines to Lebanon to maintain the Chamoun government in power.

The Nixon Doctrine

By 1967, over 200,000 American troops were fighting in South Vietnam. Casualties began to rise, reaching 15,000, and the war had cost the U.S. economy $25 billion. During the presidential election campaign of 1968, when American troop strength in South Vietnam suddenly reached 500,000, Republican candidate Richard Nixon (see Figure 10-5) proclaimed that he would cut back American troop strength. After being elected and becoming president in 1969, Nixon decided it was time to act. He established the Nixon Doctrine to justify and accomplish his goals of withdrawing American troops from South Vietnam.

FIGURE 10-5:
Richard M. Nixon.

Yanker poster collection/Library of Congress/
Public domain

On July 25, 1969, during a press conference held in Guam, President Nixon proclaimed that from now on Asian countries fighting communist aggression would have to rely more heavily on their own manpower instead of American troops. Nixon stated that instead of sending troops to countries facing communist aggression, the United States would supply these countries with military advisors and military hardware, but not with troops.

In an address to the nation on November 3, 1969, Nixon polished up his new doctrine, directly relating it to the situation in South Vietnam. According to President Nixon:

"First, the United States will keep all of its treaty commitments."

"Second, we shall provide a shield if a nuclear power threatens the freedom of a nation allied with us or of a nation whose survival we consider vital to our security."

"Third, in cases involving other types of aggression, we shall furnish military and economic assistance when requested in accordance with our treaty commitments. But we shall look to the nation directly threatened to assume the primary responsibility of providing the manpower for its defense."

Using the Nixon Doctrine, President Nixon was able to recall 90,000 troops by the end of 1969. By 1972, only 30,000 American troops remained in South Vietnam.

The Nixon Doctrine still affects American foreign policy today. It was most recently used by Presidents Bush and Obama and President Biden. President Obama pulled out most American troops from Iraq after rebuilding an Iraqi military, and President Biden did the same in Afghanistan.

The Bush and Obama administration's goals in Iraq were exactly what the Nixon Doctrine advocates: Build up a country's forces militarily so that it can defend itself against foreign or domestic aggression. Only then will you be able to withdraw your own troops.

The Carter Doctrine

The Carter Doctrine of 1980 was a direct response to the Soviet invasion of Afghanistan. After the fall of the monarchy in 1973, Afghanistan had been taken over by a communist party, which established a pro-Soviet government. By 1979, the ruling communist leadership in Afghanistan experienced a change of heart and tried to move away from the Soviet sphere of influence. This led to the Soviet invasion of the country in late 1979.

President Carter (see Figure 10-6) felt that he had to act. Besides boycotting the 1980 Olympic games in Moscow and imposing a grain embargo against the Soviet Union, Carter outlined a new policy towards the Middle East. The United States was especially afraid that the Soviet Union would use Afghanistan as a springboard into Iran where the pro-American government of the Shah had just been replaced with a hostile Islamic fundamentalist government.

In his State of the Union address on January 23, 1980, President Carter stated what would be termed the Carter Doctrine. He said:

"An attempt by an outside force to gain control of the Persian Gulf region will be regarded as an assault on the vital interests of the United States of America, and such an assault will be repelled by any means necessary, including military force."

President Reagan later on added what is termed the Reagan Corollary to the Carter Doctrine. It proclaims that the United States would also use military force to protect Saudi Arabia if threatened.

The Reagan Doctrine

By the time President Reagan took over, U.S. prestige and power worldwide had suffered greatly. The Soviet Union had used the Ford and Carter years to expand and rearm, while the U.S. stood by idly. By 1981, the Soviet Union had penetrated Africa; communists were now in power in Angola, Mozambique, and Ethiopia. A second country in Latin America, Nicaragua, went communist and was destabilizing its neighbor El Salvador. In Europe, the Soviets were installing new nuclear missiles targeting Western Europe. The U.S. was perceived as weak, whereas Soviet power was growing in the world. Reagan proceeded to change all of this. He was especially concerned with growing Soviet power in Latin America, and he proceeded to act.

To counteract this growing Soviet expansion, President Reagan (see Figure 10-7) announced what was to become the Reagan Doctrine in his State of the Union address in February 1985. Reagan said:

FIGURE 10-7:
Ronald Reagan.

Ronald Reagan/Library of Congress/Public domain

"We must not break faith with those who are risking their lives . . . on every continent, from Afghanistan to Nicaragua . . . to defy Soviet aggression and secure rights which have been ours from birth. Support for freedom fighters is self-defense."

The objective of the Reagan Doctrine was to undermine communist governments and groups by supporting anti-communist movements around the globe. Soon, military and economic aid started flowing to many groups opposing communist governments. The Mujahedeen in Afghanistan, UNITA fighting the communist government in Angola, and especially the Contras fighting the communist government in Nicaragua were the groups that benefited the most from the Reagan Doctrine.

The Clinton Doctrine

The Clinton Doctrine was created to justify the American intervention in the Federal Republic of Yugoslavia in 1999. Beginning in 1998, the Federal Republic of Yugoslavia was committing genocide against its Albanian minority located in the province of Kosovo. Under American leadership, NATO acted, and President Clinton (see Figure 10-8) ordered air strikes against the Federal Republic of Yugoslavia. By the summer of 1999, the Federal Republic of Yugoslavia agreed to stop committing mass murder and even allowed UN peacekeepers into Kosovo.

In 2000, the people rose up and toppled their long-time communist dictator, and the Federal Republic of Yugoslavia joined the rank of democratic nations in the world. Since 2006, the Federal Republic of Yugoslavia is known as just Serbia.

FIGURE 10-8:
Bill Clinton.

Library of Congress/Public domain

The Clinton Doctrine was best enunciated in a speech on February 26, 1999. President Clinton said the following:

"It's easy . . . to say that we really have no interests in who lives in this or that valley in Bosnia, or who owns a strip of brushland in the Horn of Africa, or some piece of parched earth by the Jordan River. But the true measure of our interests lies not in how small or distant these places are, or in whether we have trouble pronouncing their names. The question we must ask is, what are the consequences to our security of letting conflicts fester and spread. We cannot, indeed, we should not, do everything or be everywhere. But where our values and our interests are at stake, and where we can make a difference, we must be prepared to do so."

Later, after the successful resolution of the Kosovo conflict, President Clinton added the following:

"We can say to the people of the world, whether you live in Africa, or Central Europe, or any other place, if somebody comes after innocent civilians and tries to kill them *en masse* because of their race, their ethnic background, or their religion, and it's within our power to stop it, we will stop it."

According to President Clinton, the United States will from now on use military force not only to prevent genocide, but also to settle conflicts creating political instability throughout the world. The reasoning behind the doctrine is to settle international conflicts before they can threaten the United States. What may seem remote and irrelevant right now could become a major problem for the United States in the future. The president, however, only selectively enforced the Clinton Doctrine. A major conflict in Liberia in 2000, for example, was ignored.

The Bush Doctrine

The Bush Doctrine is a result of the terrorist attacks on the United States on September 11, 2001. The public got a first glimpse of the new doctrine in the president's address to Congress on September 20, 2001. For the following eighteen months, the Bush administration put together a set of responses to the new terrorist threats, which became the Bush Doctrine. President Bush (see Figure 10-9) unveiled the new policies in a speech given to the graduating class at West Point on June 1, 2002.

FIGURE 10-9:
George W. Bush.

Draper, Eric/Library of Congress/Public domain

The Bush Doctrine states that the United States will make no distinction between terrorists and states that harbor them. Furthermore, the doctrine proclaims that the United States will destroy any terrorist threat to it and its population before it can reach the United States. While preferring to act with the international community to eliminate any such threats, the United States will not be afraid to act alone if necessary. According to President Bush:

"Every nation, in every region, now has a decision to make. Either you are with us, or you are with the terrorists."

The Bush Doctrine advocated preventive measures, such as war to protect the American public from any terrorist threat. The administration's new foreign policy in regard to terrorism was anticipatory in nature and not reactive, as American foreign policy used to be.

The Bush Doctrine was first used in the attack on Afghanistan in October 2001, which removed the Taliban regime from power, because it had sponsored terrorism and harbored Osama Bin Laden.

The 2003 invasion of Iraq was heavily influenced by the Bush Doctrine's emphasis on preemptive self-defense and the global war on terror. However, the decision to go to war was driven by a mix of motivations, including disputed claims that Iraq possessed weapons of mass destruction and had ties to terrorist groups. In addition, longstanding U.S. policy favoring regime change in Iraq, and broader strategic goals in the Middle East played a role. Although the Bush Doctrine provided the framework for unilateral action, the justification and execution of the Iraq War remain deeply controversial and were based on intelligence later found to be inaccurate.

Ironically, after finding no weapons of mass destruction in Iraq, a better doctrine to justify the invasion of the country would have been the Clinton Doctrine, which protects people from genocide.

The Trump Doctrine

The Trump Doctrine, as outlined in speeches by President Trump (see Figure 10-10) and Secretary of State Marco Rubio, is a step back in time.

FIGURE 10-10:
Donald J. Trump.

*Craighead, Shealah/Library of Congress/
Public domain*

As Secretary of State Marco Rubio said:

"The postwar global order is not just obsolete; it is now a weapon being used against us."

The doctrine rejects the old post-WWII bipolar system of two great powers, the U.S. and the Soviet Union, and returns the U.S. to the multi-polar world of the 19th century. The doctrine states that the U.S. has overextended itself being the world's policeman. The U.S. cannot afford to police the world anymore and it's time for the United States allies to do their fair share protecting themselves and not just relying on the U.S.

When it comes to Europe and Russia, the Trump Doctrine states that Europe needs to be able to defend itself and, if not, it will fall under the dominance of Russia. Europe cannot just expect the U.S. to protect it for free anymore. It has to contribute and learn how to protect itself one more time.

The Trump Doctrine further reemphasizes the Monroe Doctrine claiming that the Western Hemisphere (Latin America) is a zone of U.S. interests, and the U.S. will intervene and protect its interests. A good example is the pressure put on Panama, threatening to take the canal back, unless Panama reduces Chinese presence in the country.

Finally, the Trump Doctrine targets China. For the Trump administration, China, not Russia, has become the major threat. For that reason, most of U.S. foreign policy will be designed to contain China and to stop Chinese influence globally.

5

Participating in Politics

Examine how people acquire their political beliefs and values. Then study U.S. public opinion and see how it can be measured by polls.

Observe the history of the U.S. media and study its powers over the U.S. public. Next, discover the many ways to participate in politics and analyze the U.S. voter.

See how candidates get nominated for office, how campaigns are run, and where the money for a successful campaign comes from.

Learn about the uniqueness of U.S. political parties, take a look at their history and functions, and see why political parties are still necessary today.

Define interest groups and analyze their functions in U.S. society. See why people join and how interest groups lobby our policymakers.

IN THIS CHAPTER

» **Studying public opinion**

» **Socializing the public**

» **Being an agent of political socialization**

» **Taking a look at the media**

» **Having powers**

» **Being controversial**

Chapter **11**

Regarding Public Opinion and the Media

Public opinion is usually defined as the preferences of the adult population on matters of relevance to the government. Although adults have opinions on many matters, from sports to the weather, only opinions on political matters are relevant here. For political leaders and political activists, what the public thinks is a matter of grave interest. Political leaders need to know how the public feels about issues and politicians themselves so that they can please the public and get re-elected.

The Greek term *democracy* refers to rule by the people. Our Founding Fathers believed that the government should serve the will of the people. To be able to do this, government needs to know what the public wants. Today, every politician knows that public opinion often decides important political issues and battles.

The term *public opinion* was popularized by the famous French philosopher, Jean-Jacques Rousseau, who used it in the 1740s to refer to the opinions of the French population. This was in contrast to *elite opinion*, which refers to the opinions of a government elite making policy, in his case, the French king and the French aristocracy. For Rousseau, seen in Figure 11-1, it was the population, the public, that mattered and should impact policymaking in a country.

In the U.S. over time, the concept of public opinion changed from a small group of educated who could communicate their preference to their country's leadership, to a majority of the population. In a democracy, the public suddenly consisted of most of the people who can express their opinions and influence policymaking through political participation.

Perhaps the best definition of public opinion and the one used in this book was developed by political scientist V.O. Key, Jr. It states simply: "Public opinion are those opinions held by private persons which government find prudent to heed."

Measuring Public Opinion

Public opinion polls have become a mainstay in American politics, and rarely a day goes by without a new poll being released about candidates running for office or about the way people feel about certain policies. Some polls are taken by reputable polling firms trying to measure how the U.S. public feels about a candidate or a certain political issue. Other polls are published by irreputable organizations just trying to push an issue. Therefore, it is important to distinguish between scientific and unscientific polls.

Measuring public opinion was easy in the beginnings of the republic. Only a few educated voters mattered, and they were usually found in large cities or on large estates, and many were your friends, relatives, or fellow politicians.

When more people became enfranchised, it became a little tougher to measure public opinion. Now, an elected official could read letters to newspaper editors, talk to people in the streets, attend political rallies, or start a discussion in local restaurants and bars. None of this was very scientific.

Polls to measure public opinion had been around since the early 19th century when newspapers conducted straw polls on all kids of topics, including politics. These polls were usually inaccurate because only people who cared about the topic participated. Then, with the popularization of the discipline of statistics in the 1920s, scientific polls became a possibility.

A public opinion poll is a method of measuring the opinions of a large group of people and generalizing the findings to the whole population.

Using scientific polls

Polling has a long history in the U.S. Early in the republic, newspapers conducted straw polls. Straw polls can be conducted in convenient places such as bars or grocery stores; you just ask the people a question, like who are you going to vote for. Then, you publish the unscientific results in newspapers. Often this resulted in big polling errors.

The most famous polling error in U.S. history occurred in 1936, a presidential election year. By then, scientific techniques to measure public opinion had been developed and nobody foresaw the polling disaster coming. The incumbent President Franklin Delano Roosevelt was running against Republican challenger Alf Landon, the governor of Kansas. The *Literary Digest*, one of the oldest and largest circulation magazines at the time, took a poll to try to predict the winner of the election. It sent questionnaires to 10 million people, whose names and addresses came from its own subscriber lists, telephone books, and automobile registrations. When the questionnaires were returned, the return rate was a little over 20 percent. The results showed that the Republican candidate would get 57 percent of the vote and easily defeat FDR. The actual result, however, was FDR winning reelection with 62.5 percent of the vote. What went wrong?

The *Literary Digest* was founded in 1890 and had been taking presidential straw polls for decades. It correctly predicted the winners of the 1920, 1924, 1928, and 1932 elections. After the 1936 polling disaster, the magazine went under in 1938.

The problem was the sample that was used. It was 1936, and the country was still undergoing the Great Depression. At this time, most Americans were dirt poor and only the wealthy could afford magazine subscriptions, telephones, and automobiles. The Literary Digest sampled wealthy Americans, and they supported the

Republican candidate. In addition, the return rate was very low and consisted of people who disliked FDR the most.

1948 proved to be another bad year for polling. The candidates were incumbent President Harry Truman, who had succeeded FDR after he passed in 1945, and Republican challenger Thomas Dewey, the governor of New York. After several mistakes happened, polls, including one from the Gallup organization, predicted that Dewey would easily defeat Truman. However, President Harry Truman, seen in Figure 11-2, won reelection. What went wrong?

The Washington Post/Wikimedia Common/Public Domain/https://commons.
wikimedia.org/wiki/File:Dewey_Defeats_Truman.jpg/
Last accessed on Last accessed on October 06, 2025

FIGURE 11-2:
President Truman celebrating victory in 1948.

First, the pollsters stopped polling over a month before the election took place, believing that U.S. voters would not change their minds. They did, and there was a late surge for Truman that polls therefore missed. Second, several third-party candidatees had polled quite well, but in the end, third-party supporters from the Progressive Party headed by FDR's former vice-president, Henry Wallace, moved to Truman. Polls had not predicted this and thus missed increasing electoral support for Truman in the last weeks of the campaign. Today, all serious polling firms continue polling up to the night before the election takes place.

Not screwing up

So how can pollsters avoid mistakes and produce scientific polls? First, they have to pick a representative sample. This means that the poll has to mirror the population accurately. The pollster then must take a random sample of the population. This refers to everybody in the population having the same chance of being selected.

The size of a poll also matters. The more people are sampled, the lower the sampling error will be. For example, if a pollster samples 1,200 people, the sampling error is plus or minus three percent. A sampling error is the difference between poll results from a sample and what the results would be if the entire population was surveyed. It is rare that a pollster samples more than 1,200 people because to do so is expensive and the sampling error does not change that much after a certain number of people sampled is reached.

Random sampling refers to a method of selecting people from the population for a poll in which everybody in the population will have to have the same chance of being selected.

Creating a good poll

A good poll, properly conducted, is able to measure the opinion of the U.S. public on any topic. So, by sampling 1,200 people, we can know how the whole population of over 300 million thinks. How is this possible? Random sampling has to be used. Literally every adult American has to have the same chance of being selected for the poll. Polls today are conducted by phone, landline or cell phone. Even so, there will always be a slight difference compared to the actual population, and this is called a sampling error.

To get an acceptable sampling error of about three percent, pollsters have to sample about 1,200 people. The larger a sampling size, the smaller the sampling error is. A very small sample of about 200 people has a sampling error of plus/minus seven percent at 95 percent level of confidence. This means that the researcher is confident that if the poll were to be repeated, the results would be the same (within seven percent) 95 percent of the time. By increasing the sample size to 600, the sampling error goes down to +/-4 percent. Finally, when sampling 1,200 people, the sampling error goes down to +/-3 percent.

A sampling error is the difference between the results of random samples and the actual population. The level of confidence refers to how many polls produce the same result. For example, when the level of confidence is at 95 percent, it means that if the same poll was repeated many times, 95 percent of the results would fall within the margin of error.

Polls have been very accurate from 1952 until 2016, when most polls predicted that Hillary Clinton would easily beat Donald Trump. Polls were correct in predicting Clinton would win the popular vote, which she did, but did not see her losing the Electoral College vote.

One of the reasons that happened was response bias. People gave pollsters the answer they thought the pollster wanted to hear. People tried to be politically correct and did not want to publicly admit that they would vote for candidate Trump. They did not want to be labeled racist or sexist for doing so. So they just lied.

Second, there is nonresponse bias. Many people who were selected by pollsters to be interviewed just did not answer the phone or hung up before taking the poll. Polls, yes, it is ironic, have shown that people who have a tendency not to answer polls tend to lean more conservative.

Third, polls under-sampled non-college educated white voters who heavily voted for Trump.

Question wording is another problem. To create a good, scientific poll, the right type of questions must be used. Questions have to be written clearly so that the average person can understand them. In addition, loaded language, which gives the pollster a predetermined result, cannot be used. Good questions are always carefully worded to avoid confusion and are pre-tested to see whether the question gives the data expected.

Question wording refers to the way questions are phrased. This can influence how persons answer them.

REMEMBER

Types of polls

There are many unscientific polls out there today. Unscientific polls are designed to manipulate public opinion. They are not representative of the public at all but are marketed as being so. For example, an unscientific poll would be a political party sampling its supporters and then proclaiming that there is overwhelming support for a certain candidate. Such a poll could come from interest groups sampling members, like the Sierra Club publishing a poll showing overwhelming support for environmental policies in the U.S., while in reality the interest group sampled only its members, who of course support environmental policies. Many unscientific polls today are taken online.

Push polls are another type of these polls. They are usually found online and designed to get a person to vote against a certain candidate. Pretending to be from a legitimate polling firm, the poll will ask questions such as did you know that candidate X beat his wife? Then the follow up question is: Do you still support candidate X? The poll is designed to "push" people into a certain way of acting, in this case voting.

Socializing Politically

Political socialization is the process by which people acquire their political values or political ideology. These values shape people's political opinions and political behavior in the U.S. For this reason, governments are interested in political socialization. It is a way to shape people politically. The objective for any country, be it a democracy or any other form of government, is the same: create a loyal citizen, a population that is well socialized and supports the form of government in place. Not surprisingly, governments will interfere in the political socialization process, which is usually accomplished through education and religion.

Political socialization refers to the process of how people acquire political values. It teaches children values and norms that impact their political behavior.

A political ideology affects people's outlook on the world and the role they play in it. It is a belief system that shapes how people see and analyze politics and who they support or vote for. It determines how people act within the political system and how they see everything and everybody.

The goals of political socialization are simple. Create a loyal citizen. So, three types of loyalty must be achieved:

>> **Loyalty to the state or country.** This is the most important level of loyalty. If people are not loyal to their country and believe in it, the country collapses. Recent examples are Yugoslavia and Czechoslovakia, two countries that do not exist anymore. Loyalty towards the country is created through patriotism and nationalism. The objective is to instill pride for a country into a people, which can be achieved through patriotic activities such as singing the national anthem before sports events, pledging allegiance to the country and the flag in school, and teaching schoolchildren about the great history a country has. By all measures, the U.S. has been very successful in achieving this objective. Most U.S. citizens are proud to be Americans and support their country.

>> **Loyalty to the form of government.** The U.S. has a democratic form of government and a capitalist economic structure. Loyalty towards these two concepts, democracy and capitalism, is taught in civic education classes at the lower and higher school level. In civic education classes, students are told how great democracy is and of the benefits capitalism produces. At the same time, the evils of other forms of government are discussed. Again, the U.S. does a good job socializing it citizens into being loyal to a form of government and economic structure. Not too many Americans reject democracy and capitalism.

>> **Loyalty to the current government.** A citizenry must be well socialized and accept election outcomes they do not like personally. In other words, if your candidate loses an election, a loyal citizen does not go out in the streets to engage in violent activity, trying to overthrow the new government. Instead, they accept the election loss and hope for a better election result in four years. People have to consider the new government legitimate and not turn against it. Only then can a government survive.

Becoming an Agent of Political Socialization

How do citizens become socialized in a society? What are the institutions and who are the people who can transmit political values? *Agents of political socialization* refers to the various institutions and people that can transmit political norms and values. These are the most influential:

>> **Having a family:** The family is still the most important agent of socialization today. Parents are closest to children early in life and have the most contact with them. This allows them to pass on values and beliefs. Therefore, families do matter, and parents do influence political behavior. A majority of children look at politics the same way their parents do, and almost 80 percent have the same party identification their parents do. This can be positive or negative. When parents have a distrust or dislike for the government, this can be transmitted to children, and if parents are apolitical, this can be transmitted, too.

REMEMBER

Most parents are unconscious agents of political socialization. This means that they do not transmit their political beliefs and values on purpose. Children just listen and learn their political values that way.

>> **Getting educated:** Government has the best chance to politically socialize children through school. Often, governments will make a serious attempt to indoctrinate children and create loyalty towards the country and the current form of government. During civic education classes, governments can instill civic pride, nationalism, and patriotism into children. For countries that contain ethnic minorities, education can have a unifying effect, overcoming a separate culture or language to bring people together. In other words, educational structures can create a common culture for ethnically divided countries.

>> **Finding friends:** Friends and peers can be quite influential in socializing young adults, especially if a young person comes from an apolitical family.

If your best friend takes you along to political meetings, discusses politics with you, and introduces you to more prospective friends who are all political, you will try to fit in, become one of the group, and soon become political yourself.

>> **Going to church:** Religion can be an important agent of socialization. If a person is deeply religious and their religion takes particular stances on political issues, this can obviously shape a person politically. For example, a deeply devout Catholic will take their cues from the Catholic Church on abortion.

>> **Listening to the media:** The media has become a major source of political socialization. With more and more U.S. children growing up in a one-person household, the media has an opening to socialize. Living in a one-parent household allows for children to be more exposed to the media, be it television, the Internet or social media. When children come home from school, they may be alone, with no adult supervision, and may end up exposed to media — TV shows, websites, or social media influencers peddling political ideas. Especially for a child from a nonpolitical family, this can result in the child adopting the beliefs and values they find.

TECHNICAL STUFF

In most societies, the government regulates parts of the media and controls the flow of information to the public. In authoritarian and totalitarian societies, the government directly controls the media and allows only for certain information to be passed to the public. This gives the government the ability to control and manipulate people.

>> **Belonging to groups:** Group membership can determine how people are socialized politically. If a person is born into a certain group, be it ethnic or economic, they acquire political values and beliefs from this group. For example, people born into union households used to vote Democratic. This, of course, has changed today. Black Americans are born into a specific ethnic group, and they acquire certain group values. Today, politically speaking, African Americans are the most loyal group supporting the Democratic Party. Certain political ideas are socialized into black children, such as being careful of police and voting Democrat. These ideas stick with them for the rest of their lives.

>> **Experiencing life-changing events:** Certain catastrophic events can change people's political values and political behavior. For example, the Great Depression changed American values and in turn political behavior. The previous majority party, the Republican Party, became the minority party for several decades (see Chapter 14 on political parties). Before the Great Depression, most Americans believed in a small government and voted Republican. This all changed. After the Great Depression, the Democratic Party was the majority party and an era of government intervention in the economy with the welfare state had begun. The next major event that changed U.S. political values and behavior would be the war in Vietnam and the conflict over race relations in the 1960s.

Most people are politically socialized by the time they become adults. However, later changes in political beliefs are possible. We call this *adult socialization*. A person might grow up poor in a Democratic family. His parents are lifelong Democrats, and all the family are Democrat. Then this person acquires wealth, moves out of the neighborhood into a country club, and makes new friends. The person is now surrounded by conservative Republican peers. This can change his political attitudes, especially on economic issues. For example, the person paid very low-income taxes in the past, but now they are high, and taxation becomes an issue they are concerned about. So they now vote Republican for low taxes.

Examining the Media

Media is defined as any means by which communication takes place. Mass media, on the other hand, is defined as communication that reaches large numbers of people. This includes newspapers, magazines, television, the Internet, and, of course, social media.

The media in the U.S. started in the form of newspapers before the Revolutionary War. There were about 40 newspapers and all were weekly papers. That is how most Americans who lived in large cities and were literate got the news. These newspapers had a small circulation, small advertising revenue, and few subscribers. They were usually tied to political groups and political parties and were not trying to be non-partisan. They definitely had a political bias.

TECHNICAL STUFF

Newspaper circulation had to be small because transport was expensive and producing newspapers was still done by hand; the type was set by hand, and the presses printed very slowly. There were no large advertisers to pay the bills, and the readership was only the American elite who were literate and could afford high subscription prices. Papers existed only because they were subsidized by political parties or even the government itself.

Starting out partisan

After the republic had been founded, competing newspapers supporting the Federalists and the Anti-Federalist causes appeared. The Federalists, led by Alexander Hamilton, created the *Gazette of the United States*, while the Jeffersonian Republicans created the *National Gazette* and even made its editor a part of the Jefferson administration. He became clerk for foreign languages and received an annual salary for his job.

After Jefferson became president, he created his own newspaper, the *National Intelligence*, and gave it government contracts to print government documents to keep it profitable. Andrew Jackson helped to set up the *Washington Globe* and employed several journalists who were on the government payroll. Not surprisingly, these newspapers were highly partisan.

By the time Andrew Jackson became president in 1829, it was not uncommon for major politicians and officeholders to also serve with newspapers in some capacity. All government printing contracts were given only to newspapers supporting the current administration. This slowly changed in the 1830s with the invention of the printing press, which allowed for the mass production of newspapers. Newspapers further received tax free status and low postal rates.

In the 1830s, the *New York Herald* started to be printed. It cost only a penny, starting the era of the penny press, and it for the first time included human interest stories, not just political news. The people loved it, and other newspapers began to emulate it.

The U.S. public slowly became educated and politically active after being enfranchised by the Jackson administration. Now there was a market for newspapers. Journalism grew, the penny press developed, and the new media would encourage Americans to politically participate; so, voter turnout increased.

The invention of the high-speed rotary press in the 1840s enabled publishers to print thousands of copies of newspapers quickly and cheaply. In addition, the invention of the telegraph allowed for news stories to be available throughout the country relatively quickly. In 1846, the Associated Press (AP) was founded. It allowed for unbiased news stories to be disseminated quickly all around the U.S.

Sensationalizing the media

With the U.S. public becoming educated, demand for newspapers increased and businesses noticed. Suddenly, advertising revenue flowed to newspapers, and the papers did not have to rely on political partisans and groups anymore.

Publishers also noticed that the way to attract readers was through sensationalism, violence, romance, sex, and patriotism. The average citizen loved these stories, and soon some of these sensationalized stories became powerful political forces in themselves.

This was the case with the war on Spain. The Hearst newspaper empire agitated for war against Spain over Cuba for years. When Cuba rebelled against Spanish rule in 1895, the Washington establishment wanted to stay out of the war. However, stories by the Hearst papers about Spanish brutality against the Cuban population, mostly unfounded, got the public going, demanding U.S. intervention in Cuba. After the U.S. battleship Maine blew up in Havana Harbor, killing 260 U.S. soldiers, the public wanted war, blaming Spanish sabotage for the incident. President McKinley gave the public what it wanted. The U.S. declared war on Cuba in 1898.

TIP

To this day, there is disagreement over the sinking of the battleship Maine. Some believe that it was an internal coal bunker fire that sank the ship whereas others blame a mine.

REMEMBER

After the Civil War, *yellow journalism* developed in a desperate attempt to sell newspapers. Stories involving sex and violence appeared to grab the attention of the reader and sell more papers. Using photographs, comics, and publishing stories on yellow paper, thus the term yellow journalism, the Hearst and Pulitzer conglomerates tried to sell as many stories as possible. A mass media was born. These were stories that grabbed the attention of the reader and were written in plain English so that everybody would understand.

Becoming professional

The next phase of journalism started in the late 19th early 20th century. The educated middle class were disgusted by yellow journalism, which they associated with lower-class people. So, they started to read magazines that often supported the progressive movement (see Chapter 14 for a discussion of the progressive movement), which wanted reform in the U.S. Some of these magazines, like *Harper's* and *The Atlantic Monthly*, are still around. These magazines discussed public policy problems and issues such as business regulation and reform to the American bureaucracy. Investigative reporting was born. So, audience interest had changed, and nationally known reporters were created. These magazines and writers were not associated with political parties anymore but with social causes instead. Being objective and politically unbiased was the new norm. The old partisanship of journalists and their papers disappeared.

The times had changed, and the so-called muckrakers took over. They dug up stories on government corruption and other government scandals. They wanted political and economic reform in the U.S. and with the invention of the telegraph and telephone, investigating was now easier and high-speed printing presses allowed for increased circulation to grab the attention of as many people as possible.

In 1909, the number of daily newspapers peaked in the U.S. and almost all small cities had a newspaper and big cities even published newspapers in languages other than English. National newspaper chains were born and newspaper circulation topped 15 million. By 1935, the Hearst publishing empire published forty newspapers, and every fourth American read one of its papers.

However, steadily both radio and especially television resulted in a decline of newspapers. Instead of reading about the news, people preferred to listen to it on radio and, later, watch it on television. Today, the number of daily newspapers has declined from 2,200 to about 1,100, a trend that is sadly continuing.

Next came the radio

Breakthroughs in electronic communication revolutionized American politics beginning in the 1920s. Radio networks were established in the 1920s, and President Warren G. Harding was the first president to address the nation by radio in 1922. By 1930, forty percent of all American households owned a radio, and by 1940, that number increased to 80 percent. It was Democratic President Frankin Delano Roosevelt, seen in Figure 11-3, who perfected the use of radio in the 1930s and used it as a political tool. During the Great Depression, FDR's famous fireside chats, where he addressed the nation on political and economic problems on the radio, updated the public on political news and calmed down the nation.

FIGURE 11-3:
President Franklin Delano Roosevelt giving one of his fireside chats.

Harris & Ewing/Library of Congress/Public domain

Radio is still influential today. Instead of listening to long, professional news programs, however, political news is dominated by talk radio. Talk radio does not pretend to be nonpartisan in nature and has become a major draw for radio stations.

Television became the next big mass media medium. In 1939, only about five percent of the U.S. public owned a television set. By the mid-1950s, many more American households had television sets and politicians began to experiment using TV to communicate with the public. President Eisenhower was the first to use television for campaigning and later for press conferences. The press conferences, however, were taped and then televised later so they could be edited. By the 1960s, almost 90 percent of all American households had a TV, and it now became the preferred way to communicate with the American people.

In 1952, the Eisenhower campaign commissioned Walt Disney to make cartoon TV campaign commercials for him. To this day, they are the cutest campaign commercials ever made.

By the 1980s, television had become the major source of the news for most Americans. Two-thirds of the public stated that they received all their news from television and only one-third of all Americans still read newspapers for the news.

Until the 1990s, the big three television networks, ABC, CBS, and NBC, dominated the U.S. television market. About 80 percent of all Americans watched these three networks and received their news from them. The three covered campaigns, televised nominating conventions live, and covered presidential debates. Then things changed. Less time was given for political coverage of events. Presidential candidates used to receive 42 seconds in sound bites; today its 8 seconds. So, a presidential candidate today knows they have 8 seconds to get a message across to their voters.

In addition, the audience for the big three news networks fell by 50 percent since 1980. Today there are other sources to use, cable TV stations such as CNN, MSNBC, and Fox News, online content, and social media.

98 percent of all Americans own at least one television set. Interestingly, the average U.S. family has more television sets in their homes than toilets.

Going online

Online campaigning and fundraising began in the early 21st century. It was the Howard Dean campaign for president that used online fundraising for the first time in 2003 for a major national campaign. He was able to raise $41 million from 600,000 online donors, which showed everybody that the Internet was a viable medium to contact the U.S. public and even ask it for donations. Even though Dean did not receive the Democratic nomination, online campaigning was born.

In 2008, Democratic candidate Barack Obama used the Internet to collect record amounts, and, for the first time, political ads and even speeches were put online and even transmitted to people's cell phones. Online ads are cheap compared to television ads, can be easily uploaded, and changed quickly at any time, and are not covered by campaign finance reform laws.

Today, the Internet has become the major source of political information for almost forty percent of all Americans. This includes political websites and social media. Unlike television and radio, there is not much control over the Internet. There exists a free market in political news online. There are no bans on content, and no one checks facts. There are blogs where people express their opinions on political issues, often making up stories to convince people politically.

REMEMBER

A *blog* is a log or series of discussions on the World Wide Web.

Dealing with social media

Then there is social media. It is easily accessible by smartphones and companies like TikTok, Facebook, YouTube, Instagram, and X (formerly Twitter) dominate it. Politicians have realized how many people are using social media and how easy and cheap it is to reach out to them, and they have fully taken advantage of it. Former President Obama was the first one to have a team of social media special-ists who promoted his policies on social media. President Trump is a great fan of Twitter (now X) but has switched to his own social media organization, Truth Social,. He is on it almost nightly. Has social media revolutionized U.S. politics? Yes, it has, but not necessarily for the better.

It is easier than ever to get access to political information and events. People can easily find just about everything online. If one visits a credible source of informa-tion, the news will be fairly unbiased. However, often people go to sites that spread fake stories. They receive what we call *fake news*. Fake news is manufactured news to support a particular candidate or viewpoint. It is thus up to the reader to check the source of a story, compare it to other stories to see if it could be true. This takes time and effort, and most people do not do it. It is easier to believe fake news.

Second, the assumption was that the online and social media user would check for political news and information often. That is sadly not the case. Only about 3 percent of all social media users actually look for political stories daily. Four times as many look for pornography daily. So, sadly most people are not better informed because of the Internet.

Now, on the positive side, social media has made a difference when it comes to political activism and political participation. It is easier to reach people, especially young people, on social media and one can reach them at all times of the day.

Many political groups, including political parties, interest groups, and social justice groups, reach out to social media users. They do not just ask for money but also attempt to mobilize them. Social media can be used to organize communal affairs, to organize for political causes, such as political demonstrations, and also to mobilize voters. This helps to increase political participation in the U.S.

Getting the news

Television has been the dominant source of political information for Americans for decades. About sixty percent of U.S. citizens still get their news from television; however, it is not just the big three anymore. Today, cable television news networks have become dominant. The big three are CNN, MSNBC, soon to be renamed MS NOW, and Fox News.

The Internet has now become a widely used source of political information. In the near future, it may overtake television as the number one source of information in the U.S. At the same time, newspapers are on the decline, as is radio. Instead of providing information to millions of Americans, newspapers have assumed more of a watchdog function, investigating politicians and political events.

Not surprisingly, a person's age determines where they get their news from. Older Americans (50+) still rely mostly on television for their news, whereas young Americans (18-29) mostly rely on the Internet. For newspapers, it is the oldest group, sixty-five and older, that still reads them, whereas the young generation has given up on them.

U.S. citizens used to be exposed to various sources of politics. Most read newspapers in the 1950s, some listened to the radio, and by the 1960s, most watched television. When there were only three channels on television, all political events were covered live, and a person watched a presidential address, coverage of nominating conventions or a presidential debate. They had no choice. That is all that was on television. Not anymore. Today you can switch to a cable channel or go online to be entertained.

In addition, news coverage was more balanced by the big three networks. They could not be too partisan because they would lose viewers and subsequently advertisers. The network bosses made sure that the news was presented fairly and in an unbiased way. Today, there are partisan news channels and all you get on them is biased news information. If someone watches only CNN, or MSNBC, or Fox News, they will never get to hear both sides of a story. Using the Internet, which can be hyper partisan, can make a situation even worse.

REMEMBER

People today engage in *selective exposure*. This refers to getting only the news you already agree with. A Democrat watching MSNBC or a Republican watching Fox News engages in selective exposure. They are listening to stories they agree with, and this only makes their convictions stronger.

Having Powers

The media has three great powers in regard to U.S. public opinion:

>> **Setting the agenda.** The media reports on certain stories but ignores others. The public will only know and be concerned about stories covered by the media. So, if the media covers the conflict in the Middle East people will know about it, have opinions on it and might even be able to base their vote on it. At the same time the conflict in South Sudan is not covered and so nobody knows about it and wants action taken to help to resolve it. Thus, the media can impact public opinion and also policymaking by setting the agenda.

>> **Priming.** Here, the media tells the U.S. public not just what to think about but what factors to use to judge our political leadership. For example, there are many issues you can use to evaluate a U.S. president, ranging from economics to foreign policy to even personal traits. However, the media, by telling you what to think about, also indirectly tells what factors to use to evaluate a leader. If the media focuses only on the personal problems a president has and ignores economic or foreign policy successes, the U.S. public will judge the president only on this.

President Nixon was purely judged by the U.S. public on the Watergate scandal because that is all the media focused on. The public then used this information and judged Nixon on it. Nobody judged him on his foreign policy successes, like opening up China or ending the Vietnam War, because the media did not cover this. Ironically, when he left office, President Nixon was quite popular in global circles but not at home.

>> **Framing.** This refers to the way the media presents a story. It is the way the media focuses on some aspect of one story but not others. This shapes how the American public views an issue. Let's take the issue of offshore oil drilling. If the media reports on the many high-paying jobs created by increasing offshore oil drilling, the public tends to support more drilling. If, on other hand, the media focuses on the environmental destruction and negative impact on tourism, the public opposes more drilling. The story is the same but presented in different ways, and this clearly impacts U.S. public opinion.

What protects you from the media and its powers?

>> **Education.** The more people know about a person, event, or problem, the less likely people will be impacted by media reporting. So being well educated and knowing facts can protect from media manipulation.

>> **Partisan identification.** A strong Democrat or Republican will simply ignore and not believe any news stories that conflict with their own beliefs. So even if a story is true, strong partisans will not believe it if it conflicts with their beliefs.

Impacting politics and elections

A traditional function of the media is the watchdog function. In this role, the media acts as an overseer of government officials to ensure that political leaders do what they should be doing, representing the public's interest. The media performs this function fairly well, but that puts it straight into conflict with politicians, government bureaucrats, and interest group leaders.

Political stories today tend to focus on coverage of elections. The media loves polls, and they have allowed them to cover the political races as a horse race analyzing who is ahead by how much and why.

In addition, the media has to attract an audience and negative news sells. So, many stories are negative and sensational, which attracts viewers. In 2016, 77 percent of all stories covering candidate Trump were negative and 64 percent covering candidate Clinton were negative. Most stories tend to be negative in the news. The old saying is: "Bad news is news; good news is no news." So, there is a barrage of bad news, such as violence, wars, scandals, and health crises, and never any stories about something that turned out well. Not surprisingly, distrust of government is at an all-time high.

Trusting the media

Over time, Americans have lost trust in the media. Back in 1973, 23 percent of all Americans had a great deal of trust in the media and 62 percent had some confidence in the media. Only 15 percent did not trust the media.

By 2018, trust had fallen. Only 13 percent of Americans still had great confidence in the media whereas the number of Americans who distrust the media increased to 45 percent. Today, a record 66 percent of all Americans have no or little trust in the media.

Also, when it comes to trusting the media, a partisan split has appeared. Sixty percent of all Republicans do not trust the media whereas only 6 percent of

Democrats distrust it. Finally, an age gap has appeared, with older Americans more likely to trust the media than younger Americans.

So, is the media biased? According to the Pew Research Center, only 26 percent of all Americans believe that the media was fair and unbiased. Almost three quarters believe that the media was one-sided and biased. By 2016, 80 percent of all Americans believed that the media favored Hillary Clinton over Donald Trump. Although studies have not shown a big media bias towards one of the two major parties, they have shown that the media favors incumbents. Do keep in mind, if the mainstream media gets too biased, they lose viewers and advertisers. In the end it is all about money.

Regulating the media

All media in the U.S. face some type of regulations and restrictions. Newspapers and magazines, the oldest form of media, are almost free of government restrictions. Anyone can start a newspaper or a magazine; there are no licenses to acquire or permissions to receive. All you need is money to get a newspaper or magazine going. However, newspapers can be punished for violating libel laws (refer to Chapter 7). They can be sued for libelous and pornographic materials published.

Radio and television are a little different. Public broadcasting is regulated in the U.S. It is illegal to start a radio or television station without getting a license from the Federal Communications Commission (FCC). The license has to be renewed every seven years for radio stations and every five years for TV stations. The FCC also has the power to force station operators to change certain shows by asking them to tone down violence and sex and run more public service programs.

Beginning in the 1980s, radio and television began to be deregulated. The idea was that with so many television and radio stations in the U.S., natural competition between all the stations would allow for them to self-regulate. As of 1996, when the Telecommunications Act was passed by Congress, a company could own up to eight media outlets in a large market and as many as they wished nationally. The result was that a few large companies now control most media markets in the U.S.

TECHNICAL STUFF

The Telecommunications Act of 1996 allowed companies to own media outlets in multiple markets (television, radio, and newspaper) and removed limits on how many of these outlets companies can own. This resulted in a consolidation of the U.S. media.

In the early 1980s, 50 companies controlled most media outlets in the U.S. Today it is six. Consolidation is continuing and changing the market model used for radio and television. Maybe it is time for the FCC to regulate some of the media markets again.

IN THIS CHAPTER

» **Participating in politics**

» **Not wanting or being able to vote**

» **Shaping the vote**

» **Determining the vote**

» **Explaining the vote**

Chapter **12**

Partaking in the Political Process

P *olitical participation* refers to the many ways U.S. citizens can get involved in politics and government in the U.S. Many people vote for candidates running for office, but that is not the only form of political participation. People can give money to candidates and political parties; they can volunteer for campaign activities such as putting up yard signs or handing out flyers; they can contact lawmakers, sign petitions, engage in protests, or just talk to friends about politics. All these activities count as political participation. Although U.S. citizens do not vote in high numbers compared to voters in other democracies, they are politically more active than most other citizens in compatible democracies.

Participating in Politics

Although voting is the most prevalent form of political participation, it is not the only one. People can give money to candidates and campaigns, they can volunteer door to door, they can staff phone banks and put up yard signs. Most importantly, being active in your local community also counts as a form of political participation. Running for school board or just attending a school board meeting is political participation. So is protesting and making political comments on social media. In their seminal work *Participation in America*, published in 1972, Sideny H. Verba and Herman H. Nie argue that the American public can be divided into six groups of participants based upon their various forms of political participation:

>> **The completely inactive.** They do absolutely nothing political. They do not vote, do not get involved in local organizations, and do not discuss politics much. They usually have little education, are young, and tend to be minorities.

>> **The completely active.** They are political animals, interested in all levels of politics, local, state, and national. They love to discuss politics, vote in high numbers, and even run for office. They volunteer for candidates, give money, put up yard signs, and place bumper stickers on their cars. The completely active have higher levels of education, a higher income level, and tend to be middle-aged.

>> **Voting specialists.** As the term implies, they vote and that's about it. They are not engaged in politics, but they do vote. They tend to have lower levels of education and are older.

>> **Communalists.** They love and live for local politics and local community engagement. They do not like partisan campaigns and battles and are more interested in non-partisan politics and want to deal with local problems. National-level politics is less of a concern to them.

>> **Campaigners.** They not only vote but get involved in campaign activities. They identify closely with a political party and candidate. They take strong, often controversial positions, and enjoy a good political debate. For them national politics matter whereas local politics is often a bore. They tend to be well educated and have a higher level of income.

>> **Parochial participants.** They really are not engaged in any form of political participation unless it affects them personally. Then they will get off the sofa and get active. A local problem like the garbage not being picked up will get them going. However, as soon as the problem is resolved, they will go back to being inactive.

To vote or not to vote

Political participation takes many forms in U.S. politics, not just voting. However, voting is at the core of U.S. democracy, so elections link the government and the people.

Voters are supposed to be knowledgeable about political issues and the candidates' stances on those issues. These voters cast rational ballots to elect people who reflect their political and policy preferences. Elected officials will then initiate voters' favored policies, and if voters are satisfied with the elected official's record, they will reelect the official. If the voters are unhappy with their representatives, they will vote them out of office.

Compared to voters in other democracies, U.S. voters have a lower voter turnout than many other democratic societies, as Table 12-1 shows.

TABLE 12-1

Recent voter turnout in select democracies

Country	Most recent election	Turnout as % of registered voters
Australia	2025	90.70
Canada	2025	68.65
Denmark	2022	84.2
France	2022	73.7
Germany	2025	82.5
Italy	2022	63.8
Japan	2024	53.85
Netherlands	2023	78.2
Norway	2021	77.2
Sweden	2022	84.2
United Kingdom	2024	60.0
United States	2024	63.7

Source: Data assembled by Author

As the table shows, many democracies have a turnout higher than the U.S. Only Great Britain, Japan, and Canada have a lower voter turnout. Why is this the case? Are there some underlying reasons for the U.S. voter not to turn out in higher numbers?

Despite voting being at the core of U.S. democracy, why do Americans not vote at higher numbers? Over the last century and a half, many new groups, from former slaves, women, to the 18–21-year-olds have been enfranchised, but voting as a percentage of eligible population has actually seen a decline.

The U.S. system has made it easier to vote, too. Residency requirements have been shortened or eliminated, ballots are printed in many languages, people in all states can register to vote when applying or renewing a driver's license, and absentee ballots have been widely available. Some states even allow a voter to register to vote on Election Day, and some states now conduct their elections entirely through mail. How much easier can it get?

Between 1860 and 1900, turnout rates in the U.S. were as high as 80 percent. Today's turnout has been averaging around 55 to 65 percent. One-third to almost one-half of all U.S. citizens do not vote in presidential elections, and midterm elections see turnout in the 40-percentage rank. In 2014, midterm elections hit a low of 33 percent.

Voting in the U.S.

The right to vote is known as *franchise* or *suffrage*. The Constitution in Article I, Section 4, assigns the procedures for voting, including who is enfranchised and who is not, to the states. Therefore, states decide questions on voter registration, voter eligibility, methods of casting ballots, and selecting candidates.

In 2020 and 2024, voter turnout increased, as Figure 12-1 shows. In 2020, turnout reached 66 percent, the highest since 1908. In 2024, turnout came close, reaching 64 percent, the second highest turnout, tied with the voter turnout in 1960. The increase in turnout is mostly attributable to the increasing polarization of the U.S. electorate. It is not just growing partisan identification but also more partisan antipathy, where one side loathes the other so much that they vote just to block them from winning. It was especially former nonvoters and voters who rarely cast a ballot who turned out in 2024, increasing overall turnout. Only a small share of voters actually switched parties in the election. President Trump benefited mostly from those voters who had not voted in the last election.

Not voting in the U.S.

To study the low voter turnout in the United States, we must compare the U.S. to the rest of the democratic world. First, however, we must understand three terms when it comes to measuring voter turnout.

The *voting-age population*, or *VAP*, refers to the whole population, eighteen or older, in the United States. This includes non-citizens and felons. The better measure is *VEP*, or *voting eligible population*, which refers to adult citizens in the U.S. who are actually eligible to vote. Finally, the term *registered population*, or *REG*, refers to eligible adults who are registered to vote.

2020 and 2024 presidential contests were two of the highest-turnout elections in the past century

% of voting-eligible adults who turned out in each election

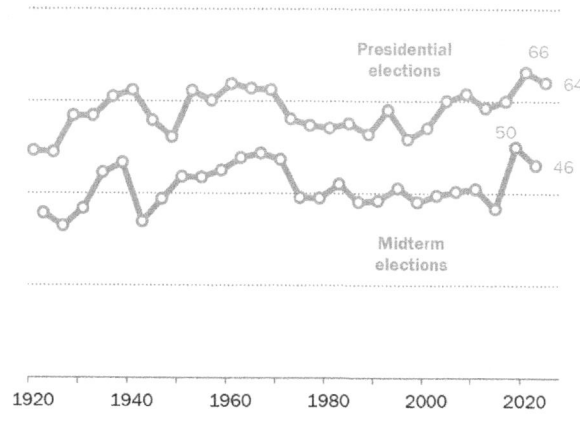

Note: Turnout data for presidential and midterm years compiled by University of Florida Election Lab, accessed June 2025. https://election.lab.ufl.edu/voter-turnout/

PEW RESEARCH CENTER

Pew Research, 2025/Pew Research Center

FIGURE 12-1: Voter turnout in the 2020 and 2024 presidential election.

In the United States, a discrepancy exists between the three numbers, which reflects poorly on American voter turnout. In 2024, for example, the VAP, the number of Americans eighteen years and older, stood at 267 million people (the number is rounded). Of these, about 245 million were eligible to vote. Only 173.854 million, or 71.0 percent of the VEP, were registered to vote, and only 154.308 million of the VEP, or 63.0 percent, actually did vote. When looking at VAP turnout, the number is actually only 57.6 percent.

Using the VAP number, it looks like a big majority of Americans do not care about voting, and the voter turnout numbers look comparatively low. However, when using VEP numbers, it looks a little better for the U.S.

Preventing voting in the past

The U.S. has a long history of disenfranchising groups of voters. When the Constitution was ratified, only white property owners and taxpayers could vote. It was not until the Jackson administration (1829-1837) that all white males received the right to vote; still a few states, such as New Jersey and North Carolina, did continue property requirements. However, by the time the Civil War broke out, virtually all white males could vote. It is estimated that by 1880 about 85 percent of all adult males in the U.S. could vote. The corresponding number in Great Britain was only 60 percent.

In the beginning, the states controlled federal elections. Over time this changed. In 1842, Congress passed a law that all members of the House of Representatives had to be elected by districts, which was not done in some states, and later on, Congress required that all federal elections had to be held on Tuesdays following the first Monday in November.

Restricting voting still impacts voting today. Long-disenfranchised groups of voters historically experience lower voter turnout rates when they finally become enfranchised. Voting is a habit people must develop, and it takes time to acquire this habit. After being enfranchised, many new voters do not believe they should vote or are unfamiliar with the practice of voting. It usually takes a generation or two for newly enfranchised groups to reach the turnout levels of other groups with a history of voting.

For example, women were disenfranchised in the U.S. until 1920, when they received the right to vote with the 19th Amendment. Female turnout did not catch up with male turnout until 1980, 60 years later, and today women are more likely to vote than men.

The largest decline in overall electoral turnout occurred in 1972, when eighteen- to twenty-year-olds received the right to vote with the 26th Amendment to the U.S. Constitution. Overall turnout declined dramatically, and to this day, this age group has the lowest turnout of any age group.

Restricting voting for minorities

The legacy of voting restrictions also impacts voter turnout. Many Southern states adopted poll taxes beginning in the 1890s. A *poll tax* is a fee people must pay before casting a ballot. For example, the poll tax in Texas at the turn of the 20th century was $1.75 plus an additional $0.25 fee Texas counties levied. This amount represented an average daily wage for Texans in 1902. The poll tax did not just disenfranchise African Americans and Hispanics, who tended to be poor, but also poor whites who could not afford to pay a fee for voting. In 1964, the 24th Amendment to the Constitution declared poll taxes at the federal level unconstitutional, and poll taxes at the state level were finally declared unconstitutional by the United States Supreme Court in 1966 in the case of Harper v. Virginia Board of Elections.

Many Southern states also used the *white primary* to prevent the non-white population from voting. First used in South Carolina in 1896, the white primary disenfranchised African Americans and Hispanics in the general election. How did it work? All Southern states were one-party states at this time, and the Democratic Party controlled all aspects of government. The white primary stipulated that only white residents could join and vote in the Democratic

Party's primary. Because the Democratic Party controlled the state, the Democratic Party primary winner was then assured election during the general election. The white primary was coded into state law and was not declared unconstitutional by the Supreme Court until 1944 in the case of Smith v. Allwright.

Literacy tests were another method used to prevent minorities from voting. Literacy tests assess the ability to read and write English. Because many former slaves could not read and write, and it was illegal to teach slaves to read and write in many Southern slave states, they had no chance to pass the tests and could not vote. Even worse, the tests were different for white and black voters, and tests for black voters were often more difficult to pass. Literacy tests were introduced in the 1890s and often poor, illiterate whites were excluded from taking them. A method to exclude them was the grandfather clause. It stated if your grandfather voted before 1867, so could you. So, a poor, illiterate white person whose grandfather voted was able to vote without having to take the literacy test whereas a black person whose grandfather had been a slave and unable to vote, could not. The grandfather clause was declared unconstitutional in 1915 in Guinn v. United States, but literacy tests lasted until 1965 when the Voting Rights Act of 1965 made literacy tests illegal in the U.S.

TECHNICAL
STUFF

In 2020, it was estimated that five million U.S. citizens were disenfranchised because they had committed felony-level crimes. Many states prohibit felons from voting if they are in prison, on probation, or on parole.

Mandating voter registration

Voter registration in the U.S. began in 1800 in Massachusetts. The voter registration law did not gain a lot of traction, and most states did not adopt voter registration laws until after the Civil War, between the 1870s and 1890s. Voter registration laws were pushed by the progressive movement, a movement of white, middle-class protestants targeting immigrants, mostly Catholic and Chinese. The progressive movement further attempted to weaken political party machines, organizations that manipulated enough votes to control a city. Voter registration reduced the ability of political party machines to commit voter fraud, such as allowing their supporters to vote more than once and have non-citizens vote. (See Chapter 14.)

Voter registration decreased voter turnout among recent immigrants, mostly Catholic, and made it tougher for political party machines to commit voter fraud. In addition, young and mobile voters who moved frequently for job requirements were disenfranchised.

TECHNICAL STUFF

Cumbersome voter registration laws are a major reason for low voter turnout. In the United States, voters must put effort into registering to vote before they can actually vote. Studies have shown that registration requirements lower turnout by about nine percent nationwide. Some states have imposed fairly stringent voter requirements whereas other states have made voter registration easier. North Dakota has even eliminated voter registration requirements, but a person has to show ID at the polls to be able to vote.

Registration requirements for voting by state are shown in Figure 12-2.

In many states, registering to vote is automatic

States that have implemented, or plan to implement, automatic voter registration

Implemented

Will fully implement in next two years

No voter registration requirement

No automatic voter registration

ME

AK | VT | NH | MA

WA | MT | ND | SD | MN | WI | MI | NY | CT | RI

OR | ID | WY | NE | IA | IL | IN | OH | PA | NJ

CA | NV | UT | CO | KS | MO | KY | WV | MD | DE | DC

AZ | NM | OK | AR | TN | VA | NC

HI | TX | LA | MS | AL | GA | SC

FL

FIGURE 12-2: Registration requirements for voting by state.

Note: Data as of January 2022.
Source: National Conference of State Legislatures.

PEW RESEARCH CENTER

Pew Research, 2022/Pew Research Center

Getting the Australian ballot

The Australian ballot, a government-printed ballot that was cast in secret, was a game changer. States began to use it around 1890. It replaced the old party ballots, which were cast in public. By 1910, just about every state was using it.

The Australian ballot is a ballot of uniform dimensions that is cast in secret. Previously, ballots were printed by political parties and people had to vote in the open, making it easy for political parties to control how people voted.

By having a ballot cast in secret, not printed by political parties, voter fraud became less common, especially in larger, party-machine–controlled cities.

Decline in Voter Turnout

Why don't U.S. citizens vote in high numbers? First, there is the decline and weakening of political parties. In the 19th century, political parties were strong and were able to turn out the vote for their candidates. There were party caucuses and conventions that allowed people to participate and, until the late 19th century, people could even get a job from participating in politics (this was known as the *spoils system*).

Legal barriers to voting were kept to a minimum by political parties, voter registration was unheard of, and elections were close and exciting. This all changed in the late 19th century when both the South and North became one-party regions, and the progressive movement weakened political parties and implemented voter registration laws and, later, direct primaries (see Chapter 14).

With regions of the U.S. becoming dominated by one party, elections became less exciting, and people turned away from politics. If you know in advance that your candidate will lose, why bother to vote? At the same time, if you know your candidate will win, why get engaged and vote? If you are a Democrat in Wyoming what are the chances that your candidates will ever win? The same goes if you are a Republican in Massachusetts. In both instances, voters will stay home, and voter turnout goes down. As long as parties are competitive and elections are close, turnout rises. Having noncompetitive elections in many states results in lower turnout.

Another explanation focuses on the number of elections held in the U.S. No other democracy has as many elections as the U.S. With the U.S. being a federal country, elections are held at the federal, state, and local levels. Americans vote for everything from president to local sheriff and members of Congress to the state legislature. But it does not stop there. In addition, there are primaries, run-off elections, elections on constitutional state amendments, and even referenda in some states. This means elections are not special; there is always one around the corner. Voters get sick of them and stop voting, or if they do vote, they vote only at the highest level, for president.

To make matters worse, U.S. ballots can be long and confusing. If there are initiatives on the ballot, they are attached to the ballots themselves in some states like California. The California voter guide in 2016 was 224 pages long. This turns voters off.

In addition, the U.S. holds elections on Tuesdays, a workday. So, voters are supposed to vote after having worked for 8-9 hours. Again, this is a major imposition, and many voters are unwilling to do it. In most democracies, elections are held on Sundays when people are off work.

In the U.S., being able to vote requires a voter to register to vote, unless you live in North Dakota. Most democracies register voters automatically after they turn 18; then, you just show up on Election Day at a voting station and have a ballot waiting for you. This means that 100 percent of all voters are registered. In the U.S., where voters register themselves, the number is closer to 75 percent. It was 73.6 percent in 2024.

REMEMBER

Automatic voter registration modernizes the voter registration process by automatically registering eligible voters through their interactions with state agencies, most commonly when they apply or renew their driver's license.

Finally, as mentioned earlier, extensions of the franchise to previously disenfranchised voters have resulted in lower voter turnout.

TIP

Many social scientists claim that voter turnout numbers were overstated until 1896. Especially in large cities, party machines turned out the vote with fraudulent measures. Often, party members were allowed to vote more than once. For this reason, the number of ballots cast often exceeded the number of voters.

Providing identification to vote

Thirty-six states have voter identification laws. In these states, voters have to present a government-issued photo identification, such as a driver's license or passport to vote. Studies have shown that about 10 percent of all voters do not possess such a form of identification. For this reason, most of the voter identification laws contain provisions for voters to use another form of ID, such as utility bills or school identifications.

Ironically, studies have shown that the voter identification laws really have no impact on electoral fraud, because electoral fraud is rare. At the same time, studies also show that the 10 percent of citizens who cannot present a form of identification are evenly split between parties and candidates and their participation does not impact electoral outcomes in the U.S.

Making voting easier

The federal government and many states have recently attempted to make voting easier to increase voter turnout in the U.S. Early voting is an example of this. Forty-seven states and the District of Columbia allow for early voting without an excuse before Election Day. Early voting periods range from the Friday before the election to up to 45 days in advance.

Absentee voting is legal in all states for military personnel, their voting age dependents, and U.S. citizens living abroad. For civilians, the ability to absentee vote is state dependent. Twenty-eight states and the District of Columbia allow absentee ballots to be mailed with no excuse necessary. Nineteen states demand an excuse for absentee ballots. Three states, Washington, Oregon, and Colorado, conduct their elections fully by mail.

In 2024, 39.6 percent of all voters voted in person on Election Day, 30.7 percent voted in person during the early voting period, and 29 percent voted by mail.

REMEMBER

Determining the Vote

What determines who votes? Who does not vote? Which political party is favored by U.S. voters? Studying voting behavior reveals several characteristics that determine the way people vote, among them ethnic background, education, income, age, and gender.

When studying ethnic background, one notices that white citizens have the highest turnout of any ethnic group. They are closely followed by African Americans and Asians Americans. Citizens of Hispanic descent have the lowest voter turnout rate. Reasons include a lower level of education, being first-generation immigrants with limited English skills, lower levels of income, and youth (the Hispanic population is the youngest group of voters in the U.S). Combined, these result in a low voter turnout. However, after a generation or two, voting levels increase. By then, Hispanic voters will have become older, better educated, and better situated financially. All this should result in a higher voter turnout.

When it comes to party difference, 2024 was quite different from previous elections. The Hispanic vote, except for Cuban Americans, had been solidly Democratic for decades. This has slowly changed. In 2020, President Biden won the Hispanic vote by a 25-point margin. In 2024, President Trump almost won it, getting 48 percent of the Hispanic vote, the best showing ever for a Republican candidate. Looking at the white voter, President Trumps's support remained the same compared to 2020 and even 2016, sitting at 55 percent.

Analyzing the black vote, a similar result can be observed. President Trump received 15 percent of the black vote, up from 8 percent in 2020, the best showing of a Republican candidate since Richard Nixon in 1960. Black men actually gave him 21 percent of their vote. Kamala Harris still won the black vote, however, with a substantial 83 percent of the vote.

Looking at the Asian vote, we see a similar result. President Trump lost the Asian vote but improved his standing by ten percentage points. In 2024, he won 40 percent of the Asian vote compared to 30 percent in 2020.

Studies show that education is another major determinant of the vote, and more educated people are more likely to vote. They have the resources to participate in politics and the knowledge of how to register and vote. People who attended college are also more likely to feel a civic duty to participate. A low educational level leads to low voter turnout. U.S. citizens with a bachelor's degree or higher have a turnout rate of almost 78 percent. Those with less than a high school degree see their voter turnout rate drop to 41.5 percent.

When it comes to voting preference in elections, the 2024 results showed that the college-educated group voted for Vice President Kamala Harris by a 57 percent to 41 percent margin, whereas President Trump carried noncollege voters by a similar 56 percent to 42 percent margin.

Income and education are correlated. The more education a person has, the higher the income. To participate in politics not just by voting but by donating money and time, income comes into play. Further, higher income people have more to lose in elections. They are more affected by higher taxes like income or property taxes, and are willing to base their vote on these issues.

A third major determinant of the vote in the United States is age. Many studies show that voter turnout tends to increase with age. Among eighteen- to twenty-four-year-olds, voter turnout was a measly 27.3 percent in the 2016 general election that President Trump won. On the other hand, the sixty-five and older group had a turnout rate over 65 percent. Why does this voting discrepancy exist? The explanation is situational; older voters have higher incomes, own homes, and are more likely to be married and have children. Thus, they are more interested in issues such as property and income taxes and the quality of schools in their neighborhoods, which causes them to become politically active and thus vote. Older voters also are more likely to have a history of voting and involvement in previous campaigns. Finally, older voters are more likely to identify with a political party and have a more coherent ideology. These factors all contribute to higher voter turnout.

For example, in the 2020 election, turnout among the oldest voter group (65 plus) was 74.5 percent. The youngest voter group (18-24) had a voter turnout rate of 51.4 percent.

Geographical location has become a major determinant of the vote. Living in rural areas versus living in larger cities makes a big difference, voting-wise. President Trump won the rural vote by 40 points in 2024 (69 to 29 percent) while

Vice-President Kamala Harris won urban areas by a similar margin (65 to 33 percent).

The final determinant of voting is gender. For several decades, one of the hottest topics in political science has been the gender gap. In 1980, women became more likely to vote than men, and differences in turnout numbers and in political party and candidate preferences appeared.

In the 2024 general election, major differences appeared between men and women regarding political issues and voting. Women were more likely to vote in the 2024 general election, with 66.9 percent reporting that they voted. Of men, 63.7 percent reported that they voted.

Interestingly, the turnout gender gap also appears with other ethnic backgrounds. For example, more African-American women reported voting than African-American men, and more Hispanic women voted than Hispanic men.

For party preferences, minority female voters tend to mirror white female voters because they are more liberal than minority male voters. Women nationwide tend to be more liberal on many economic and social issues like abortion and the death penalty, so they tend to support the Democratic Party and its candidates more than men do.

Men, on the other hand, seem to be getting more conservative. In 2020, about half of all men voted for President Trump. This increased to 55 percent in 2024. At the same time, President Trump lost the female vote, receiving 44 percent in 2020 and 46 percent in 2024.

Now, did we see a major switching of party and candidate preferences by existing voters in 2024? Not really. President Trump's increase in support did not come from partisans. They stayed with the party they had always supported. It actually came from nonvoters. More nonvoters and voters who rarely vote turned out to vote for President Trump. Looking at the increase in Hispanic support for President Trump, one notices that it did not come from voters switching sides. Sixty percent of Hispanic voters who voted in 2024 but had not voted in 2020 voted for President Trump. The question is, will these voters be one-time voters or will they continue to participate in politics, especially after President Trump leaves office in January 2029? Figure 12-3 shows changes in President Trump's support based on ethnic backgrounds and gender.

In conclusion, white Americans are more likely to vote, but African Americans have made great strides and are now almost even with white voters when it comes to turnout. Hispanics, on the other hand, still trail badly in all age groups and have the lowest voter turnout of any major ethnic group. This should change over time, as it has in the past.

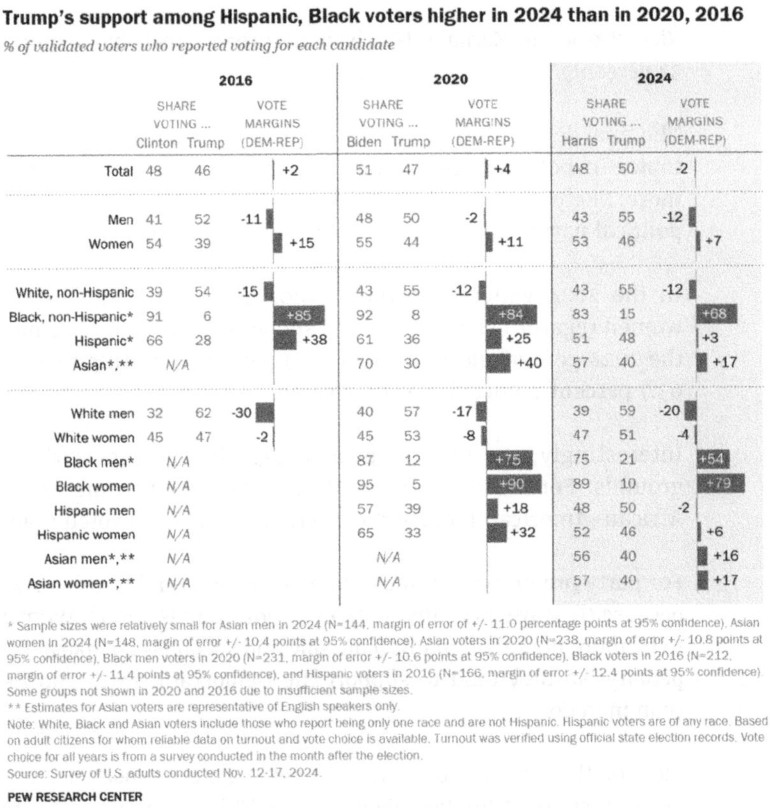

% of validated voters who reported voting for each candidate

	2016			2020			2024		
	SHARE VOTING …		VOTE MARGINS (DEM-REP)	SHARE VOTING …		VOTE MARGINS (DEM-REP)	SHARE VOTING …		VOTE MARGINS (DEM-REP)
	Clinton	Trump		Biden	Trump		Harris	Trump	
Total	48	46	+2	51	47	+4	48	50	-2
Men	41	52	-11	48	50	-2	43	55	-12
Women	54	39	+15	55	44	+11	53	46	+7
White, non-Hispanic	39	54	-15	43	55	-12	43	55	-12
Black, non-Hispanic*	91	6	+85	92	8	+84	83	15	+68
Hispanic*	66	28	+38	61	36	+25	51	48	+3
Asian*,**	N/A			70	30	+40	57	40	+17
White men	32	62	-30	40	57	-17	39	59	-20
White women	45	47	-2	45	53	-8	47	51	-4
Black men*	N/A			87	12	+75	75	21	+54
Black women	N/A			95	5	+90	89	10	+79
Hispanic men	N/A			57	39	+18	48	50	-2
Hispanic women	N/A			65	33	+32	52	46	+6
Asian men*,**	N/A			N/A			56	40	+16
Asian women*,**	N/A			N/A			57	40	+17

* Sample sizes were relatively small for Asian men in 2024 (N=144, margin of error of +/- 11.0 percentage points at 95% confidence), Asian women in 2024 (N=148, margin of error +/- 10.4 points at 95% confidence), Asian voters in 2020 (N=238, margin of error +/- 10.8 points at 95% confidence), Black men voters in 2020 (N=231, margin of error +/- 10.6 points at 95% confidence), Black voters in 2016 (N=212, margin of error +/- 11.4 points at 95% confidence), and Hispanic voters in 2016 (N=166, margin of error +/- 12.4 points at 95% confidence). Some groups not shown in 2020 and 2016 due to insufficient sample sizes.
** Estimates for Asian voters are representative of English speakers only.
Note: White, Black and Asian voters include those who report being only one race and are not Hispanic. Hispanic voters are of any race. Based on adult citizens for whom reliable data on turnout and vote choice is available. Turnout was verified using official state election records. Vote choice for all years is from a survey conducted in the month after the election.
Source: Survey of U.S. adults conducted Nov. 12-17, 2024.
PEW RESEARCH CENTER

FIGURE 12-3: Changes in President Trump's support based on ethnic backgrounds and gender.

Pew Research, 2025/Pew Research Center

Explaining the Vote

For decades, political scientists have tried to explain the voting behavior of the U.S. public. Many theories were created but none fully explain it. All of these explanations have contributed to our knowledge of voting behavior, but not one is able to explain it all. Possibly the best option is to combine aspects of all and come up with a new, more comprehensive theory.

The first theory is the classical democratic theory of voting behavior popular until the 1940s. It stated that in a democracy, voters are rational, aware of issues and how candidates stand on these issues. They then base their vote on this knowledge. The theory was never tested because the assumption was that in a democracy voters were rational, and the U.S., being a democracy, thus had rational voters.

Beginning in the 1940s, this changed. Suddenly, studies were conducted that showed that most U.S. voters were not rational voters. One of these studies was the Columbia Model. This stated that group behavior determined how people voted. According to this theory, a person is born into a certain group, ethnic, economic, or religious, and membership in this group determines how those people vote. So someone in an economic group such as a union voted Democratic because of union membership. Someone belonging to a Christian fundamentalist group voted Republican because of group membership. Today, ethnic background and gender constitute group membership and can still determine how people vote. A vast majority of African Americans vote Democratic, whereas most white voters are Republican supporters.

The major study on voting was conducted in the 1950s. It was conducted by social scientists from the University of Michigan and is appropriately titled the Michigan Model. This model is based on psychology and analyzed the 1952 and 1956 presidential elections in the U.S. It found that people had a party identification, which was a psychological attachment to a political party. It was this party identification that determined how people voted in elections. Party identification, not knowledge is how people cast their vote. The study, published in a seminal work entitled *The American Voter* in 1960, further claimed that political socialization, the process of acquiring one's political beliefs and values, determines party identification (for a discussion of political socialization, refer to Chapter 11). In other words, you are a Democrat or Republican because you were born and raised in a Democrat or Republican household. Party identification is still a major predictor of the vote today. In 2024, 95 percent of all Democrats favored Vice President Kamala Harris and 94 percent of all Republicans voted for former President Trump.

REMEMBER

An *independent* is a voter who does not identify with a political party and a *partisan* is someone who identifies with a political party.

As soon as the Michigan Model was published, political scientists set out to disprove it. This was not an easy task. Famous political scientist V.O. Key came up with the Echo Chamber Effect Theory to do so. The theory states that the Michigan Model was a good, solid theory. However, it was time-bound. It reflected only the U.S. political scene of the 1950s, when both political parties were close on issues and the president, Dwight D. Eisenhower, was a moderate Republican beloved by the American public. With no major issues dividing the public, people had to base their vote on party identification. There was nothing else left.

However, the 1960s changed all of that. With the war in Vietnam, civil rights and expansion of the welfare state with the Great Society programs, new issues arose that divided the public. Now, instead of basing their vote on partisan identification, the public was able to base their vote on issues. Issue voting came to the forefront. Voters overcame partisan identification, as with Southern Democrats, who actually voted Republican in 1964 over the issue of civil rights.

Key claims that the American electorate reflects, or echoes, the political environment. If issues arise and the public cares about those issues, the public will engage in issue voting. If the political climate is dull, the parties are similar on issues, and no divisive issues are out there, they will base their vote on partisan identification.

In the 1950s, economic theories of voting behavior became widely known. They stated that voters are rational, and when voting they look at the state of the economy and their pocketbook. If they and the economy are doing well, voters will vote for the incumbent candidate and party. If they are dissatisfied, they will vote to replace them. Therefore, voters will base their vote on who they expect to provide more economic benefits for them. This obviously makes voting rational. If they receive what they expect, they will reelect a candidate; if they did not get their expected utility, they will vote against the incumbent candidates.

TECHNICAL STUFF

There are two ways to analyze a vote, *retrospective* and *prospective* voting. Retrospective voting happens when an incumbent is running for reelection. If the voting public believes the incumbent has done a good job they will reelect the candidate, On the other hand, if the public does not approve of the incumbent's handling, the voter can vote them out and replace them. The last retrospective election was in 2020. Prospective voting happens when there is no incumbent. Now the voting public has to take an educated guess who the better candidate would be. The last prospective election happened in 2016.

IN THIS CHAPTER

» **Setting a precedent**

» **Running for the nomination**

» **Having different type of primaries**

» **Winning the nomination**

» **Running a general election campaign**

» **Hiring experts**

» **Needing lots of money**

Chapter **13**

Participating in Campaigns and Elections

R unning for federal office, especially the presidency, has become time-consuming and expensive. A campaign starts right after the last election is held. Some social scientists say it even starts the day after a previous presidential election.

Running for federal office involves more than just declaring yourself a candidate for office and receiving a party nomination. It includes winning caucuses and primaries and succeeding in the invisible primary, better known as the money primary. Candidates, after deciding to run for office, must build an organization to run their campaign. If running for president, such an organization must be nationwide. Candidates must raise money, debate other candidates, and campaign just about everywhere. Then, the state contests to select a presidential nominee begin. It all started out so simple.

Setting a Precedent

Campaigning for federal office has dramatically changed over the last two centuries. Until 1840, candidates for federal office had to appeal to a small segment of the population, those literate and able to vote. This all changed with the Jackson administration (1829-1837) and the extension of the franchise to all white males. Instead of just giving speeches and occasionally writing a small essay to support a candidacy, modern campaigning now emerged.

We have the presidential election of 1840 to thank for this. The incumbent president was Martin Van Buren, a traditional, long-time Democratic politician. Although he himself did not campaign personally, which was considered undignified at the time, he had his supporters campaign for him. He did release letters on issues such as states' rights and tariffs, which were then reprinted in newspapers all over the country. His opponent was the hero of the war of 1812 and the Indian wars, General William Henry Harrison. The Whig Party had selected him because, first, the party could not agree on any important issue of the day, and second, he had great name identification. So they picked a famous person who really did not care much about issues. Every American knew of the great Indian fighter. Instead of talking about issues, as President Van Buren did, the Whigs focused on Harrison's image. The modern-day image campaign was born.

The party played up Harrison's war record and added that he, like most Americans at the time, was born in a small log cabin. He was a common man, just like most Americans were, and because of this, he was familiar with the issues America cared about. They attacked Van Buren for being an out-of-touch aristocrat. His name Van Buren sounded foreign and aristocratic. That was good enough to attack him.

Van Buren did not dignify the attacks, did not defend himself, but continued talking about economic issues such as tariffs. Harrison campaigned with a life-size log cabin at his side, drinking hard cider and talking about his military victories. The campaign became known as the famous "Tippecanoe and Tyler Too" campaign (Tippecanoe was a battle that Harrison had won and John Tyler was his vice-presidential candidate).

When the results came in, Harrison won in a landslide. Van Buren did not know what had hit him. By the way, the whole campaign was based on a lie. Martin Van Buren was the son of a small innkeeper in New York, whereas William Henry Harrison was born in a mansion on a large plantation in Virginia. He came from a prominent English family, and his father had been governor of Virginia and his brother a member of the U.S. House of Representatives.

With the image campaign being successful in 1840 (see Figure 13-1), politicians took note, and image campaigning has been with us ever since.

FIGURE 13-1: William Henry Harrison campaign poster from 1840.

Ironically, William Henry Harrison was the first U.S. president to die in office and became the president with the shortest tenure. He died after four weeks in office. He delivered his inaugural address in March of 1841, in freezing rain, without wearing a hat or a coat. He further delivered the longest inaugural address in U.S. history, talking for almost two hours. He caught a cold, which turned into pneumonia, and he died.

The nominating campaign

As soon as one presidential election is over, future candidates for the presidency begin to get involved in the prenomination campaign for the next presidential election. They begin to test the waters, talking to political leaders and, of course, big donors.

To win a presidential nomination, a lot of money is needed. Candidates need to line up campaign staff, including campaign managers, and give speeches, run television ads, and make social media appearances to see whether there is interest in their candidacy. If there is a little bit of interest, they set up an exploratory committee, and then, if they decide to go for it, they formally announce their candidacy for the presidency.

This long process has one advantage. It weeds out candidates who are not popular with the U.S. public and have not received party leadership support or the necessary funds to run for the presidency.

The invisible primary is the next stage. Here candidates compete for financial support and support from party leaders. They also need to show popular support by taking polls. As soon as a candidate receives frontrunner status, they receive more coverage by news organizations, which enhances their name identification among the public and potential donors, which leads to more financial resources and in turn more support by the public.

Name identification refers to voters' ability to identify a candidate due to a certain amount of previous exposure to a candidate's campaign.

Running for the nomination

Now comes the decisive phase of running for the presidency. Over a period of a little over half a year, candidates have to run in primaries and caucuses.

Most states use presidential primaries today. A *primary* is a statewide election in which voters select delegates to attend the national nominating convention for a political party. These delegates then go to the national convention and cast their ballots for the candidates the voters in their state have selected. In 2020, 45 states used primaries to pick delegates for the convention.

A few states still use a *caucus system*. The most famous is the Iowa caucus. Using this method to select candidates for the presidency, party members attend local meetings at which they choose delegates who pledge their support for candidates. These delegates then attend county/regional meetings where they select delegates for a state convention, which then selects the final delegates for the national convention.

The first contest for delegates to the national nominating convention is always Iowa. In 2024, it held its caucuses on February 5, 2024. One week later comes the New Hampshire primary, which is the first primary of nomination election season. Other states' primaries follow. This goes on until the last states or territories, such as Guam, meet in June of election year.

Why do Iowa and New Hampshire, small states with few delegates that aren't very representative of the U.S. population, go first?. The reason is simple: They have traditionally been the first two states to pick delegates.

The media focuses on them. They get nonstop coverage, and often the two states make and break candidates. Over the years, other states have become jealous and have started to hold their primaries or caucuses earlier to get similar attention from candidates and the media. This is called *frontloading*. By 2024, this reached a point where most delegates were selected between February 5 and March 19, 2024. In other words, the two parties selected a majority of delegates for the nominating convention in a six-week period. Back in 1988, it took more than 20 weeks to pick a candidate.

In 2016, Bernie Sanders, seen in Figure 13-2, the progressive senator from Vermont, came in second to frontrunner Hillary Clinton in the Iowa caucus. The media, instead of focusing on winner Hillary Clinton, gave Bernie Sanders all the coverage, and he went on to narrowly beat Clinton in the popular vote in the New Hampshire primary the following week. A serious candidate had suddenly been born. Sanders ended up winning 23 primaries and caucuses and received 46 percent of all delegates.

FIGURE 13-2: Senator Bernie Sanders of Vermont.

Palácio do Planalto/Flickr/CC BY 2.0/ https://www.flickr.com/photos/ palaciodoplanalto/52680144037/Last accessed on Last accessed on October 06, 2025

Loving primaries

Reform occurred during the progressive era in the nominating process. The progressive era of the late 19th century gave the country the direct primary system, which allowed voters to pick a party candidate. The voters pick delegates pledged to candidates in a primary. These delegates are then sent to the nominating convention to pick a presidential nominee. Florida was the first state to hold a primary in 1900, and the practice spread rapidly. Today, to win the presidential nomination, a candidate must win a majority of delegates in states through primaries.

Most states use various types of primaries to select their presidential nominee. New Hampshire is the first state to use a primary in the presidential nominating process. Then, in March of a presidential election year, Super Tuesday is held, during which multiple states, many in the South, hold primaries. Super Tuesday often gives a party a nominee.

Direct primaries are the most popular way of selecting party nominees in the U.S. today before they run in a general election. As mentioned previously, the U.S. Constitution allows each state to decide how the public chooses its elected officeholders. Some states use state conventions or caucuses to select their party's nominees for office. Most states use the direct primary to do so. Three types of primaries exist in the United States:

>> **Closed primary:** Most states use closed primaries, in which voters must declare their party affiliation in advance. Only then can they vote in that party's primary. For example, only registered Republicans can vote in the Republican primary. This allows for some party control by ensuring that only registered partisans can vote in a party's primary.

>> **Modified closed primary:** One of the newer methods of selecting delegates is a *modified closed primary*, during which voters show up on primary Election Day, declare a party affiliation, and then vote in that party's primary.

>> **Open primary:** In an open primary, registered voters decide on the primary Election Day which party's primary to vote in. For example, a Democrat can choose to vote in the Republican primary on a primary Election Day. However, voters can vote in only one party's primary — not in both. This allows for *raiding* a primary. Republicans, for example, might have only one candidate in a primary, making the result a foregone conclusion. So, the Republican Party might urge Republican supporters to vote in the Democratic primary to select the weakest possible Democratic candidate. This would make it easier for the Republican candidate to win in the general election.

One great advantage of open primaries is that they allow for independents, voters not registered with any party, to request a ballot and vote in the primary.

>> **op-two primary:** Several states, including California and Washington, use a top two primary system. In this type of primary, voters receive only one ballot listing all the offices and all the candidates from all the parties. This often includes more than one candidate from the same party. The top two

candidates, even if they are from the same party, will move on to the general election.

TECHNICAL STUFF

The United States Supreme Court ruled in 2000 in Democratic Party et al. v. Jones that a blanket primary must be truly non-partisan, meaning that all candidates, including those from third parties, must be listed on the ballot. This ruling resulted in the top-two primary.

Other types of elections

U.S. citizens can engage in many types of elections. At the national level are general elections for the presidency, the U.S. Senate, and the House of Representatives. Next, state-level elections include those for governor, for state executive positions, for the state legislature, and for many local offices.

Besides local, state, and national elections, many states also hold occasional special elections. These elections fill local, state, and national level vacancies when a state legislator dies, resigns, or retires.

Many Southern states use runoff elections. In most states, whoever wins the most votes in a primary is declared the winner and moves on to the general election. In some Southern states, such as Texas, however, a candidate must receive an absolute majority of the votes. If no one receives an absolute majority of votes in a primary, the top two primary candidates will move on to a runoff election, and whoever wins will be the nominee for the general election.

Holding a nominating party

The National Nominating Convention introduces a party's candidate to the U.S. public. It is also a time to get high-level party officials and thousands of delegates from the state parties together to celebrate and have fun. Attendees include corporate sponsors, members from conservative or liberal interest groups, and, often, famous Hollywood stars and music performers. Every group, economic or political, wants to introduce itself to the potential president. A successful convention usually produces a small electoral bounce for a candidate. This bounce is temporary, but if their candidate is now better known and liked by the U.S. public, it shows a party how successful their convention was.

TECHNICAL STUFF

Party conventions used to be an important part of U.S. politics. It was here where presidential nominees were selected. In the infamous smoke-filled rooms, party leaders got together to pick a presidential nominee. They had to bargain, compromise, strike a deal, and then finally agree on a candidate. Today, national nominating conventions are a mere formality, and everybody already knows who the presidential nominees are before the convention takes place. However, they still perform a few functions, like drawing up a party platform and the selection of the presidential nominee's vice presidential running mate.

Formally Campaigning

A candidate's campaign for the presidency can be determined by several factors. First is whether an incumbent is running. If there is an incumbent, voters look at the incumbent's record and determine if they are happy with the incumbent. If they are, they will reelect the incumbent. If not, they will vote the incumbent out of office.

Although statistics show that incumbents have an advantage, being an incumbent for the presidency is not a shoo-in. Since 1800, twelve incumbents have lost reelection. It started with John Adams in 1800, and most recently, President Trump lost reelection in 2020. He then won the presidency back in 2024, which had only happened once before in U.S. history, when Grover Cleveland won the presidency back in 1892, after losing reelection in 1888.

Then there are open elections where there is no incumbent. The most recent of these happened in 2016 when Hillary Clinton lost to Donald Trump. In an open election, voters must make an educated guess: Who would be the better candidate of the two? There is no established record at the presidential level, so voters look at candidates' records at lower levels of office or in the private sector. Some votes are even swayed by things such as the morals of a candidate or even just how a candidate looks.

Today, candidates look at an electoral map of the U.S. to determine which states decide the election. Most states are reliably Democratic or Republican and do not need to be targeted. Why waste your money in a state where a candidate already has won or lost? Then there are the battleground states that decide elections in the U.S. In 2024, it came down to seven battleground states. The other 43 states already had been considered safe for one of the two candidates.

REMEMBER

The battleground states in 2024 were Arizona, Nevada, Georgia, North Carolina, Pennsylvania, Michigan, and Wisconsin. Former President Donald Trump won all seven and the presidency.

Presidential debates have become an important part of political campaigning. Usually, presidential candidates debate three times and the vice-presidential candidates once. Presidential debates can make or break a candidate. The first debate televised on TV was in 1960 between Vice-President Richard Nixon and his democratic opponent John F. Kennedy, and televised presidential debates have been with us ever since.

REMEMBER

In that first televised presidential debate in 1960, Nixon had just come out of the hospital and looked haggard. John F. Kennedy looked young and energetic. People who watched the debate on television believed Kennedy won the debate. People who listened to it on radio gave the debate win to Nixon. This clearly shows how important image and looks have become in campaigning. Today, make-up artists travel with campaign teams to make sure their candidates look good.

Running a campaign

The most expensive part of a campaign is still television advertising. TV commercials are used to introduce a candidate to the public, to increase name identification among the public, and, of course, to convince the public to vote for a candidate and against another candidate. Often negative advertisements are used to attack an opponent. TV commercials can target a certain group of voters who have not yet decided who to support. TV commercials are great for candidates because they can target potential voters by their viewing habits. If you want to target older voters, for example, you just run ads during a show that is watched by older voters.

Hiring specialists

To run a successful campaign, many specialists need to be hired. The following list highlights some of the most significant:

>> The **campaign manager** is one of the most important specialists. They handle day-to-day operations of a campaign and set the tone for the campaign. Together with the candidate, the campaign manager decides what type of campaign is run. Will it be a positive campaign highlighting a candidate's great successes or a negative campaign viciously attacking your opponent? Or maybe a combination of the two?

This in turn determines what type of commercials the campaign runs on television, the radio, and social media. The campaign manager determines where commercials will be run, what locations the candidate travels to, who the candidate addresses, what campaign events to attend, and so on.

>> Then the campaign needs to hire a **field operations specialist**. This person organizes campaign appearances. They check out sites, organize travel, and even bring some supporters along, in case the turnout is not what was expected. The field operations specialist also trains campaign volunteers.

>> **Campaign volunteers** are those people who campaign for the candidate by going door to door, coming in close contact with the voter. Campaign volunteers need to know how to interact with people without alienating them.

>> Candidates have to hire **speechwriters**. Today, candidates no longer write their own speeches.

>> Hand in hand with a speech writer goes a **speech coach**. The speech coach shows a candidate how to address people properly on television and in the field. They teach candidates how to pronounce words, how to emphasize terms, and even how to stand and move their arms when they deliver a speech. You do not want your candidate to deliver a great speech in such a way that the audience is either tuning out or going to sleep.

>> In addition, a presidential campaign has to hire **experts in policy**. A candidate must be familiar not just with domestic events but also foreign events. The candidate cannot mispronounce a foreign leader's name and has to know the newest economic data for the country.

>> **Opposition research specialists** are needed. They look into your opponent's past to try to discover if there were any indiscretions. They also analyze every speech ever given and every comment ever made by a candidate. This arms you to contradict your opponent by saying, well, that is not what you said in college 30 years ago.

>> A **professional fundraiser** is a must. Campaigns cost millions today, and the money has to come from somewhere — unless the candidate is independently wealthy and can finance his own campaign, as Ross Perot did in 1992. The fundraiser has to target donors, organize fundraising dinners and also design fundraising messages, many of which run on social media today.

>> The most important person next to the campaign manager is the **pollster**. Today a candidate is likely to hire more than one pollster, usually a polling firm. Pollsters provide the data to run a campaign. The first thing a potential presidential candidate does is to have a pollster take a pre-election poll. This poll shows if the candidate actually has a chance of winning.

After the candidate decides to enter the race, the pollster conducts a benchmark poll. It is a large-scale poll, quite expensive and involving thousands of people, which provides the campaign with four types of data:

- *Information on issues:* The poll shows which issues people care about so the candidate can focus on these issues.

- *Image:* The poll can provide information about a candidate's image and, more important, about the opponent's image.

TIP

Occasionally, a candidate might come across as too intellectual. That is not a good thing in campaigning for office. So, the candidate might shoot a commercial showing him going hunting to show the voting public that he is a regular guy and not a nerdy academic.

- *Swing voters:* Pollsters provide information about the nature of swing voters. A candidate has a built-in base of support and does not have to do too much to get their vote. Swing voters decide elections. Pollsters provide information on the message to be used to target these voters and can also tell if the message is working.

- *Fundraising:* Pollsters are invaluable for fundraising. They can tell you what groups of people are willing to contribute to a candidate's campaign so that you can target them directly and do not waste money targeting people who will not donate.

>> Campaigns also hire **press relations specialists,** who handle any contact with the media. These professionals coordinate press releases, respond to press inquiries and help coach a candidate before a debate or a press conference.

Needing Big Money

Running for the presidency and Congress has gotten extremely expensive. In 2024, the two presidential candidates, Kamala Harris and Donald Trump spent $3.1 billion on political ads in the general election campaign. Ad money spent by Congress, both House and Senate, totaled $4.3 billion. Overall, campaign spending on political ads in the U.S. in the 2024 election totaled a little over $11 billion, a sharp increase from the $9 billion spent in 2020. So where is all this money coming from?

Campaign contributions come from various sources, including the following:

>> Regular U.S. citizens.

>> Interest groups, political action committees (PACs) and super PACs (see Chapter 15). About a third of all contributions come from political action committees, which are the financial arms of interest groups, including business and unions.

>> The political parties themselves still help out financially. Both political parties have national and state committees that raise money. Typically, these committees support congressional candidates and the occasional governor's race in an important state.

>> Incumbent members of Congress have become major sources of funds. Some of them even establish their own PACs. Many are in safe districts and still raise money they put aside. They can use this money to support fellow congress-people or candidates running for office.

>> Occasionally, some candidates use their own money to run for office. They are wealthy candidates who tap into their fortune to finance their own campaigns. For example, Donald Trump, a billionaire, used $66 million of his own money to run and win the presidency in 2016 and Senator and former governor of Florida, Rick Scott, spent $64 million of his own money to run successfully for the U.S. Senate.

>> A new form of fundraising is the Internet and social media. In 2000, Internet fundraising was used for the first time, and by 2004, it had become common. Candidate and future president Barack Obama perfected Internet fundraising in 2008, raising over $200 million. By 2012, the Obama campaign was able to raise monies from over 3 million people online.

Regulating fundraising

In 1896, the regulation of fundraising became a hot topic. Republican William Mckinley won the presidency and had his whole campaign bankrolled by a few large businesses. Overall, business gave McKinley $3.5 million to spend on his campaign, whereas his Democratic opponent William Jennings Bryant ended up spending $50,000.

Not surprisingly, many thought that business bought the new president. The public wanted reform, and Teddy Roosevelt, who became president after McKinley's assassination, gave it to them. In 1907, Congress passed the Tillman Act, with the president's support, which made it illegal for businesses to give money directly to federal campaigns. In 1925, the Federal Corrupt Practices Act followed, making indirect contributions, such as paying for campaign travel, illegal. The Smith Connally Act in 1943 applied the Tillman Act to unions, which had become quite powerful by the 1940s. Then the issue of campaign financing went away until the early 1970s.

Restricting campaign contributions

In the early 1970s, a progressive Congress decided to tackle campaign finance reform again. It passed the Federal Election Campaign Act of 1971, which set limits on how much a candidate could spend of his own money on his own campaign. The Supreme Court ruled this to be unconstitutional. So today, candidates can spend as much money as they want to on their own campaign. In addition, an overall limit on campaign spending was declared unconstitutional.

Congress tried again in 1974, passing the Federal Election Campaign Act Amendments of 1974. It changed the way candidates raised money in the U.S. and impacted U.S. politics for decades. From then on, the following rules applied to campaigns:

>> The Federal Elections Commission (FEC) was created and consists of six members appointed by the president and confirmed by the Senate. The FEC monitors compliance with all federal laws regarding campaign fundraising and expenditures.

>> All federal election campaign contributions and expenditures have to be reported to the FEC.

>> All contributions over $100 have to be reported by name to the FEC. Contributions under $100 can be pooled, and no names are reported.

>> Cash contributions over $100 are illegal. All donations over $100 have to be made by check or credit card.

>> Foreign contributions are illegal.

>> Individual contributions are limited to $1,000 per candidate per election for an overall contribution limit of $25,000.

>> Contributions to political parties are limited to $20,000 per election cycle.

>> Political action committees are limited to $5,000 per candidate per election (for more information on political action committees, see Chapter 15).

Public funding at the presidential level was established in 1974. At the general election level, candidates who accept public funding, which is voluntary, receive a grant. However, after they take public money, they are not allowed to raise any more money for their campaign. In 2008, John McCain, see Figure 13-3, became the last presidential candidate to accept public funding. He received about $85 million. His opponent Barack Obama refused public funding and raised over $700 million privately.

TECHNICAL
STUFF

There is public funding available for major party candidates running in the general election for the presidency. John McCain was the last presidential candidate to accept public funding in 2008 and since then all candidates have rejected it because they can raise much more privately.

Since the 1971 FECA laws were passed, many amendments have been made to them. In 1979, *soft money*, money that is spent on party building, including voter registration, getting-the-vote-out drives, issue advertising for a political party and not a candidate, and administrative party expenses, was legalized. Soft money did not have to be declared until 1992 and could be raised in unlimited amounts. By 2000, both parties raised close to half a billion dollars in soft money.

United States Congress/Wikimedia Common/ Public Domain/https://commons. wikimedia.org/wiki/File:John_ McCain_official_portrait_2009_ (3x4_cropped).jpg/Last accessed on Last accessed on October 06, 2025

FIGURE 13-3: Senator John McCain.

REMEMBER

Hard money is money given directly to candidates running for federal office and their campaign committees. *Soft money* is money given for party activities.

In addition, *independent expenditures* became common. These are monies spent by a third party to support or defeat a candidate. The Supreme Court in 1996 ruled that independent expenditures are legal if they advocate for issue positions and if the monies spent are not tied to a specific candidate's campaign. The Supreme Court ruled in Colorado Republican Federal Campaign Committee v. FEC in 1996 that political parties were allowed to engage in independent expenditures as long as they were made independently from specific candidates and their campaigns.

Trying again

In 2002, the Bipartisan Campaign Act was passed by Congress. It was sponsored by Arizona Republican Senator John McCain and Wisconsin Democratic Senator Russ Feingold. It was first used for the 2002 federal election, and it stipulated:

» Soft money was banned at the federal level.

» Individual contributions were increased from $1,000 to $2,000 per candidate per election, and contributions were indexed to inflation. Today, the limit is $3,500.

>> Overall limits for individuals on how much they can give to candidates increased to $95,000 per two-year election cycle.

>> A person could now give $44,300 to a national political party committee per calendar.

The section on setting a time limit on third-party campaign ads was struck down by the Supreme Court.

Contributions to state-level candidates for governor or state legislature or local offices, such as mayor, are regulated by state laws and vary by state. They are not impacted by federal campaign finance regulations.

Going crazy

The role of third-party groups in U.S. campaign politics has increased quite dramatically. Third-party groups today bypass campaigns and are not affiliated with them. They can take unlimited contributions, often from unnamed donors, and spend the money however they wish. They are not accountable to candidates or political parties.

These third-party groups are often called *527 organizations*, named after the tax code that governs them.

In 2010, in Citizens United v. FEC, the Supreme Court ruled that it is unconstitutional to limit or ban corporate or union funding of candidates. Corporations and unions could now freely spend money to support or defeat candidates as long as they are not directly affiliated with a candidate's' organization.

Now the question is, do interest groups favor one party over the other? Studies have shown that labor unions favor the Democratic Party whereas industries such as oil and gas favor the Republican Party. However, overall, most business groups split their money between the two sides. They want to make sure that they cover all their bases.

In federal races, incumbents do raise most of the money. In 2018, incumbent senators raised $14.6 million on average. Their challengers raised a measly $1.9 million. Clearly, monies do go to incumbents, which accounts for their overwhelming reelection rate.

Getting 527s

527 groups are organizations that can raise and spend unlimited amounts of money for issue advocacy, but they cannot coordinate with any candidate or

campaign. So, they cannot explicitly support or oppose a candidate, but they can run ads focusing on an issue a candidate supports or opposes.

527 groups are so named after the section of the U.S. tax code that regulates them and makes them tax-exempt organizations. They are primarily created to influence the nomination, selection, or appointment of candidates for federal, state, or local public office. They are not regulated under state or federal campaign finance laws, but they cannot clearly advocate for the election of or defeat of a specific candidate or party.

There are no upper limits on contributions to 527s and no restrictions on who can contribute. They have to register with the Internal Revenue Service (IRS) and must disclose their donors and file reports on contributions and expenditures. Although they cannot expressly advocate for specific candidates or coordinate with a candidate's campaigns, they can raise money to advocate for policy issues and voter mobilization.

In July 2010, the U.S. Supreme Court struck down fundraising limits on independent-expenditure–only committees or Super PACs, which, like 527s, can raise unlimited amounts of monies from individuals, unions, and corporations to influence elections. Super PACs must also disclose their finances but can clearly advocate for or against candidates. Suddenly 527 groups became less valuable, because they cannot advocate for and against specific candidates, and they have been on the decline ever since.

Creating super PACs

In 2010, we see the birth of the super PAC. Super PACs are independent-expenditure–only committees that can raise and spend unlimited amounts of money from individuals, corporations, and unions. Although they cannot directly give money to campaigns and candidates or coordinate with political campaigns, they can engage in independent political expenditures.

Independent expenditures include communications like television ads, radio spots, social media advertising, direct mail, and voter mobilization efforts that advocate for the election or defeat of clearly identified federal candidates or a specific political issue.

REMEMBER

Super PACs are also known as independent-expenditure–only committees that can raise unlimited money from any source to support or oppose a candidate.

However, super PACs are not allowed to contribute directly to a candidate or coordinate with a candidate's campaign. Super PACs are subject to the same rules and public disclosures as regular PACs (see Chapter 15) and must report to the Federal Election Commission.

Super PACs can thus receive contributions of any amount, including from corporations and unions. They are supposed to operate independently of candidate camps, but they are often established by a candidate's friends, allies, and even former party operatives.

Super PACs cannot accept money from foreign nationals or national banks.

Candidates running for president can even outsource some of their campaign activities to super PACs. This happened in 2024, when former President Trump outsourced canvassing and getting-out-the-vote drives to a super PAC run by his then-ally Elon Musk in all swing states.

Super PACs must report their donors to the Federal Election Commission like regular PACs, unless they take dark money from groups. *Dark money* refers to election spending and contributions by nonprofits and shell companies that are not legally required to and do not disclose the political identities of their donors. These companies engage in U.S. campaign politics by contributing to super PACs, as well as doing their own TV and online spending. If super PACs take dark money, then they cannot be aware of who actually donated that money and just know how much they received, and this they must report.

Super PACs must disclose contributing organization's names. However, if those organizations are 501(c)(4) social welfare groups, trade organizations, or shell LLCs, Super PACs are not required to disclose their original donors or funders.

Raising record levels of money in 2024

The Citizens United Supreme Court decision back in 2010 allowed corporations and unions to raise and spend unlimited amounts on elections. In 2020, these groups spent $1 billion on elections, and by 2024, this amount nearly doubled to 1.9 billion.

A lot of this money was so-called dark money. Dark money groups give money to super PACs to attack and support candidates and even run their own ads, many of them online, which have to be worded in such a way as not to openly attack candidates.

Television ad spending

Dark money groups spent $242 million on TV ads in 2024. Most did not have to be reported because the ads did not directly advocate support or opposition to a candidate. Interestingly, a lot of money was spent on streaming applications such as Hulu. Online ad spending also increased to $325 million. Again, no reporting to the FEC is necessary unless the campaign commercial advocates for supporting or defeating a specific candidate. The major platforms that reported political ad sales in 2024 were Facebook, Instagram, Google, YouTube, X, and Snapchat.

Untraceable spending

Both parties benefited from dark money. Dark money tends to benefit Democrats more than Republicans. Up to $1.2 billion in dark money was given to the Democratic Party and its super PACs in 2024, whereas close to $700 million went to Republicans. The major Democratic dark money group was Future Forward USA Action. It is a nonprofit group that poured a little over 300 million dollars into the election by running ads and giving money to its super PAC Future Forward USA. On the Republican side, there was Building America's Future, a nonprofit that received funding from billionaire Elon Musk. It spent $35 million on a super PAC that ran fake ads on behalf of Kamala Harris suggesting she supported controversial policies.

With super PACs and dark money coming to dominate U.S. campaign financing, it looks like 2028 will be another record year for billions spent on campaigning without knowing where the money came from.

IN THIS CHAPTER

» **Being necessary for a democracy**

» **Being different**

» **Still functioning**

» **Slowly declining**

» **Evolving over time**

» **Organizing third parties**

Chapter **14**

Examining Political Parties

F or decades, the field of political science has debated whether political parties are necessary for a democracy to function properly. Many argue that political parties are found in every working democracy, and that they are necessary to organize political participation, aggregate interest, and to serve as the link between social forces and the government.

What is a political party? James Madison gives the classical definition of a political party in Federalist Paper No. 10. According to Madison, who perceived political parties negatively, believing that political parties were divisive and could lead to political conflict, a party — or as he calls it, faction — can be defined as follows: "By a faction, I understand a number of citizens, whether amounting to a majority or a minority of the whole, who are united and actuated by some common impulse or passion, or of interest, adverse to the rights of other citizens or to the permanent aggregate interest of the community."

Modern definitions of political parties do vary. However, most political scientists agree that a political party is a group that seeks to elect candidates to public office by supplying them with a label by which they are known to the electorate. A more detailed definition states that political parties are: "a team of men and women seeking to control the governing apparatus by gaining office in a duly constituted election."

Both definitions agree on two major characteristics: First, political parties want to elect people to public office. Second, political parties provide a label or cue to their supporters facilitating voting in elections.

A political party is a group of citizens who organize to contest elections, win public office, and impact policymaking.

REMEMBER

Analyzing Political Parties

Famous political scientist V.O. Key Jr. suggested political parties need to be studied as structures composed of three different components:

>> **The party in the electorate.** The party in the electorate includes all the individuals who identify with a political party and support the party on Election Day. Examples are Republicans who voted for President Trump and Democrats who voted for Vice-President Harris.

>> **The party as an organization.** Here, one examines the party's structure at the national, state, or local level. For example, local, state, and national party offices, staff, and budgets can be analyzed. In addition, the party's organizational view also includes an analysis of the party's involvement in the recruitment of candidates and the organization of primaries, conventions, or caucuses to nominate candidates for office.

>> **The party in government.** This third and final component of political parties consists of elected party officeholders at all political levels. This includes members of Congress, governors, state legislators, mayors, and city council people. Studies involving this component include, for example, the voting behavior of United States senators.

Describing political parties

When studying the Constitution of the United States, an interesting phenomenon concerning political parties is apparent. Unlike other democratic constitutions, such as the German or French constitution, political parties are not mentioned or regulated by the U.S. Constitution. Believing that parties were a source of corruption and an impediment to the freedom of the people to judge issues on their own merits, as James Madison argues in Federalist Paper No. 10, the Founding Fathers perceived parties or factions as a threat to the survival of the newly formed democratic governmental system in the United States.

George Washington perceived political parties as so dangerous that he even mentioned them in his Farewell Address in 1796. In the address, Washington warned the country against factions because they divided the country along partisan lines. He believed that political parties undermined the spirit of cooperation so necessary for the new country to survive. This negative attitude towards political parties has persisted in the United States, and many Americans still perceive political parties as a necessary evil and a source of corruption.

Being different

American political parties are unique in nature. Some claim that the United States has the oldest political party still in existence in the world, namely the Democratic Party, whereas others give that distinction to the British Conservative Party, or the Tories. Despite this disagreement, everybody agrees that American political parties are very different from traditional or European parties.

The first characteristic of the American party system is the endurance of a two-party system. Following Duverger's Law, which states that single-member district election rules result in a two-party system, the United States has found itself with a two-party system for most of its history.

TECHNICAL
STUFF

Duverger's Law states that electoral law determines whether a democracy has a two-party system or a multi-party system. U.S. electoral law, single-member district electoral law, creates a two-party system.

With a few exceptions, usually in times of crisis, such as before the Civil War, the United States always had a two-party system. Why is this the case?

The first reason is electoral law. The United States uses British electoral law, also referred to as a single-member district electoral law. British electoral law is simple; the person who wins the most votes in a district wins office. At the same time, this type of electoral law discriminates against third or minor parties. Only the two major parties have a shot at winning seats, whereas a third party getting 20 percent of the vote receives nothing.

Most of the democratic world uses proportional representation, where political parties receive seats in legislative chambers based on the proportion of the vote they receive. If a political party wins ten percent of the vote, it automatically receives ten percent of the seats in the legislature. This type of electoral law aids smaller or third parties, allowing them to win seats even if they do not come in first. In turn, a multi-party system, where more than two parties are represented in the legislative chamber, results.

Being all-encompassing

A second major characteristic of American political parties is that they are *all-encompassing*. All-encompassing political parties are not very ideological or extreme and represent a plethora of political viewpoints. For example, the Democratic Party historically has been open to both liberal, moderate, and conservative Democrats. In Europe, each faction within the Democratic Party, conservative, moderate, and liberal, would have its own political party. In the United States, they are packed into one party. This results in party leaders constantly having to mediate between the various factions, resulting in more moderate policies acceptable to all factions within the party. In other words, the concept of pluralism also works within political parties. This reflects the moderate, non-ideological nature of the American electorate.

Being regulated at the state level

Unlike European parties, American parties are regulated at the state level. Therefore, they are decentralized, and instead of having a national party structure with millions of dues-paying members, like many European parties do, American parties differ from state to state. Every state (but not the national government) has the power to regulate state parties, and every state party must follow different sets of rules. In Texas, for example, political parties are regulated by the state constitution; it regulates Texas political parties and sets guidelines. For this reason, in Texas it is the state constitution that determines how nominees for elections are chosen, and it also sets limits on many party activities, such as holding elections and raising funds.

Being negative

Another unique characteristic of American political parties is that they face a public that perceives them negatively. Many trace this back to the warnings of our Founding Fathers, such as Washington and Madison, who considered political parties divisive and bad for democracy. Today, the American public distrusts political parties and doubts that they are useful and necessary for a democracy.

Classifying political parties

Political parties can be characterized as mass or cadre parties. Political parties that are decentralized, with power vested at the local level, and are led at the national level only by informal committees, are *cadre* or *electoral parties*. Cadre parties have no dues-paying mass membership at the national level, and their functions are purely electoral. In other words, they are in it to win elections at all cost. An electoral party has one overarching objective, which is to win office. It sacrifices everything, including its soul, to win. Its policies tend to be moderate, favoring the status quo.

Mass parties are very centralized at the national level. All power is vested in a small leadership group, which runs the party with an iron fist. They have a large dues-paying membership, which can run in the millions. Their main purpose is not just to win elections but to stay true to their vision. Although winning elections is a major function, it is not the only function. Mass parties would rather lose elections than compromise on issues. If elected to power, mass parties tend to be very doctrinaire and uncompromising in nature. The British Labour Party is a good example of a mass party today.

Functions in a Democracy

As discussed earlier in the chapter, political parties are considered by many to be essential for a well-functioning democracy. Why is this the case? To provide an answer to this question, the next section of the chapter deals with the functions political parties perform in a democratic political system.

According to a 2024 study by the Pew Research Center, about two-thirds of all U.S. citizens identify with a political party, meaning that they are partisans. The other third identifies as independent. However, most independents profess support for one of the two parties when asked. So, they are not true independents but they are called *partisan leaners*. They share the same political views and political behavior as partisans. Of these partisans and partisan leaners combined as of 2024, 49 percent are or lean Democrat, and 48 percent are or lean Republican. Only three percent are truly independents. Clearly, partisan identification still matters today and is a major predictor of election outcomes.

Determining the vote

Political parties have become a major determinant of the vote through a process called *party identification*. The concept of party identification is psychological in nature. There exists a psychological attachment to a political party by most voters and this attachment in turn determines how people vote. Therefore, party identification, whether a person identifies as a Republican or Democrat, determines how they vote. It is not knowledge that determines the vote for most Americans but party identification.

One of the core functions of political parties is to facilitate voting for the average voter. Most voters are unfamiliar with the details of many issues, especially complex economic ones, and are unaware of how candidates stand on these issues. That is one of the reasons voters opt not to vote. However, identifying with a political party, or, in other words, having a partisan identification, allows voters to still cast a ballot. Political parties facilitate voting by providing voters with cues and symbols that make it easier to vote.

Political parties allow voters to identify with a political party that represents their political wishes. A Republican voter, even though he or she does not know about a Republican candidate on a ballot, knows that the candidate very likely will have values and beliefs similar to the voter, making voting for the candidate rational.

Socializing the U.S. public

Political socialization is another function of political parties. Political socialization refers to the process of acquiring political beliefs and values. A person's political beliefs and values determine how that person acts within the political system.

Agents of political socialization are responsible for a person acquiring their political values and beliefs. They are structures that pass on values, shaping political beliefs. These include the family, friends, religion, the media, interest groups, and political parties. Political parties have an interest in instilling political values into the public. By socializing voters, political parties can create lifelong supporters who will support the party during good and bad times.

However, to become an agent of political socialization, political parties must have close and personal contact with the public. The public in turn must perceive them as being necessary in their lives. American political parties performed this function in the 19th century, and European political parties still perform it today.

In the 19th century, American political parties engaged in many political and social functions. They organized meetings, provided entertainment such as party picnics and dances, and were in close contact with the average person. In addition, political parties published newspapers and were a major provider of information for the average voter.

Today, political parties have ceased to be an agent of political socialization for most Americans. Most of their traditional socializing functions have been taken over by the media in the United States. In Europe, on the other hand, parties still perform this core function. It is common for European political parties to publish newspapers or to control other parts of the media.

Recruiting and nominating candidates

The traditional function of political parties is to recruit and nominate candidates for political office. A party recruits the strongest possible candidate to run for office and then nominates that candidate. This in turn gives the party control over the candidate. If a candidate deviates from party policy, votes against the party, or in any other way opposes the party, the party can punish the person by denying re-nomination, which can end a political career.

Although American political parties performed this function a century ago, times have changed. With the introduction of the direct primary (see Chapter 13), candidates can recruit and nominate themselves and even run their own campaign if they have the necessary resources. This has ended party control over many politicians and has led to less party discipline in U.S. politics.

Running and financing campaigns

Running for office in the U.S. has become prohibitively expensive. In 2024, candidates running for Congress spent $10.3 billion on their respective campaigns. Historically, political parties provided candidates with the funds to run for political office and provided staff and campaign specialists.

Due to the direct primary (see Chapter 13), all of this has changed. Candidates today raise their own funds and establish their own campaign organization without party support during primary campaigns. This favors wealthier candidates who can finance their own campaigns. It also takes the party out of campaigning, which decreases the control political parties have over their own candidates.

After winning the nomination without a party's help, candidates are unlikely to scrap their winning campaign teams and let the party take over. Today the party still provides some financial help as well as indirect support. It can provide candidates with campaign support, such as campaign specialists like pollsters.

At the local level, parties are even more important, because they provide needed help by registering voters and providing volunteers to help candidates' campaigns.

Informing the public

Since their inception, political parties have been a major source of political information in democracies — that is, in most democracies, but not the U.S. In the early years of the republic, that was quite different. The two major parties of the time, the Federalists and the Democratic–Republicans, published not only leaflets and campaign information, but actual newspapers. This provided supporters with information, albeit biased in nature. More recently, in the 1980s, there even was a GOP TV cable channel in the U.S. All of this is gone.

Today, neither party publishes newspapers nor runs a news channel as is done in many European countries. American parties' only activity is during election times, when they run campaign commercials and provide handouts, pamphlets, and leaflets, which provide voters with a limited amount of information.

Mobilizing the public

Political parties can mobilize voters on Election Day. Political parties not only help to register voters but also try to get them to vote. Voting is not a priority for many U.S. citizens, so it is important to have an organization that tries to get as many registered voters to the polls as possible. Political parties initiate contact with voters by calling them, stopping by their homes, or even texting and emailing them, not just on Election Day, but weeks before an election, to make sure that voters will go out and vote. This is one of the core functions political parties still perform.

Providing policy proposals

One of the most important functions of a political party is to provide the voters with information they can use to make a rational decision on Election Day. Political parties formulate ideas and propose policies and programs to the voters in their party platforms. Every four years, both major parties, as well as most minor or third parties, create party platforms containing policy proposals. Voters are supposed to read the platform, familiarize themselves with the policy proposals, and then vote for or against the party. Studies show that most voters do not bother to read party platforms. This proves to be a big problem, because winning political parties implement close to 75 percent of the policies outlined in their party platforms. People are then shocked when political parties suddenly begin to implement policies they have never heard of and often oppose.

Organizing government

One of the reasons political parties were created is to organize the policymaking machinery at all governmental levels. In other words, this function is being performed at the local, state, or even national level. Could you imagine the House of Representatives, which has 435 legislators, without any kind of machinery in place to run its affairs? How likely is it that 435 individuals could run a legislature and write, debate, and pass bills? This is very unlikely. It is here where political parties come in. They organize the policymaking process by making sure its members support the party policy line and vote for its bills.

Aggregating interests

Similar to interest groups (see Chapter 15), political parties are a way to aggregate interest for citizens. Most U.S. citizens are powerless by themselves but when they get together with like-minded people, they will suddenly acquire political power. A good example is a petition to change a policy. If only one person signs it, elected officeholders have a tendency to ignore it. If one million people sign the petition, then suddenly elected officeholders take notice and act on the petition. So, if people aggregate their interests, get together with like-minded people, they can acquire political power and get things done.

TECHNICAL STUFF

Political power is the ability to make people engage in a political act that they would not engage in out of their own free will.

Political parties perform many functions in a democratic society. Some of these functions are historical in the U.S. such as providing information by publishing newspapers or organizing social functions such as picnics and dances. Most functions parties perform are still needed in a democracy. Without parties organizing government, little gets accomplished in Congress. Facilitating voting by providing a party identification increases voter turnout, necessary in a democracy. Aggregating interests gives average people political power in the U.S., and creating party platforms creates a link between government and citizens.

Declining Over Time

American political parties do not perform many of the traditional functions they used to perform. What happened? A century and a half ago, the American party system looked similar to the European one. Today, American political parties have become weaker, perform fewer functions, and are less powerful than their European counterparts.

The decline of American parties can be traced back to the progressive movement of the late 19th century. A white middle-class movement designed to take on powerful political machines in many large American cities, the progressive movement not only managed to weaken political machines but also to weaken our two major parties at the same time.

Relying on political machines

A *political* or *party machine* is defined as an organization that uses tangible incentives to recruit its members. These tangible incentives include jobs and money. The machine is hierarchically structured with a party boss controlling the whole city. Machines were commonly found in the larger cities in the Northwest and Midwest and most party bosses were Irish in origin. This should not be too surprising because the concept of a political machine is Irish in origin, too. The classical machines of the late 19th and early 20th century have disappeared today, but during their times they provided many needed services to immigrants and were powerful brokers at presidential-nominating conventions. Some of the functions they performed included the provision of housing, jobs, and food to new immigrants, as well as the teaching of English, so immigrants could become citizens and vote for the machines.

The concept of *patronage* was at the bottom of the machine network. Patronage is defined as the reward of jobs based on party ties instead of merit. For many, joining a political machine was necessary to get an acceptable job within a party dominated city.

Political machines were controversial because machines engaged in certain illegal activities, like the selling of permits and licenses, as well as tolerating crime for fees in their cities. One of the last powerful machines in the United States was the Daley machine in Chicago. Lasting into the 1970s, the machine controlled about 40,000 jobs, and its recipients were expected to deliver ten votes apiece on Election Day by mobilizing voters and to donate five percent of their salary back to the Democratic Party. The Chicago machine was weakened with the death of Mayor Daley in 1976, but some elements of machine-style politics are still around today.

Going progressive

The progressive movement, made up of the white middle class, did not benefit from machines and was not able to exercise political power in machine-run cities, so it decided to attack the political machines. It pushed for major reforms, which destroyed many party machines, and weakened American political parties.

First, the progressive movement gave the country non-partisan elections at the local level. In states such as California, where many local elections are non-partisan, meaning candidates cannot run for office with a party label attached to them, this destroyed the local party organizations. Having no purpose in local politics, the party lost its reason for being.

Second, the progressive movement introduced the concept of direct primaries to most of the country, except for many Southern states where primaries were already used. The direct primary had a devastating effect on political parties. It was the most destructive weapon against strong political parties. The primary hurt political parties in the following manner:

>> The power to nominate candidates for political office now rested with the people, mostly party identifiers. Previously, local, state, and national party leaders were able to nominate candidates for office. This resulted in the party being able to control elected officeholders by being able to deny them renomination for office if they did not follow the party's wishes. The primary took away this power. Less party cohesion in bodies such as Congress was the result.

>> The party often is split by primaries. Instead of having the party leadership getting together to nominate a candidate, who then enjoys the support of all the party's supporters, a primary allows for many candidates from the same party to run. This can be very divisive, especially if the primary gets nasty. Intra-party factionalism can hurt the party in the general election. Today, the party usually stays out of the primary until the public has picked a nominee.

>> The primary took away a powerful incentive to join or support a party. Previously, loyal party supporters could expect to be nominated for office sooner or later to repay their support and loyalty. The primary took away a party's power to reward party loyalists in such a manner.

>> The primary took the party out of campaigning. During the primary, the party usually stays out of the campaign. This forces the candidates running in the primary to set up their own campaign organization and raise their own funds. After winning the primary, it is unlikely that a candidate will scrap their winning campaign organization and let the party take over. Instead, they will keep the organization and rely on some (but not much) help from the party.

>> The primary is also responsible for increasing the length of campaigning and the associated campaign costs. Instead of running in only one campaign, candidates must win two elections, a primary and a general election, to get elected. This leads to increased dependence on political action committees (PACs) and large-scale donors for funds. Candidates today are much more reliant on sources of funds coming from wealthy donors and interest groups

than they were previously when the parties shielded them from these sources by running candidates' campaigns.

>> Finally, the power to nominate, given to the people by primaries, has today been taken over by party activists to the left and right of the public. Previously, parties nominated the candidates most likely to win, meaning they had to be moderate in nature to appeal to the widest possible spectrum of voters. Today, with party activists picking the nominees, the chosen candidates are often too liberal or too conservative for the average voter, resulting in electoral defeats for the respective parties.

Changing times

Civil service reform was another progressive reform that hurt the political parties in the United States. Started by the Arthur administration and the Pendleton Act of 1883 (see Chapter 6), it targeted patronage, or the power to hand out jobs based upon party ties. Previously, patronage could be used to reward party loyalists with jobs, which in turn helped to recruit people to the party. With this power gone, it became more difficult to attract supporters and funds for the parties.

The advent of the media, especially television and the Internet, had an unexpected negative effect on political parties. Previous campaigning involved literally walking door-to-door and holding campaign rallies, which required the help of party volunteers. Today, it is possible to campaign for office purely on television or social media without ever meeting the voting public and still do well. Parties do not seem to be imperative for a candidate if they have the necessary financial resources.

Finally, education has taken a toll on political parties. With higher education becoming more readily available after WWII with the GI Bill, more Americans went to college. Studies have shown that college graduates are less likely to identify with political parties and are more likely to consider themselves independent or at least willing to split their ticket on Election Day.

Studying Five Party Systems in U.S. History

When looking at the evolution of U.S. political parties, five distinct party systems, or eras of party dominance can be found.

Developing early despite Washington's warnings (1792–1828)

In 1792, George Washington, the first U.S. president, was reelected. Soon, policy disagreements broke out in his cabinet between his secretary of the treasury, Alexander Hamilton, and his secretary of state, Thomas Jefferson (see Figure 14-1). Both were trying to get Washington's support for their policies and were secretly hoping to become his successor. By 1792, supporters of the two began to organize to push for their policy preferences and the U.S.'s first political party system was born.

The supporters of Alexander Hamilton called themselves the Federalists. They advocated for a stronger national government with an active role in the economy. For this reason, they favored higher tariffs, duties on imports on foreign goods, to protect native industries from foreign competition. Foreign policy wise they were close to Great Britain.

Thomas Jefferson and his followers called themselves the Democratic-Republicans. They believed in a smaller national government and advocated for states' rights. They stood for lower tariffs so that the average American could buy cheaper foreign goods. Finally, they were closer to France in foreign policy.

The Federalists were poorly organized and appealed to a smaller group of Americans, mainly businesspeople. Their support was concentrated in New England. The Democratic-Republicans represented the U.S. farmers and artisans. The Federalists won only one election, in 1796, when John Adams was elected president. He was subsequently defeated in 1800 by Thomas Jefferson, and the Federalist Party started to slowly wither away. It was gone from American politics by 1820. The Democratic-Republicans ended up dominating American politics from 1800 until 1824 and, by 1820, became the only viable party in the U.S.

Getting a dominant party: The Jacksonian Democrats (1828–1860)

The disputed presidential election of 1824 ended the first party system. Four Democratic-Republicans ran for the presidency. The two frontrunners were Secretary of State John Quincy Adams (see Figure 14-2) and General Andrew Jackson, the hero of the battle of New Orleans. Jackson came in first, winning the popular vote and 99 Electoral College votes. But it wasn't enough. Jackson needed 131 votes for an absolute majority. With no candidate winning an absolute majority of the Electoral College votes, the election went to the House of Representatives, where each state had one vote.

FIGURE 14-2:
John Quincy Adams.

Durand, A. B. (Asher Brown)/Library of Congress/Public domain

At this point, the Speaker of the House, Henry Clay, who came in fourth, threw his support behind John Quincy Adams, who had won 84 Electoral College votes and came in second. However, with Clay's support, Adams had votes from 13 states, whereas Jackson had only 7 states backing him. Adams won the presidency.

So, despite coming in first and winning the popular vote, Jackson lost the presidency. His supporters were furious. When John Quincy Adams appointed former opponent Henry Clay as his secretary of state, Jackson and his supporters cried foul, accusing Adams of a "corrupt bargain."

Bitter over their candidate's loss, Jackson's supporters left the Democratic-Republican Party and formed the Jacksonian Democrats, later known as just the Democrats. The new party's platform continued the tradition of the Democratic-Republican Party, representing the common man and called for liberalizing electoral laws, favored states' rights over the federal government, and expressed opposition to tariffs.

John Quincy Adams and his supporters also changed the name of their party to National Republicans, now supporting a stronger federal government, which could actively promote economic development.

REMEMBER

in 1824, approximately 350,000 U.S. citizens could vote. That was about six percent of the population. To be able to vote, a person had to be a white property-owning or tax-paying male. By 1828, the property-owning requirement was dropped, but some states continued the tax-paying requirement. Suddenly, about 80 percent of all white adult males could vote.

In 1828, Andrew Jackson got his revenge when he beat John Quincy Adams easily. This also signaled the end of the National Republicans, which were soon replaced with the Whigs, partially organized by Henry Clay. By 1836, the Whigs became the major opposition party to the Democrats. After electing two presidents, William Henry Harrison in 1840 and Zachary Taylor in 1848, the Whigs began to fall apart over the issue of slavery in the 1850s and disappeared after the end of the Civil War.

The issue of slavery came to the forefront in the 1850s and pushed the country towards its third-party system. The battle over the extension of slavery into new states and the Dred Scott Decision of 1857, stating that slaves could not be American citizens and thus were not protected by the Constitution, drove the country towards a bloody civil war. It also took a toll on the existing party system. By 1860, the Democratic Party had split over the issue of slavery into the Northern and Southern Democrats, with both parties running candidates for the presidency. The Whigs, renamed the Constitutional Unionists, ran a candidate for the presidency for the last time.

Finally, the Republican Party, a new party, founded in 1854, as an anti-slavery party in the Midwest, ran a candidate for the second time in its short history. Its standard bearer was Abraham Lincoln (see Figure 14-3), a former member of the House of Representatives from Illinois. His election in 1860, with 39.9 percent of the vote, led to the outbreak of the Civil War and the creation of the third-party system.

FIGURE 14-3: Abraham Lincoln.

J.H. Bufford & Sons./Library of Congress/Public domain

Moving on to a new dominant party: The Republican Party (1860–1932)

The election of 1860, won by Lincoln and the Republican Party, started an era of Republican dominance. Although in 1860 the Republican Party and its standard bearer Abraham Lincoln won the presidency with only 39.9 percent of the vote, by the end of the Civil War it became the majority party in the United States. After the war, the Republican Party, (these days also called the Grand Old Party or GOP), established its dominance in the East and Midwest, whereas the Democrats came to dominate the Southern parts of the United States.

Until 1896, national elections were competitive, with the Republican Party winning narrow victories. However, in 1896, the Republican Party managed to convert the urban working classes to Republicanism emphasizing economic development. The Democrats in turn ran on an agrarian populist platform appealing mostly to farmers and the solid Democratic South.

This led to an era of Republican dominance of American politics. From 1860 until 1932, the Democrats managed to win only four presidential elections. Grover Cleveland won two nonconsecutive terms because he was more conservative than the Republican candidate, and Woodrow Wilson won two terms only because the Republican Party had split in 1912 (see the section, "Third Parties," later in this chapter).

Staging a comeback: The Democratic Party (1932–1968)

It was the Great Depression that brought the Democratic Party back to dominance in American politics. Dissatisfied with Republican President Hoover's handling of the economic crisis, many core Republican groups turned away from their party and joined the Democrats headed by Franklin Delano Roosevelt. This created the New Deal Coalition, which now established Democratic dominance until the 1960s. The New Deal Coalition consisted not only of groups that switched from the Republican Party, such as Jewish voters and African Americans, but also of new voters who were mobilized by FDR's New Deal programs. An example would be recent immigrants, who were mostly southern- and eastern-European and were Catholic. Overall, the New Deal consisted of the following groups: unionized voters, Jews, African Americans, Catholics, the Solid Democratic South, the working class, and intellectuals.

Reaching stalemate (1968–present)

Beginning in 1964, the New Deal Coalition began to fall apart. First, the Solid Democratic South moved out of the New Deal Coalition. Incumbent Democratic President Johnson, favoring civil rights and voting rights, drove white Southerners to the Republican Party, whose standard bearer Barry Goldwater had voted against the Civil Rights Act in the Senate. After voting for the American Independent Party in 1968, white Southerners became solidly Republican by the 1980s and today constitute one of the most heavily Republican voting groups in the United States. Ironically, the Solid Democratic South is now the Solid Republican South.

At the same time, Catholic voters changed. Today, the Catholic vote, which was solidly behind Democratic candidates, has slowly moved into the Republican camp. By 2024, President Trump and the Republican Party won 56 percent of the Catholic vote. The same has happened with the white working class, a core Democratic group, which has moved to the Republican Party.

African Americans and Jews, on the other hand, have continued to be of the most solidly Democratic voters. Hispanics, however, are almost evenly split, with 45 percent voting for President Trump and 53 percent for Vice President Harris (see Chapter 13 for a detailed discussion of the voting behavior of the U.S. public).

Stalemate between the two major parties has been the characteristic of the fifth party system since 1969. During this time, the Democratic Party controlled the White House for 21 years and the Republicans did so for 32 years. However, the Democratic Party controlled both chambers of Congress for 26 years and the Republicans did so for only 14 years. Thirteen years saw split majorities with one party controlling one chamber while the other party controlled the other.

With the New Deal Coalition falling apart, both parties are equally competitive in presidential and Congressional elections today. The characteristic that is most noticeable today is U.S. voters turning away from political parties, dealigning themselves from the U.S. party system. Depending on the poll, up to a third of all U.S. voters consider themselves independent today.

Realigning Over Time

When studying political parties, voters, and elections, one of the most widely used concepts is the concept of *realignment*. The concept was developed by political scientist V.O. Key Jr. in an article in 1955 and can be used to explain the shifting of party dominance in the U.S.

The theory states that all political parties are made up of various groups who support a party for different reasons. These groups can be based on ethnicity, religion, or various economic characteristics. U.S. parties are not homogeneous but very heterogeneous. For example, the New Deal Coalition, which maintained the Democratic Party in power for decades, consisted of many different groups such as unionized voters, Jews, Catholics, African Americans, the Solid Democratic South, the working class and intellectuals. They all supported the Democratic Party for different reasons.

After WWII, white Southerners began to slowly leave the Democratic Party. Many moved to the Republican Party. This is called realignment. One core group of supporters of a political party leaves its old party and aligns itself with a different party. Realignments are usually caused by issues. Whenever a political party takes a stance on a specific issue, it will gain and lose support. For example, when the Democratic Party embraced civil rights in the 1960s, it gained support from many more African Americans and Northern liberal voters. At the same time, it lost support from white Southerners who continued to believe in segregation.

White Southerners began to leave the Democratic Party, which led to realignment in the former Solid Democratic South.

On rare occasions — it has happened only four times in American history — this switch by a core group from one political party to another can create a new majority party. If this happens, a *critical realignment* occurs.

Hand in hand with the terms *realignment* and *critical realignment* goes the term *dealignment*. Dealignments occur when one core group leaves a political party but fails to realign itself with a new political party. Instead, the group is non-partisan for the time being and often engages in ticket-splitting and varying their votes depending on candidates and elections.

For example, white Southerners moved away from the Democratic Party in 1964, when they voted for Republican Barry Goldwater. The reason was the issue of civil rights. However, in 1968 they voted for the American Independent Party, headed by Governor George Wallace of Alabama, and then in 1972 they voted for Republican Richard Nixon. However, in 1976 many voted for fellow Southern Democrat Jimmy Carter of Georgia, and in 1980 they supported Republican Ronald Reagan. It is at this time that they decided to remain with the Republican Party, and they finally became realigned. Today, white Southerners constitute one of the most heavily Republican voting groups in the United States.

Third Parties

Throughout the history of the United States, literally thousands of third or minor parties have participated in American politics. Most were short-lived and made no visible impact on American politics. Some, however, did make a difference, impacting American voters and even changing how the major parties stood on issues.

Usually, a third party is formed by a group of voters who become dissatisfied. They believe that issues of importance to them are not addressed properly or even at all by the major parties, and for this reason they form a new party that better addresses their issue concerns.

Some third parties tend to be ideological in nature, meaning that for them winning is not the most important aspect of political life. Instead, they are satisfied to stick with their political beliefs, even if this means that they will lose an election. The Libertarian Party exemplifies this type of third party.

Another type of third party is the splinter party. Here, a section of one of the two large parties breaks off because it is dissatisfied with the larger party and especially how it stands on certain issues dear to the group. So, the splinter group creates its own party to push for its issues. This usually involves the selection of a strong personality to head the new party. Teddy Roosevelt and his Bull Moose Party would be an example of this.

Finally, third parties can be the extension of a certain person. In other words, a popular, strong personality sets up his/her own political party to push for a certain cause. Ross Perot and his Reform Party are an example of this.

It is also imperative to distinguish between single-cause and multi-cause third parties. A single-cause third party runs candidates based on one major issue, remaining silent on other issues. The Prohibition Party of the late 19th century, which advocated the banning of alcohol, would be an example of a single-cause party. Multi-cause parties, on the other hand, are parties, which like their two big siblings, run candidates on a whole platform with issues spanning from social to economic to foreign policy.

Coming in third

The following section provides a brief overview of the most influential and important third parties in American history.

>> **Anti-Mason Party:** An early major third party in the United States. The Anti-Mason party was active from the 1820's to the 1840's and elected members to the House of Representatives. It opposed Masons, because of their secret meetings, which were suspect to the party. The Anti-Mason party did give the country the first presidential nominating convention.

>> **The American Party:** Also called the Know-Nothings, because its members were required to answer "I know nothing" whenever outsiders asked about its specifics, was a major third party from 1849 until 1860. The party was anti-Catholic, anti-black, anti-Semitic, and anti-immigrant. Despite these racist overtones, the party elected governors in states such as Massachusetts and Delaware in the 1850s. Former President Fillmore was its standard bearer in the 1856 presidential election, winning almost 900,000 votes and carrying one state, Maryland.

>> **The Socialist Party:** Founded in 1901, the Socialist Party became a mainstay in American politics until the end of WWII. Running on a platform of union rights, the creation of a welfare state and the nationalizing of certain core industries, such as public utilities, the party appealed to the American working class and many intellectuals. By 1912, the party had almost 120,000 members

and received close to a million votes, or 6 percent of the vote, in its quest for the presidency. The party began to decline when the Democratic Party under President Franklin Delano Roosevelt took over most of its agenda. After the welfare state was created und unions achieved political power with the Wagner Act, the Democrats absorbed many of the former Socialist supporters and the party disappeared by the early 1970s.

>> **The Bull Moose Party (Progressive Party):** In 1912, the Republican Party split. Former president Teddy Roosevelt had decided to run for the presidency one more time, but the incumbent Republican President William Howard Taft also threw his hat in the ring. When Roosevelt did not receive the nomination at the Republican National Convention, he ran as a third-party candidate, setting up the Progressive Party, more commonly referred to as the Bull Moose Party. He received 27.4 percent of the vote and 88 Electoral College votes, actually beating the incumbent Taft, who only received 23.2 percent of the vote. However, due to the Republican split, Roosevelt lost to the Democrat Woodrow Wilson. By 1916, the two Republican factions fused again, and Roosevelt was the frontrunner for the 1920 nomination. However, he died before he could run one more time for the presidency. Roosevelt's showing in 1912 is still the best third-party showing in the history of the United States. (See Figure 14-4)

>> **The Communist Party of the United States (CPUSA):** The extreme left of the Socialist Party established the CPUSA in 1919. Emboldened by the victory of communism in Russia, the party advocated a violent class rebellion to establish a communist state in the United States. Strong in the 1930s and 1940s, especially in unions, the party started to decline with the onset of the Cold War and collapsed after the break-up of the Soviet Union in 1991.

FIGURE 14-4: Campaign button for the Progressive Party (Bull Moose Party).

WorthPoint Corporation

>> **The Dixiecrats:** In 1948, incumbent president Harry Truman emphasized the issue of civil rights, such as, for example, integrating the U.S. armed forces, and became the first president to address the NAACP (National Association for the Advancement of Colored People), thereby angering the Solid Democratic South. They nominated the governor of South Carolina, Strom Thurmond, to run against Truman as a third-party candidate. To this end, white Southern Democrats founded the Dixiecrats, also referred to as the States' Rights Party. The party ran on a segregationist platform in 1948, winning four Southern states, Alabama, Louisiana, Mississippi, and South Carolina.

>> **The American Independent Party:** George Wallace, the Democratic Governor of Alabama, set up the American Independent Party in 1967. He was dissatisfied with the way the Democratic Party was handling the issue of desegregation. Being a segregationist himself, he decided to run against the Democratic Party on a segregationist platform. He carried five Southern states (Alabama, Arkansas, Georgia, Louisiana, and Mississippi) and almost took the election away from Republican Richard Nixon by winning 13.9 percent of the vote. He ran again in 1972 but dropped out of the race after an assassination attempt left him paralyzed.

>> **The Libertarian Party:** The Libertarian Party closely follows the ideals of small government set out by Adam Smith in his book "*The Wealth of Nations*. The party advocates a very limited government role in the economy and people's lives. Besides defense, the provision of law and order, and a working infrastructure, the government should do little more. Today, the party calls for the privatization of healthcare, social security, and education. More controversial, the party also wants to legalize drugs and prostitution.

>> **The Green Party:** Founded in the 1980s, the Green Party advocates environmental awareness, corporate responsibility, and gender equality. The Green Party did not play a major role in American politics until 2000 (see Figure 14-5). In the presidential election of 2000, its standard-bearer Ralph Nader managed to win close to 3 percent of the vote, which proved decisive in many close states, like Florida, where Nader won 97,000 votes and arguably took the state and the presidency away from Democrat Al Gore, giving the presidency to Republican George W. Bush. In the 2024 presidential elections, it received .6 percent of the vote, coming in third after the Republican and Democratic candidates.

>> **The Reform Party:** Established in 1995 by H. Ross Perot. The party stood for campaign reform, a balanced budget, and term limits. More controversially, the Reform Party also advocated immigration reform and took a protectionist stand on international trade. It received 8.4 percent of the vote in the 1996 election. The party has since declined and today has become another small

third party in U.S. politics. In 2024, its nominee was Robert F. Kennedy, Jr., who later endorsed President Trump and is currently serving as President Trump's secretary of health and human services.

Ralph Nader/Wikimedia Common/Public Domain/
https://commons.wikimedia.org/wiki/
File:Bush_%26_Gore_Make_Me_Want_Ralph!.
jpg/Last accessed on Last accessed on October 06, 2025

FIGURE 14-5:
Campaign button for the Green Party in 2000.

Effects of third parties

Even though it is virtually impossible for a third party and its candidate to win national political office, third parties have played an important role in American politics.

>> **They have brought important new issues to the forefront of American politics.** Many of these have received popular support and the two major parties felt compelled to absorb these issues in their own platforms. This undermined and even destroyed many third parties. A good example of this is the adoption of a prohibition platform by the Republican Party in turn destroying the Prohibition Party. The previously mentioned adoption of parts of the Socialist Party's platform by FDR and the Democratic Party led to the decline and ultimate demise of the Socialist Party.

>> **Third parties allow for dissatisfied voters and previous party supporters to express their opinions legally through the political system.** In other words, third parties channel dissatisfaction peacefully in the United States. Occasionally, third parties can also mobilize new voters or dissatisfied voters who would have normally stayed home on Election Day. In 1992, voter turnout in the United States increased by almost five percent, mostly due to Ross Perot bringing back dissatisfied voters to the polls.

>> **Minor parties can decide elections.** Many times, in the history of the United States third parties decided hotly contested elections. Most recent,

Ralph Nader and the Green Party siphoned off enough votes from the Democratic nominee Al Gore to allow for the Republican George W. Bush to win the election. In 1992, Ross Perot took the election away from the Republican President George Herbert Walker Bush. Studies have shown that almost two-thirds of all Perot voters would have voted for Bush if Perot would not have been running. In 1968, George Wallace and his American Independent Party almost sent the election into the House of Representatives by winning several Southern states, which normally would have gone for the Republican nominee, Richard Nixon.

The Structure of American Political Parties

Unlike European political parties, U.S. parties are not structured hierarchically. There is no national leader of the two major parties, who exercises total control over party members including elected officeholders. Some say the president is the national party leader; however, this is questionable. For example, President Biden was unable to prevent Democratic Senator Joe Manchin from West Virginia from leaving the Democratic Party and becoming an independent in the Senate. U.S. parties are more like loosely coordinated networks where state and local parties have independent powers and come together once every four years to nominate a candidate for the presidency.

The national party

The closest we have in the United States to a national party is the national convention held every four years to nominate a candidate for the presidency. The convention brings together national, state, and local party leaders and delegates from every state.

REMEMBER

A national nominating convention was put in place for the first time during Andrew Jackson's term as president in 1832. Previously, members of the congressional caucus for each political party nominated the president.

In addition to nominating a presidential and vice-presidential candidate, the convention draws up a national party platform, in which the party outlines national policies for the next four years.

Finally, at the convention a national committee, comprised of delegates from each state and territory, is chosen. This national committee, referred to as the Republican or Democratic National Committee, has the obligation to direct and coordinate party policies, including the planning of the next party convention. In addition, the national committee raises money for elected officeholders and state parties, provides support for candidates, and acts as the national spokesperson for the party for the next four years, until the next convention chooses a new committee.

Usually, the presidential nominee picks a person to chair the national committee. The major responsibility of the national chairperson is to raise funds for the party, tour the country as the party's spokesperson, and act as liaison between the national and the state and local parties.

The state parties

There are 50 state parties for each one of the major parties in the United States in addition to various territorial parties. Each state party has different structures and therefore varies from state to state. Despite these differences a few similarities are visible. First, each state party is headed by a party chairperson and is run by a state committee. The state committee is comprised of representatives from the state's congressional and state legislative districts and even county districts. The committee's major function is to carry out policies set forth by the party's state convention. The committee raises funds for candidates running for local or state office, and often recruits members; however, in most states the state committee has no real powers.

The local parties

Local parties have changed dramatically in the last century. As mentioned earlier, city machines dominated by party bosses were the norm in most large northeastern and Midwest cities. Today, most machines have disappeared. Local parties often operate independently of state and the national party; their only contact with the two structures is before elections.

Today, local parties are found wherever elected offices are available. For example, local party organizations are active at the county, city, town, ward, or even precinct level. At each level, local party leaders dominate. At the lowest organizational level, such as a voting precinct, which can be a block within a city or part of a rural county, the party selects or appoints precinct captains who take care of party business. This might include organizing or supervising polling places or registering new voters. It is here where the average person has contact with the party. Local parties recruit the volunteers needed to run for office, and many future partisans have their first taste of politics at this level.

IN THIS CHAPTER

» **Being necessary for democracy**

» **Looking at different types of interest groups**

» **Having different sources of power**

» **Performing many functions**

» **Studying lobbying**

Chapter **15**

Discovering Interest Groups

nterest groups, defined as organizations that seek to influence public policy, have become a major player in American politics. Currently, the U.S. leads the world in the number of interest groups and in no other democracy have interest groups become as influential as in the U.S.

Reasons for the large number of interest groups in the U.S. include the decentralized nature of our governmental structures; in the U.S. interest groups can lobby at the national, state, and local level, whereas in other countries, such as Sweden, one only lobbies at the national level. Further, the U.S. is a very diverse country, being divided along economic, religious, ethnic, and ideological lines. This division leads to people organizing along those lines, resulting in thousands of economic, ideological, religious, and ethnic interest groups, all of which hope to impact policymaking. For example, the U.S. sees hundreds of religious groups whereas a country like Germany has only a few.

Most Americans do not talk about or discuss interest groups, but some of your friends and family very likely belong to one. Many do not even know that they benefit from interest groups. A college professor, for example, is likely unaware that professors in the U.S. are represented by several interest groups.

Popular interest groups today include the National Rifle Association (NRA), the Sierra Club, the American Federation of Teachers, and many unions and business organizations.

Embracing Diverse Interests

As early as 1830, the famous French philosopher Alexis de Tocqueville (see Figure 15-1), while touring the United States, noted that Americans are a nation of joiners. This is even truer today. Currently, the United States has more than 200,000 interest groups attempting to influence public policy. Sweden in comparison has a little over 1,000.

FIGURE 15-1: Alexis de Tocqueville.

Château de Tocqueville/Wikimedia Common/Public Domain/https://commons.wikimedia.org/wiki/ File:Cl%C3%A9ral_de_Tocqueville.jpg/ Last accessed on Last accessed on October 06, 2025

Our Founding Fathers were aware of the inclination of Americans to get together, organize, and push for policies they favor. James Madison even addressed the issue in Federalist Paper Number 10, where he states that the Constitution provides for the right of the people to organize to pursue their own interests. He further proclaims that humans are social creatures and so it is natural that they are drawn together and pursue their group interests.

At the same time, he warned that *factions*, as he called interest groups, could become dangerous by undermining democracy, if they serve only a few. He attempts to dispel this fear by arguing that factions could be controlled by elected officeholders and could further check themselves by competing for interests. This would result in bargaining and compromising among various interest groups, which in turn leads to moderate policies acceptable to everybody.

REMEMBER

Madison's writings contributed to the popularity of the concept of *pluralism in the U.S.*, which claims that interest groups can be beneficial for a democracy.

Pluralism

James Madison (see Figure 15-2) is considered to be one of the first to study diverse interests competing for benefits in a political system. His writings are foundational to what would later be called pluralism. In Federalist Paper Number 10, he tried to dispute the notion that interest groups are detrimental to democracy. Pluralism states that interest groups arise naturally in a diverse, economically complex society. People will aggregate their interests into interest groups. This gives them political power that they can use to push their governments for benefits. These benefits can be economical, professional, ideological, or even religious in nature.

FIGURE 15-2:
James Madison.

Pendleton's Lithography.Stuart, Gilbert/
Library of Congress/Public domain

In a society with many interest groups asking government for benefits, no one group is powerful enough to get everything they ask for, so the groups have to bargain and compromise. The resulting public policy will be acceptable to all. If a case arises where one interest group gets too powerful, other groups will unite against it, restoring a balance to the political system.

With pluralism, competition among interest groups shapes public policymaking.

Elite theory

Elite theory presents an opposing viewpoint. It states that not all interest groups are created equal. They differ in political power and over time, some interest groups will become so powerful that they can ignore other interest groups and push for policies that benefit only them. In such a case, the government makes policies for a few very powerful groups, ignoring the public overall. Because these interest groups represent mostly business and the wealthy, they are not representative of the majority in a democracy. The U.S. would be controlled by a small wealthy elite.

Elite theory states that a handful of powerful interest groups exercise control over policymaking.

Defining interest groups

What is an interest group? An interest group is an organization made up of individuals that share common interests and goals and seek to impact public policy. Interest groups attempt to influence all branches of government. This includes the legislative, executive, and judicial branches at the federal, state, and local level.

Often, interest groups and political parties get confused. There is a distinct difference between the two. Political parties are large, all-encompassing organizations that represent large groups of people in society. They nominate and run candidates for office and later help to organize government at the federal, state, or local level. Interest groups are narrower in scope. They represent a smaller segment of the population and push for policies that benefit only their members. Interest groups may support candidates running for office, but they don't nominate them or run government.

Interest groups attempt to create policies that are favorable to their cause and to block policies that might harm their cause. Interest groups further attempt to increase their number of members and financial muscle to increase their political power in the U.S.

Joining interest groups

There are several reasons why a person joins an interest group, including the following:

>> **Economic reasons:** Someone joins a union, for example, for better pay and better working conditions.

>> **Ideological reasons:** A person who believes in gun ownership and is an avid hunter, joins the National Rifle Association (NRA) to protect the right to bear arms in the U.S.

>> **Solitary incentives:** This concept refers to people joining interest groups to be around people who think like they do and to acquire a social life. Many interest groups organize social events such as dinners, movie nights, or even dances that allow their supporters to socialize with each other.

Recognizing types of interest groups

Not all interest groups are the same. Interest groups do vary in size, political power, and importance in the U.S. political system. Often, the number of members aren't as important as monetary resources or the prestige of interest group members. When studying interest groups, we find five different types of groups:

>> **Economic interest groups:** Most interest groups in the U.S. are economic interest groups. These groups demand economic benefits for their members. An example would be the AFL-CIO (the American Federation of Labor-Congress of Industrial Organizations), which is a conglomerate of labor unions throughout the United States. Their demands include better wages and work conditions for their members as well as benefits such as health insurance and vacation time.

On the business side, there is the United States Chamber of Commerce. Founded in 1912, it represents about 3 million U.S. businesses of all sizes. The Chamber makes sure that the business side of issues will be heard.

>> **Professional interest groups:** Professional interest groups represent a small but powerful segment within the U.S. They actively push for benefits for a small group of members such as medical professionals or lawyers. Their membership numbers may be small, but they make up for this by having plenty of monetary resources and enjoying a lot of prestige among the American public. A good example is the American Medical Association (AMA). It was founded in 1847 and has about 272,000 members today.

>> **Public interest groups:** Public interest groups push for policies that benefit a majority of the U.S. public. They are trying not only to benefit their members but also to help the U.S. public. A good example is the Center for Auto Safety. Established in 1970, the Center for Auto Safety pushes for policies such as the "lemon laws," which made auto manufacturers and auto dealerships accountable for any defective cars they sell.

Another example of a public interest group is the League of Women Voters. Although the League was originally created to push for women's suffrage, the group now focuses on increasing voter turnout in the U.S.

>> **Governmental interest groups:** Yes, you heard right. Government at all levels often organizes itself into interest groups and pushes for benefits from other governmental structures. For example, large cities, such as Dallas or Houston in Texas, are organized into interest groups to ask the Texas state legislature for benefits such as tax breaks or grants.

>> **Ideological interest groups:** Ideological interest groups push for very narrow policies. These groups hold a very narrow belief and push for policies in their areas. A good example is the National Rifle Association (NRA). The NRA only deals with gun issues and not economic or foreign policy. Founded in 1871, the NRA pushes for gun rights and currently has 4.3 million members. It is the most powerful ideological interest group in the U.S. today.

Sources of Interest Group Power

Not all interest groups are made equal. Some are more influential than others. What determines interest groups' power and influence in U.S. politics? Interestingly, it is not all about money, even though money of course matters. Besides contributing monetary resources, interest groups are active in U.S. politics by campaigning for preferred candidates, by lobbying, by providing support for candidates, by mobilizing their members to vote for a certain candidate, and by getting involved in policymaking.

Membership size

It is simple. The more members an interest group has, the more power it has in the U.S. political system. Even a lack of monetary resources can be made up for by having a large membership. For example, the American Association of Retired People (AARP) does not have a lot of monetary resources. Its influence stems more from its large, politically active membership than from monetary contributions. It does have more than 38 million members in the U.S. In addition, in order to become an AARP member, a person has to be 50 years or older. This is the age group most likely to vote in elections in the U.S.

Thus, an endorsement for a specific policy by the AARP can make a difference in any election. Our politicians are aware of this, and during an election they will not dare to cross the AARP or go against issues favored by the 50-plus group.

Monetary resources

Not surprisingly, the more money interest groups have, the more powerful they are. The most affluent of all the interest groups in the U.S. is the Chamber of Commerce. Between 1998 and 2014, the Chamber of Commerce, representing more than 3 million businesses in the U.S., spent over a $1 billion on political candidates. Just as a comparison, this amount of money equals the annual GDP of a country like Mongolia.

Intensity of members convictions

Often, small groups of dedicated members make up for their smaller size. The more strongly interest group members feel about an issue, the more powerful the interest group is. Dedicated interest group members are more likely to give money to the organization and base their vote on an issue they feel strongly about. A good example is the National Rifle Association (NRA). NRA members strongly believe in the right to bear arms and are willing to donate and base their vote on this specific issue alone. When the NRA endorses a candidate, its members will go out and vote for their candidate, without caring much about how the candidate feels about other, non-gun related issues.

Prestige of members

The prestige that an interest group enjoys also affects the power of that interest group. A good example is the American Medical Association. Even though it has fewer members than the AARP, it makes up for this by the prestige its members — medical doctors — have. The AMA also is very adept at raising money, ranking in the top ten percent of interest group spenders in the U.S.

Organizational structure

The structure of an interest group does matter. A powerful interest group has to have offices in not just the capital, Washington, D.C., but also in the capitals of the largest states. Locations throughout the country, especially in states like California and Texas, allow for interest groups to participate not just at the federal level but also the state level. Not surprisingly, a nationwide organizational structure is expensive and only the wealthiest interest groups can afford it.

Leadership skills

An exceptional leader can sometimes overcome shortcomings in other areas. An interest group may be poor, and it may not have many members, but a good leader can still make a difference. A good example is the interest group Center for Auto Safety, founded by Ralph Nader in 1970. Under his leadership, this small and poor interest group took on the U.S. auto industry and pushed Congress and the states to pass "lemon laws," which made it illegal to sell defective cars to consumers.

Taking Stock of the Most Powerful Interest Groups in the U.S.

When combining all the six sources of interest group power, five interest groups emerge as the most relevant interest groups in the U.S. These five are measured on their impact on U.S. politics and the policy successes they have had in the U.S. government and the states.

The U.S. Chamber of Commerce

The U.S. Chamber of Commerce (see Figure 15-3) is the most powerful interest group in the U.S. It is the biggest organizational spender in American politics. The group was created in 1912 at the urging of President Taft, who believed that a group was needed to speak for the interests of business and to counter the growing union movement. The group, with about 3 million members, usually supports Republican candidates for office, spending 93 percent of its campaign budget on Republican candidates. Since 1998, the group has spent over $1 billion on political candidates, about $81 million in 2022 alone.

FIGURE 15-3:
The U.S. Chamber of Commerce Building at 1615 H Street NW in Washington, D.C.

The American Association of Retired Persons (AARP)

The AARP, also known as the American Association of Retired Persons, is one of the most influential interest groups in the U.S. (See Figure 15-4.) It has 38 million members and focuses purely on issues affecting people 50 and older. It also publishes the two most widely circulated magazines in the U.S.

FIGURE 15-4:
AARP.

The AARP was founded in 1958 by Ethel Percy Andrus, a retired educator and the first female principal in California, and Leonard Davis, who later founded Colonial Penn's insurance companies. To become a member of the AARP, members pay a nominal annual fee and are then eligible for benefits such as cheaper auto and life insurance and, of course, the AARP's representation in front of our political system. Officially, the AARP is a non-partisan organization, which advocates for the 50 plus crowd in the U.S. They advocate on issues such as social security and Medicare and ask for lower prices for drugs. The AARP also educates older Americans on issues such as fraud and healthcare issues.

The AARP has become a leader in grassroots lobbying, mobilizing their supporters on certain issues. Their membership then contacts elected officeholders and expresses their wishes on certain political issues. With the organizations' members being likely to vote on Election Day, it is not surprising that our elected officeholders listen to the AARP.

The AARP was influential in creating Medicare and Medicaid in the 1960s and currently lobbies for social security cost of living increases and other benefits for retired Americans.

The American Medical Association (AMA)

The American Medical Association, or AMA, was founded in 1847 to represent U.S. physicians. (See Figure 15-5.) It is headquartered in Chicago and currently has about 272,000 members. This won't rank the AMA among the groups with the largest memberships, but it makes up for this by being well funded and by its members enjoying confidence and trust throughout U.S. society.

FIGURE 15-5:
AMA.

The organization disseminates health information to both its members and the public overall. The AMA further lobbies on behalf of its profession, setting standards for physician education and supporting a mixed healthcare system with both public and private healthcare options.

The AMA for decades has attempted to limit the supply of doctors in the U.S. by campaigning against the number of foreign doctors trained in the U.S. and allowed to practice in the U.S. and by not allowing physician assistants to perform doctor functions without physician supervision. This has resulted in a physician shortage in the U.S. The AMA supported President Obama's Affordable Care Act and opposed the Trump administration's attempt to repeal it in 2017.

The AMA spends about $18 million a year lobbying Congress and has divided its campaign expenditures fairly evenly between Republicans and Democrats.

The AFL-CIO (American Federation of Labor–Congress of Industrial Organizations)

Whereas the Chamber of Commerce represents American business the American Federation of Labor–Congress of Industrial Organizations (AFL-CIO) represents American workers. (See Figure 15-6.) It is made up of 60 different unions and represents close to 15 million American workers. The AFL-CIO calls for increased wages and better work conditions for its members as well as better healthcare benefits and vacation time. It was established in 1955 and has been politically active ever since. It specializes in electioneering, sending sample ballots and other mail pieces to members telling them what candidates favor union issues. In addition, it sends out campaign volunteers for candidates. For example, the AFL-CIO sent out 100,000 volunteers to walk door to door, campaigning for President Obama in 2012. The AFL-CIO favors democratic candidates spending almost 70 percent of their resources on democratic campaigns in 2020. Despite seeing declining membership numbers since its heyday in the 1940s, the AFL-CIO still represents 15 million workers constituting a major political force. Although membership has declined in recent years in the manufacturing center, union membership has increased in new and growing areas of the economy, such as home healthcare, taxi drivers, and domestic workers.

FIGURE 15-6:
AFL-CIO.

The National Rifle Association (NRA)

The NRA (see Figure 15-7) was founded in 1871 to improve marksmanship and firearm safety in the U.S. It currently has about 4.3 million members. The NRA early on was concerned with marksmanship training, teaching people how to aim and shoot properly, and was closely aligned with the National Guard and the U.S. military. Former President Ulysses S. Grant actually served as one of its presidents. It organized rifle clubs and held shooting competitions. The NRA was non-partisan until the 1970s and did not get involved in politics until gun control became a national issue.

To oppose gun control activists, the NRA began to align itself with the Republican Party and other conservative groups. In 1976, it created the Political Victory Fund, a PAC, to be able to give money to pro-gun rights candidates.

By 2016, the NRA became one of the most influential and successful interest groups in the U.S. It got actively involved in campaigns, targeting gun control candidates and gun control initiatives. In 2016, it raised $366 million and spent $412 million. Its PAC donated to 223 Republican Congressional candidates and nine Democrats.

By the early 2020s, the NRA was in trouble. Incompetent and corrupt leadership hurt the organization and membership dropped. A lawsuit claimed that the NRA violated campaign finance law. By 2023, the NRA started to sell off assets to pay down debt and cover legal fees.

Performing Necessary Functions in a Democracy

Political scientists and philosophers such as James Madison and Alexis de Tocqueville believed that interest groups are naturally created in a democracy and necessary for democracy. Although many belittle interest groups, claiming that they undermine democracy by influencing policymaking, others believe that interest groups are necessary for democracy to survive. So, what do interest groups do besides trying to influence policymaking?

Aggregating interests

In a democracy such as the U.S., an individual is powerless and cannot influence policymaking. This means an individual lacks political power. However, if an individual joins others and they combine resources, they acquire political power. Being alone makes a person powerless but combining with others gives them political power. Individuals in the U.S. can do so by either joining interest groups or political parties. The preference of most Americans is to join interest groups.

REMEMBER

Interest aggregation is the act of joining like-minded individuals to acquire political power.

Electioneering

Electioneering refers to the way interest groups attempt to influence who gets elected to office. By electing candidates friendly to their policy stances, interest groups enhance their chance of getting what they want from government. They can do this by providing public support for candidates. Examples include running TV commercials for and against candidates, holding rallies for candidates, producing and mailing out voter guides, getting the vote out on Election Day, and even organizing door-to-door campaigns.

REMEMBER

Electioneering is an attempt by interest groups to influence who gets elected to public office by supporting candidates who are running for office.

Providing information

An often-forgotten function of interest groups is to provide credible policy information to lawmakers and their staff. Many policymakers are not specialists on most issues they have to debate and vote on, and they need help. Other people, usually interest groups, will provide unbiased information to lawmakers so they can decide how to vote on issues. With most work being done at the committee level in Congress, it is here where interest groups come in. During committee meetings, interest groups provide information for or against certain policy proposals. Our elected officeholders then consider all the information they have been presented with and base their support on it. Often, interest groups even help lawmakers draft legislation.

REMEMBER

Interest groups present credible unbiased information to elected officeholders. They cannot afford to lie or present biased information because doing so means they will never be trusted again and will lose all contact with lawmakers. In some states, such as Texas, presenting false information to the legislature is actually a crime.

Litigating

If a policy passes that interest groups oppose, they can organize protests and demonstrations against the proposed policy and threaten a lawmaker with supporting and funding an opponent in the next election. If this does not work, interest groups are not shy about using litigation to stop the implementation of a policy they oppose. Lawsuits are expensive, however, so only well-financed interest groups can take this route.

Fundraising and providing monetary support

According to electoral law, interest groups cannot give money directly to political candidates. To do so, they must first establish a political action committee (PAC).

Up until 1971, both business and labor interests were unable to donate money to political campaigns. This changed with the Federal Election Campaign Act of 1971, which legalized political action committees or PACs. PACs are organizations attached to interest groups that are allowed to raise and spend money for political candidates. Every interest group that wants to raise and donate money to campaigns has to create a PAC and register it with the Federal Election Commission (FEC). Currently there are a little over 6,000 PACs registered with the FEC, and they contribute about a third of all campaign spending in the U.S.

REMEMBER

Members of Congress can even form PACs to raise money for political candidates, even incumbent members of Congress. These PACs are called *leadership PACs*. One of the most powerful leadership PACs was formed by former Speaker of the House of Representatives, Nancy Pelosi. With her PAC, Speaker Pelosi gained support from candidates running for office. Today, if a congressperson intends to move up the ladder in Congress, they must have a leadership PAC to gain support from their colleagues. Leadership PACs can even solicit money from the public.

Do PACs buy votes? Studies have shown that PACs are less influential than one might think. PACs are limited by law to a $5,000 contribution, and that makes it tough to buy a vote in Congress. The average PAC contribution is actually only a few hundred dollars. It is impossible to buy votes with that small a donation. More important political candidates receive money from many PACs, so the candidates can play PACs against each other. A candidate might receive monies from both labor and business PACs and so is free to vote however they want to. So, if you cannot buy votes with a contribution, why give at all? The reason is that you do not buy votes but buy access to politicians with your contribution. Members of Congress are more likely to talk to you about issues if you are a proven donor to their campaigns.

Shaping public opinion

Most of our lawmakers care about being reelected and thus are concerned with favorable public opinion. Interest groups are aware of this and know that if they can shape public opinion on an issue, lawmakers are more likely to support the issue. Thus, by shaping public opinion, interest groups can influence policymaking.

Interest groups use the media, especially ads on television and social media, to influence the public. Interest group ads provide the public with information favorable to their policy demands. If they can convince the public and the public now favors their policies, elected officeholders will fall in line and support the interest group's demands.

Lobbying

One of the major functions of interest groups is lobbying. *Lobbying* is defined as contacting members of the legislative, executive, and judicial branches of government in an attempt to influence policy or administrative decisions.

Interest groups can have their own lobbyists or hire firms that will supply them with lobbyists to lobby on their behalf. Lobbyists then contact lawmakers to get a chance to talk to them. That can happen in their office, over dinner, or even at a sports event. Lobbyists express a preference for seasoned lawmakers with good contacts on Capitol Hill who are in charge of important committees or subcommittees.

TIP

In 1954, in the case of United States v. Harriss, the U.S. Supreme Court ruled that lobbying Congress is a guaranteed constitutional right. At the same time, the government has the right to require information from the groups lobbying.

Lobbying has become big business in the U.S. In 2025, there are 13,007 lobbyists in the U.S. — about 41 lobbyists for every elected officeholder in Washington, D.C. These lobbyists spend about $3.3 billion dollars per year on lobbying. Interest groups spend more on lobbying than they do on actual campaigning.

TECHNICAL STUFF

President Ulysses S. Grant supposedly coined the term *lobbyist*, referring to the men approaching him for favors. Lobbying has been declared a legal form of people petitioning their government as guaranteed by the first amendment to the constitution. In 1876, lobbyists were required to register with Congress, so that people were aware of who was lobbying their legislature.

So, what does lobbying involve? There are many ways a lobbyist can impact U.S. politics. Take a look at what lobbyists do:

They set up meetings with lawmakers and their staff to try to influence a lawmaker. During the meeting, lobbyists discuss their clients' positions on issues and try to convince lawmakers to side with them on these issues. Lobbyists host campaign fundraisers for candidates and give interviews in support of candidates.

Many lobbyists are former members of Congress. After a member of Congress retires or is defeated, they keep some of their Congressional privileges, such as access to the gym in Congress and the dining room. This makes it easy to lobby any former colleagues and friends you run into. The only rule is that a former member of Congress has to wait for one year after they leave office before they can become a lobbyist.

There are five types of lobbying in the U.S. today.

>> **Grassroots lobbying:** This type of lobbying involves the general public. Interest groups here contact the general public through media advertisements, mail solicitation, or even on social media, and attempt to influence policymaking by getting the public on their side. In other words, interest groups manipulate public opinion to have the public support the groups' policy preferences. The public then contacts lawmakers using mail or email, or organizes demonstrations for policies. Interest groups can then go to lawmakers and claim that the American public supports their policies.

>> **Grasstop lobbying:** This type of lobbying does not focus on the public overall. Only prominent, well-known people in society matter. They can be popular film or music stars, athletes, or well-known community members. These stars then in turn endorse a specific policy or candidate the interest group favors. This is usually accomplished through TV or social media. How often have you see a prominent actor or actress endorse a certain policy or political candidate?

>> **Astroturf lobbying:** This type of lobbying involves interest groups spending money to make it appear that the public supports them and their policies. This can be done by spreading misinformation to manipulate public opinion. The public then gets upset and demands action from our lawmakers. In other words, interest groups manipulate the average American into demanding action on a problem the interest group wants a solution to.

>> **Coalition lobbying:** Here, two or more interest groups combine their financial resources or work together to bring about a specific policy they favor.

>> **Reverse lobbying:** Reverse lobbying is rare, but it does happen. Occasionally, government officials call for meetings with interest groups and lobby them.

For example, the Obama administration met with interest groups representing the insurance industry, the pharmaceutical industry, and physicians while working on the Affordable Care Act. During these meetings. the administration attempted to receive support for the upcoming healthcare reforms now known as Obamacare.

Regulating lobbying

Today, there are about 13,000 lobbyists working at the federal level. They spent 3.3 billion in 2024 on political activities.

Although interest group activity is protected by the Constitution, it has been regulated since WWII. In 1946, Congress passed the Federal Regulation of Lobbying Act, which required interest groups involved in lobbying to register with Congress. In 1995, Congress passed a follow-up bill, entitled the Lobbying Disclosure Act, which tightened rules on lobbying. It states:

>> A lobbyist is defined as someone who spends 20 percent of their time lobbying members of Congress, the executive branch and their staff.

>> A lobbyist who receives less than a $5,000 salary every six months is excluded from the Act.

>> The Act banned former U.S. trade representatives and their staffs to lobby on behalf of foreign interests after they leave their post.

>> The rules of the Act apply to any corporation or other interest group that spends $20,000 or more every six months on their own lobbyists.

>> The Act requires lobbyists to report their clients, their pay and their expenditures, and the issues they lobbied on, every six months to Congress.

Judging interest groups

Many observers, including James Madison, believed that interest groups are beneficial to democracy. They push for the interests of the people and give the average person a chance to acquire political power and impact politics. Today, interest groups represent many different economic, political, and social views.

Further, interest groups allow people to combine with people who have ideas like their own. They allow for the U.S. citizenry to be represented in our political system. Interest groups are protected by the First Amendment to the Constitution which guarantees the right of peaceful assembly. All citizens regardless of age, gender, race can organize and attempt to influence government. This allows for fair and equal representation of all U.S. citizens.

On the other hand, many believe that interest groups are detrimental to democracy. They can become a tool of the U.S. political elite and do not represent the vast majority of U.S. citizens. Interest group politics today is dominated by wealthy interest groups, mostly business groups and individuals, who push for their own narrow interests, ignoring the public will.

With the U.S. having almost 200,000 interest groups, the system has become gridlocked. Too many groups are asking for too many policy benefits and nothing gets done anymore. How can elected officeholders deal with thousands of interest group demands and still make policy for the country?

6

The Part of Tens

Examine the ten most influential court cases in U.S. history. See which cases still impact U.S. society today and which ones have been changed over time.

Study the ten most influential documents in U.S. history. Discover which documents were necessary to create a new nation and which documents over time have made the U.S. a more democratic and integrated society.

Chapter **16**

The Ten Most Influential Court Cases in U.S. History

n this chapter, I undertake an almost impossible task: selecting the top ten of the most influential court cases in U.S. history. I selected only cases that changed U.S. history and society and made the U.S. what it is today. Obviously, there are many cases I could have picked from, and narrowing it down to just ten proved to be quite a challenge. Some choices were no-brainers, but others could have easily been replaced with other choices. So, feel free to disagree. They are obviously subjective, and every social scientist or legal scholar could have come up with different choices to put into their list.

Without further ado, here are my picks for the top ten most influential court cases in U.S. history.

Marbury v. Madison (1803)

The case of Marbury v. Madison gave the U.S. Supreme Court the greatest power federal courts can have, the power of judicial review, which refers to the power of courts to declare laws of Congress and acts of the executive unconstitutional, thereby nullifying them. The power of judicial review allows for the federal judiciary not just to nullify legislative and executive actions, but also to influence lawmaking.

In 1800, incumbent President Adams lost reelection. He was furious and tried to pack the judiciary by appointing dozens of new judges. However, the appointments were not all delivered on time to the nominated judges. Newly elected President Thomas Jefferson was upset with Adams trying to pack the federal courts and refused to send out the appointments that had not yet been delivered. William Marbury was one of the appointees who did not get his appointment letter. So he sued, and the case went all the way to the Supreme Court.

Marbury based his lawsuit on the 1789 Congressional Judiciary Act, which gave the Supreme Court the power to force public officials to engage in an official act (writ of mandamus). Chief Justice John Marshall found an ingenious way out of the dilemma. He decided to declare that Section 13 of the Congressional Judiciary Act of 1789 was unconstitutional, because the Act allowed litigants to go straight to the Supreme Court for a writ of mandamus. Marshall said this was not in the Constitution. Litigants first had to go through the federal courts before they could appeal to the Supreme Court. For this reason, Section 13 was unconstitutional. Because Marbury had based his lawsuit on the Act, he lost the case.

With this ruling, Marshall had established the power of judicial review, and from then on, not just the Supreme Court but all federal and state courts received the power to declare legislative and executive acts unconstitutional, thus nullifying them.

Dred Scott v. Sanford (1857)

Dred Scott was a slave who had been taken from a slave state, Missouri, by his owner, to a free state, Illinois. When his owner went back to Missouri, Scott did not want to go back to being a slave. He sued for his freedom, arguing that because he had lived in a free state, Illinois, he was now a free man and a U.S. citizen. The Missouri State Supreme Court disagreed with Scott, so he took the case to federal court and then the U.S. Supreme Court.

The Chief Justice of the Supreme Court was Roger Taney, a Southerner whose family owned slaves themselves. The Supreme Court ruled in a 7-2 decision against Scott. The ruling stated that people of African descent, whether enslaved or not, cannot be citizens and therefore cannot claim any of the protections and privileges of the Constitution.

Taney further argued that slaves are property and not citizens. Therefore, they had no political rights, and because property had to be returned to its rightful owner, Scott had to be returned to his owner. Taney further ruled that Congress did not have the power to outlaw slavery in any state, thus opening the door to new slave states. With this decision, he overturned the Missouri Compromise, which had restricted slavery to certain territories.

The decision was applauded in the Southern slave states and decried in the free Northern states. It was one of the main contributors to the upcoming Civil War.

Dred Scott died in 1858 of tuberculosis, never having to go back to slavery. The Dred Scott decision was later overturned with the 13th, 14th, and 15th Amendments to the Constitution. The Dred Scott decision is widely considered to be the worst decision in the history of the U.S. Supreme Court.

Plessy v. Feguson (1896)

Homer Plessy, a man of mixed race, boarded a whites-only train deliberately in 1892, in New Orleans, Louisiana. He was charged under the Louisiana Separate Car Act, passed in 1890, which required separate accommodations on trains for black and white citizens in Louisiana. After the Louisiana Supreme Court upheld his conviction, he appealed to the U.S. Supreme Court. He argued that the Louisiana law was a violation of the 14th Amendment to the Constitution. The Supreme Court in a 7:1 decision sided against him, stating that it was not unconstitutional to segregate if the facilities for both white and black citizens were equal. With this decision, the U.S. Supreme Court established the Separate but Equal Doctrine, which legitimized segregation in the U.S. and allowed for the Southern states to legally reestablish segregation. Homer Plessy ended up paying a $25.00 fine.

The Supreme Court decision is widely considered one of the worst ever. The Court's decision in Brown v. the Board of Education of Topeka, Kansas, partially reversed it in 1954.

Brown v. the Board of Education of Topeka (1954)

In 1896, the Supreme Court in the case of Plessy v. Ferguson ruled that segregation was legal as long as each race had comparable amenities. This of course was never the case. The case of Brown v. the Board of Education reversed Plessy v. Ferguson in 1954 and changed American education and civil rights in the process.

Oliver Brown, who lived in Topeka, Kansas, tried to enroll his daughter into an all-white school in 1951, because it was closer to his home and provided a better education than the all black school in another part of town. His daughter was refused admission. So, Mr. Brown sued stating that segregation was unconstitutional. After a district court ruled against him, Mr. Brown, with the help of the NAACP Legal Defense Fund and its lead attorney, future Supreme Court Justice Thurgood Marshall, appealed directly to the Supreme Court.

The Supreme Court in this case ruled unanimously that racial segregation in public schools is unconstitutional because it violates the Equal Protection Clause of the 14th Amendment, even if the segregated facilities are comparable. Segregation instilled a sense of inferiority in black children and thus violated the 14th Amendment. The court did partially (in the area of education) overturn Plessy v. Ferguson in the process.

The ruling desegregated public schools in the U.S. by striking down all state laws enforcing racial segregation in public education. It proved to be the first step towards racial integration and spurned on the civil rights movement.

Loving v. Virginia (1967)

Richard Loving was a white man living in the State of Virginia. He was married to Mildred Loving, a woman of African-American and Native American descent. This was in violation of Virginia's Racial Integrity Act of 1924, which made marriages of white people and people of color illegal. They were convicted in 1959 of violating the law, but the judge offered to suspend the sentence if they left Virginia. They filed an appeal, which was denied by the Virginia Supreme Court. So, they appealed to the U.S. Supreme Court.

The U.S. Supreme Court in a 9:0 decision ruled in favor of the Lovings and struck down Virginia's Racial Integrity Act. The Supreme Court argued that the law was a violation of the Equal Protection Clause contained in the 14th Amendment. The Court stated that the law made distinctions based on race and outlawed conduct, getting married, that was generally accepted and that everybody had a right to do.

With that decision, the U.S. Supreme Court put a stop to all race-based legal restrictions on marriage in the United States.

Roe v. Wade (1973)

Norma McCorvey, who used the pseudonym Jane Roe, lived in Texas, where abortion was illegal unless maternal health was threatened by the pregnancy. She became pregnant in 1969 with her third child. She wanted to have an abortion. So, she sued, claiming that Texas's abortion law was unconstitutional. After a local district court agreed with her, the case was appealed to the Supreme Court.

The Supreme Court, in a 7:2 decision, agreed with her. The Court decided that there was a right to abortion because it was a part of the right to privacy, which was guaranteed by the Due Process Clause contained within the 14th Amendment to the Constitution. However, that right to abortion was not absolute. Certain medical restrictions existed. During the first trimester of pregnancy, the right to have an abortion was absolute. During the second trimester, the right could be restricted if maternal health was threatened. Finally, in the third trimester, states could restrict abortion. Thus, Roe v. Wade legalized abortion in all 50 states in 1973.

Roe v. Wade changed American politics. Abortion soon became one of the dominant and most emotional issues in U.S. politics. Two sides emerged: the pro-choice side, who believed a woman had the right to choose to have an abortion, and, the pro-life side, who believed that life begins at conception and that abortion was murder.

The two sides also joined different political parties. The Republican Party became the pro-life party whereas the Democrats became the pro-choice party. For the next fifty years, the two sides battled over the issue until in 2022 the issue of the right to have an abortion was given back to the states by the Supreme Court in the Dobbs v. Jackson Women's Health Organization decision.

Bush v. Gore (2000)

The election of 2000 proved to be the closest in U.S. history. The two candidates, Republican Governor of Texas George W. Bush and Democratic Vice President Al Gore, did not get enough Electoral College votes to get an absolute majority (270) in the Electoral College. It came down to the state of Florida. There, the election was so close, that a recount was ordered. For the next month, some Florida counties recounted ballots.

On December 8, 2000, the Florida Supreme Court ordered a statewide recount of all undervotes, ballots that had not been completely filled out or were just empty, about 61,000 ballots in all. The Bush campaign asked the U.S. Supreme Court for a halt of the recount. The U.S. Supreme Court granted the stay, ruling that the recounts would amount to a needless and unjustified cloud over Bush's legitimacy as the new president. Oral arguments over the recount were scheduled for December 11, 2000.

One day later, on December 12, 2000, the U.S. Supreme Court ruled in a 5:4 decision that the recount in the State of Florida be stopped. The court ruled that the recount violated the Equal Protection Clause in the 14th Amendment because Florida counties used different standards of counting and a common standard could not be established in a reasonable time. This resulted in the Republican candidate George W. Bush becoming president of the United States. George W. Bush ended up winning by 537 votes.

Bush v. Gore is one of the most controversial Supreme Court rulings in U.S. history. Some argue that the Court actually picked the president in this case, whereas others argue that a recount would not have made a difference in the outcome of the election. As a result of the election disaster, Florida switched to all-electronic voting for the state.

District of Columbia v. Heller (2008)

District of Columbia v. Heller involves the right to bear arms. The District of Columbia, which is a federal region, had imposed a ban on owning handguns at home for self-defense and had required that legally owned rifles and shotguns be unloaded and disassembled at home. Mr. Heller, a police officer in the District of Columbia, appealed these regulations, claiming that they were a violation of the 2nd Amendment. He stated that he could wear a weapon at work but could not have one at home to protect himself even though he lived in a crime-ridden neighborhood.

The Supreme Court ruled in a 5:4 decision that the 2nd Amendment to the Constitution protects an individual's right to bear arms, unconnected with service in a state militia, for lawful purposes such as self-defense. Therefore, the District of Columbia's ban on handguns was unconstitutional. However, it also stated that the right was not unlimited and certain restrictions on gun ownership are permissible. This case was only applicable at the federal level until it was incorporated (applied to the states) in 2010 in the case of McDonald v. City of Chicago (refer to Chapter 7).

In District of Columbia v. Heller, the Supreme Court made it clear that the right to bear arms does give Americans the right to own a weapon for legal purposes, although certain restrictions are permissible.

Obergefell v. Hodges (2015)

This case established the right to marry for same-sex couples. The Supreme Court ruled that denying same-sex couples the right to marry is a violation of the Equal Protection Clause and the Due Process Clause of the 14th Amendment. The Supreme Court ruled in a 5:4 decision that all states and the District of Columbia from then on had to accept same-sex marriages. Thirty-six states were already accepting same-sex marriage at that time.

Obergefell v. Hodges is actually not just one lawsuit but a combination of six lower federal court rulings between 2012 and 2014, representing 16 gay couples. Four district courts ruled in favor of legalizing gay marriage, but the decisions were appealed to the Sixth Court of Appeals, which upheld gay marriage bans in the four involved states, Michigan, Tennessee, Kentucky, and Ohio.

The case was then appealed to the U.S. Supreme Court, where in a close 5:4 vote, the court legalized same-sex marriage in all of the U.S. and its territories.

The only exceptions are some Native American tribal jurisdictions that still restrict same-sex marriage due to tribal sovereignty.

Dobbs v. Jackson Women's Health Organization (2022)

In 2022, the U.S. Supreme Court ruled in Dobbs v. Jackson Women's Health Organization that the U.S. Constitution does not contain a right to have an abortion. The court's decision overturned Roe v. Wade and gave the power over the right to have an abortion to the states. From then on, the states could decide whether to regulate abortion and how to regulate it. According to the court, based on the 10th Amendment: "the federal government has no general police power over health, education, and welfare."

In 2018, the State of Mississippi passed a new abortion law that banned abortion after the first 15 weeks of pregnancy. Previously, under Roe v. Wade, it had been 24 weeks. Jackson Women's Health Organization, the only abortion clinic in Mississippi, sued. Lower courts stayed the new law, agreeing with the Jackson Women's Health Organization that the law violated Roe v. Wade. The rulings were appealed to the Supreme Court, which reversed the lower courts' decisions in a 6:3 decision and let the new Mississippi law stand. In a 5:4 decision, the Supreme Court then overturned Roe v. Wade, giving the power to regulate abortion back to the states. As of 2025, 12 states have banned abortion, and 28 states have limited abortion bans based on gestational duration.

Chapter 17

The Ten Most Influential Documents in U.S. History

I n this chapter, I undertake another difficult task. Selecting the top ten of the most influential documents (including speeches) in U.S. history is both easy and difficult at the same time. Most are clear-cut cases, no-brainers, so to speak. Here we have the Declaration of Independence, the Constitution, and the Bill of Rights. Others are a little more difficult, such as the Gettysburg Address and the Voting Rights Act.

I picked only those documents that truly did impact U.S. history and society and made the U.S. what it is today. There are many documents to choose from, and I could have picked others. The task of narrowing it down to just ten documents was not easy. Feel free to disagree with my choices. They are obviously subjective, and other scholars of U.S. history and politics would disagree with some of my choices.

Without further ado, here are my picks for the top ten most influential documents in U.S. history.

The Declaration of Independence (1776)

At the Second Continental Congress held in 1775, the Congress commissioned a declaration to not only discuss the grievances against the British but also a reason for independence from Britain. A small committee was formed, consisting of Thomas Jefferson, John Adams, Roger Sherman, Robert Livingston, and Benjamin Franklin. Jefferson was asked to write the declaration.

After Jefferson was finished, he and John Adams and Benjamin Franklin sat down and edited the document. On July 4, 1776, the final version of the Declaration of Independence was presented to the whole Congress and officially adopted.

The Declaration of Independence outlines thoughts on democracy and the rights of the people. In the most famous section of the document, Jefferson proclaims: "We hold these truths to be self-evident, that all men are created equal, that they are all endowed by their creator with certain inalienable rights, that among these are life, liberty and the pursuit of happiness."

Jefferson then continues to argue that whenever government fails its people, the people have the right to change or even abolish a government.

The Declaration of Independence became a foundation not just for the U.S. Constitution, but also for many future democratic constitutions around the world.

The Articles of Confederation (1781-1789)

The Articles of Confederation were debated by the Second Continental Congress from July of 1776 until November of 1777 and came into force on March 1, 1781, after being ratified by all 13 colonial states.

The Articles of Confederation created a loose alliance between the 13 former colonies, now states. All powers were held by the states while the new national government, namely a Congress of the Confederation, held few powers.

It was a unicameral legislature, with one house, in which each one of the 13 states had one vote.

To pass legislation, 9 out of 13 states had to approve, and there was no executive or judiciary around. The Congress could not regulate foreign trade or levy and collect taxes. So, it did not have the money to create an army or repay war bonds.

With foreign enemies abound and war bonds to redeem, the government was unable to act. When Shay's rebellion (see Chapter 1) could not be put down because of the lack of a federal military, many of our Founding Fathers knew it was time for a change of government.

The Constitution of the United States (1789)

The U.S. Constitution was written in 1787 and was in effect by 1789. It is the longest surviving constitution in the world and also one of the shortest. It is composed of a preamble, seven articles, and 27 amendments. The first ten amendments are called the Bill of Rights.

How is it that the Constitution, now 238 years old, is still applicable to U.S. society today? The answer is in the nature of the Constitution itself. It is a brief procedural constitution. It does not go into much detail when it comes to societal matters, which are always changing, but it provides a basic structure of government. There are three branches of government, a legislative (Congress), an executive (President) and a judiciary (Supreme Court), which share powers and can always check on each other. In addition, the Constitution creates a federal political structure in which the federal government and the states engage in power sharing.

Parts of the Constitution are vague and open and can be interpreted differently by the Supreme Court over time. Therefore, the U.S. Constitution is a flexible document that can easily adapt to changing times. This makes it a living constitution.

The U.S. Constitution sets out a general vision of society, creates political structures, and establishes how these structures function.

The Bill of Rights (1791)

Constitutions discuss the distribution of power among its political structures and basic individual rights. The newly ratified U.S. Constitution had ignored discussing civil liberties. To get it ratified, the Founding Fathers promised to add a Bill of Rights. Therefore, one of the first acts of Congress and the new President George Washington was to add a Bill of Rights. The first ten amendments to the Constitution are referred to as the Bill of Rights, and they were added by 1791. They contain the most important civil liberties granted to U.S. citizens. For a full discussion of civil liberties, see Chapter 7, but here is a sample so that you can see why the Bill of Rights was added to my list of the top ten documents in U.S. history.

The First Amendment guarantees freedom of religion, speech, assembly, and the press, whereas the Second Amendment guarantees the right to bear arms. The Fourth Amendment guarantees protection from unreasonable search and seizures whereas the Fifth Amendment guarantees protection against being tried twice for the same crime (double jeopardy) as well as the right not to incriminate yourself. Amendment Six gives people a right to have counsel during a trial and Amendment Seven gives a right to a jury trial. Amendment Eight outlaws cruel and unusual punishment. Finally, the Tenth Amendment gives all powers not given to the federal government to the states.

As you can see, without a Bill of Rights, your freedoms in the U.S. would be severely limited.

The Emancipation Proclamation (1863)

The Emancipation Proclamation issued on January 1, 1863, is one of the most important and also most criticized political documents in U.S. history. Issued by President Lincoln, it states that all slaves in the Confederate areas are now free and makes it known that the Union will set slaves free and abolish slavery after winning the Civil War. However, the document applies only to the areas of the former Confederacy and leaves slavery in place in parts of the South loyal to the Union, such as the parts of Virginia that would become West Virginia and parts of Louisiana. Tennessee, which was already back under Union control, was also exempted. Of the approximately four million slaves in the U.S., an estimated 3.5 million were in Confederate territory and affected by the Proclamation.

Critics say it was designed to recruit former slaves into the Union army, and by protecting slavery on union territory it did not free all slaves or abolish slavery in the U.S. The 13th Amendment to the Constitution would do that in 1865.

The Gettysburg Address (1863)

The Gettysburg Address is the most famous speech in U.S. history. It was given by President Lincoln at the dedication of the Gettysburg National Cemetery on November 19, 1863, four months after the decisive battle at Gettysburg, which turned the Civil War in the North's favor.

15,000 people were in attendance and Lincoln spoke for only two minutes. In the speech, President Lincoln condensed the quintessence of the Civil War to a few sentences. He stressed the ideas of liberty and equality to provide justification for why slavery was illegal. Instead of relying on the Constitution, which does not mention slavery, Lincoln used the Declaration of Independence, which states that all men are created equal. He further talked about how only a Northern victory could provide a continuation of democracy and equality in the U.S.

Back in 1863, many in the media belittled the speech, but today it is considered one of the finest speeches ever given in U.S. history.

The 14th Amendment to the Constitution (1868)

The 14th Amendment to the Constitution is one of the most impactful. It states:

"All persons born or naturalized in the United States, and subject to the jurisdiction thereof, are citizens of the United States and of the State wherein they reside. No State shall make or enforce any law which shall abridge the privileges or immunities of citizens of the United States; nor shall any State deprive any person of life, liberty, or property, without due process of law; nor deny to any person within its jurisdiction the equal protection of the laws."

The 14th Amendment makes all persons born or naturalized in the United States citizens of the U.S., thus providing them with civil rights. This makes former slaves citizens of the U.S. It further states that no state in the U.S can deprive any person of life, liberty, and property without due process of law. This was later used to apply the Bill of Rights to the states. Further, no citizens can be denied the equal protection of the laws within the U.S.

The 14th Amendment was used to eliminate segregation in the U.S., to establish a right to privacy, and to legalize abortion and same-sex marriage. It truly is one of the most impactful amendments to the Constitution.

The Truman Doctrine (1947)

On March 12, 1947, in an address to Congress, President Truman outlined what would become the Truman Doctrine. In his speech he said: "I believe that it must be the policy of the United States to support free peoples who are resisting attempted subjugation by armed minorities or by outside pressures."

The Truman Doctrine called for military and economic aid for Greece and Turkey, which were fighting a communist insurgency. Congress approved $400 million to help the two countries. The communist uprisings were put down and both countries are NATO members today.

The Truman Doctrine became a part of Cold War U.S. foreign policy. It was designed to protect countries from communist insurgencies and any government threatened by communism could call upon the U.S. for both economic and military aid. The Truman Doctrine laid the ideological groundwork for future alliances such as NATO (the North Atlantic Treaty Association). It was a part of U.S. foreign policy until the collapse of the Soviet Union in 1991.

The Civil Rights Act of 1964

The Civil Rights Act of 1964 was landmark legislation that forbade discrimination on the basis of race, sex, religion, or national origin.

It was signed into law by President Johnson on July 2, 1964, and made it illegal to have separate voter registration requirements for minorities and to have racial segregation in public schools and public accommodations. Further, states and localities could not discriminate in access to public facilities.

The law further prohibited employers from discriminating in hiring on the basis of race, sex, religion, or national origin, if a business employed more than 15 people, and it barred discrimination in all public places, including privately owned ones such as hotels, motels, theatres, restaurants, lunch counters, gas stations, stadiums, arenas, and lodging houses with more than five rooms.

Further, the legislation withheld public funds from segregated schools. Within a decade, most public Southern schools were integrated.

Additions to the Civil Rights Act in 1968 banned discrimination in the sale and renting of housing and, in 1990, the Civil Rights Act became the foundation for the Americans with Disabilities Act, which applied the principle of non-discrimination to people with disabilities.

Southern Senators filibustered the bill for almost two months, but in the end, the Civi Rights Act was passed by the Senate with the necessary 2/3 majority to break a filibuster.

The Voting Rights Act of 1965

The Voting Rights Acts was passed in 1965. The Act was designed to eliminate racial discrimination in voting and get rid of barriers put in place to prevent African Americans from voting. It protected the right to vote for minorities, by outlawing literacy tests and poll taxes, and allowed for federal oversight, including onsite observers, in states where discrimination and voter suppression had been practiced in the past.

The Voting Rights Act further demanded that any kind of changes to voting laws or voting procedures, such as voter-identification requirements or restrictions on early voting, needed to be approved in advance by the U.S. Department of Justice in states with a history of discriminatory voting practices. This was called a *preclearance*. In 2013, the Supreme Court struck down preclearance, declaring it to be unnecessary.

The Voting Rights Act has had a significant impact on U.S. politics. It increased African-American voter registration levels, subsequent voter turnout, and their representation at the national and state levels.

Index

great migration, 142–143
Great Society programs, 112, 162, 235
Greece, 188
Green Party, 276
Griswold v. Connecticut (1965), 133
Gross domestic product (GDP), 171
group membership, 209
Guatemala, 187
Guinn v. United States (1963), 227

H

Hamilton, Alexander, 19, 36, 210, 267
Hancock, John, 19
Harding, Warren Gamaliel, 95, 213
hard money, 250
Harper's, 212
Harris, Kamala, 152, 165, 231–233, 254
Harrison, William Henry, 71, 238–239, 269
Hatch Act, 108–109
head of state, president as, 82–83
Hearst newspaper empire, 211
Henry, Patrick, 19
higher law, 86
high-tax states, 34
Hispanics, 149
Hispanic voters, 233
Holmes, Justic Oliver Wendell, 123
home protections, 128–129
House of Representatives, 17, 18, 20, 45, 46, 47, 50, 56, 94, 140, 152, 238
  caucuses, joining, 53
  leadership in, 50–52
  majority leader and whip, 52–53
Howe, William, 13

I

idealism, 179
ideological interest groups, 286
"imminent danger" doctrine, 124

imperial presidency
  creating, 76–77
  restoring, 78
  weakening, 77–78
implied powers, 72
incorporation, 120
independent executive agencies, 106
independent expenditures, 250
Independent regulatory commissions, 106
Indian Citizenship Act, 149
individual mandate, 170
inherent powers, 30
Instagram, 215
interdependence, 176
interest group power, sources of, 286
  leadership skills, 288
  member intensity, 287
  member prestige, 287
  membership size, 286–287
  monetary resources, 287
  organizational structure, 288
interest groups, 183, 281
  American Association of Retired Persons (AARP), 289–290
  American Federation of Labor–Congress of Industrial Organizations (AFL-CIO), 291
  American Medical Association (AMA), 290
  defining, 284
  diverse interests, 282–286
  joining, 285
  judging, 297–298
  National Rifle Association (NRA), 291–292
  recognizing types of, 285–286
  U.S. Chamber of Commerce, 288–289
interest groups, functions in a democracy, 292
  aggregating interests, 293
  electioneering, 293
  fundraising and monetary support, 294
  information, providing, 293
  litigating, 294

legislative dominance, 162–163

libel, 125

Libertarian Party, 273, 276

Lincoln, Abraham, 71, 270

literacy tests, 227

Literary Digest, 203

living constitution, U.S. Constitution as, 25

Livingston, Robert, 11

lobbying, 295–297

  regulating, 297

Lobbying Disclosure Act, 297

local parties, 279

Locke, John, 12, 179

Louisiana Separate Car Act (1890), 141

Loving, Richard, 304–305

Loving v. Virginia (1967), 304–305

low-tax states, 34

loyalty

  to the current government, 208

  to the form of government, 207

  to the state or country, 207

M

Madison, James, 16, 19, 20, 92, 93, 118–119, 121, 256, 283, 292, 297

majority leader and whip, 52–53

mandatory spending, 173

Mapp v. Ohio (1961), 128

marble cake federalism, 37

Marbury, William, 92, 302

Marbury v. Madison (1803), 91–92, 302

Marshall, John, 36, 91, 92, 93

Marshall, Thurgood, 96

Maryland, 20

Mason, George, 19

Massachusetts, 8, 11, 13, 15, 20

mass parties, 259

McCain, John, 249, 250

McCorvey, Norma, 130, 305

McCulloch, James, 29

McCulloch v. Maryland (1819), 29, 36

McDonald, Otis, 127

McDonald v. Chicago (2010), 127

Mckinley, William, 248

media, 183

media, examining, 210

  Internet, 215

  news consumption, 216–217

  online campaigning and fundraising, 214

  partisan beginnings, 210–211

  professionalization, 212–213

  radio networks, 213–214

  sensationalism, 211–212

  social media, 215–216

media, powers of, 217

  framing, 217

  politics and elections, impacting, 218

  priming, 217

  public trust, 218–219

  regulation, 219

  setting the agenda, 217

media and free expression, 125

  commercial and youth speech, 126

  libel, 125

  obscenity, 125–126

  symbolic speech, 126

Medicaid, 38, 112, 162, 170

Medicare, 38, 112, 162, 169–170

Medicare Act of 1965, 169

mercantilism, 159

Merit Systems Protection Board (MSPB), 111

Michigan Model, 235

Midnight Appointments, 91

Miller v. California (1973), 126

minutemen, 11

Miranda, Ernesto, 130

Miranda v. Arizona (1966), 130

Missouri Compromise, 138

modified closed primary, 242

modified or restrictive rule, 59

P

public opinion and media, 183
public policy, making, 157
  discretionary spending, 173–174
  economic theories, studying, 157–161
  federal budget, 161–165
  international economic policy, 174–176
  mandatory spending, 173
  social policy, 167–171
  supplemental spending, 174
public policy, studying, 165
  fiscal policy, 165–166
  monetary policy, 166–167
push polls, 206

Q

Quartering Act in 1765, 9
quasi-governmental agencies, 107
question wording, 206

R

radio networks, 213–214, 219
Raleigh, Walter, 7
Random sampling, 205
Rankin, Jeannette, 63
ratification, favoring/opposing, 19–20
ratifying new constitution, 18–19
ratifying the constitution, 20
Rayburn, Sam, 52, 53
Reagan, Ronald, 74, 96, 113, 161, 179, 188, 193–194, 273
Reagan administration, federalism in, 38–39
Reagan Doctrine, 193–194
realignment, 273
realism, 178–179
reapportionment, 47–48
rebellion, inciting, 11
reconstruction, 140–142
record fundraising (2024), 253
Reed, Thomas, 49
Reform Party, 274, 276–277

Regents of the University of California v. Bakke (1978), 148
registered population (REG), 224
Religious Freedom Restoration Act, 121
representational view, 60
representative democracy, 1
Republican dominance (1860–1932), 270–271
Republican Party, 49
reserved powers, 28–29
retrospective voting, 236
Reverse discrimination, 147–148
reverse lobbying, 296–297
Revolutionary War, 11, 12, 14, 35, 74
  battling the British, 13–14
  new government, creating, 14
  problems, having, 15
  winning a war, 13
Rhode Island, 14, 16, 20
Rights, 118
right to a lawyer, 131–132
right to privacy, 133
Roanoke Island, 7
Roe v. Wade (1973), 88, 91, 130, 305, 307–308
roll call votes, 62
Roosevelt, Eleanor, 81
Roosevelt, Franklin Delano, 36, 37, 67, 71, 73, 76–77, 79, 89, 93, 112, 168, 203, 213, 271
Roosevelt, Teddy, 248, 274, 275
Roosevelt, Theodore, 73, 186–188
Roosevelt Corollary, 186–188
Rosa Parks, 143, 145
Rubio, Marco, 197–198
Rules Committee, 49, 50–51, 58–59, 61
Russian Empire, 15

S

sampling error, 205
Sanders, Bernie, 241
Santa Fe Independent School District v. Doe (2000), 122

Supreme Court, 93
  decision-making, 97
  federal court appointments, 94–95
  justices, characteristics of, 95–97
Supreme Court justices and ambassadors,
    appointing, 70
swing voters, 247
symbolic speech, 126
systems of government, 31–35

T

Taft, William Howard, 95, 288
Taney, Roger, 139, 140
tariffs, 161
taxation, 8, 29, 32, 34, 161
taxing the colonies, 8–9
Taylor, Zachary, 269
Tea Act (1773), 10
Telecommunications Act (1996), 219
Television, 214, 216, 219
television advertising, 253–254
Tenth Amendment, 29
Texas, political parties in, 258
third parties, 273
  effects of, 277–278
  history of, 274–277
third-party groups, 251
303 Creative LLC v. Elenis (2023), 152
Three-Fifths Compromise, 17, 18
Thurmond, Strom, 56
TikTok, 215
Tillman Act, 248
"Tippecanoe and Tyler Too" campaign, 238
Townshend Acts, 9, 10
trading, 9
Treaty of Paris, 8
Treaty of Versailles, 54
Trenton, New Jersey, 13

Truman, Harry, 79, 204
Truman, Harry S., 71, 188–189
Truman Doctrine (1947), 188–189, 313–314
Trump, Donald, 57, 71, 74, 78, 80, 96, 165, 171,
    172, 188, 197–198, 219, 231–233, 244
Trump administration, federalism in, 39
Trump Doctrine, 197–198
trusteeship view, 60
Turkey, 188
Twitter (now X), 74, 215
two-party system, 257

U

unfunded mandates, 38
unicameral, 45–46
  bicameral vs., 45
unitary system, 31
  evaluating, 34
United States v. Harriss (1954), 295
Universal Declaration of Human Rights, 82
unjust prosecutions, preventing, 129–131
unscientific polls, 206
U.S. Chamber of Commerce, 288–289
U.S. Federal income taxes, 161
U.S. Steel, 175

V

Van Buren, Martin, 79, 238
Vance, J.D., 80
Verba, Sideny H., 222
veto powers, 70–71
vice president, 55, 79–80
Virginia, 11, 18, 20
Virginia Plan, 16
voice votes, 62
vote, determining, 259–260
voter identification laws, 230
voter registration, 227–228

W

X

Y

About the Author

Marcus A. Stadelmann is a professor of political science at the University of Texas at Tyler. Dr. Stadelmann received his Ph.D. from the University of California at Riverside in 1990, and has subsequently taught at universities in California, Utah, and Texas.

He presently teaches classes on American government, international relations, and comparative politics. In addition, he has given many public and academic presentations on American presidential elections and international topics such as the collapse of the Soviet Union, German unification, the rise of populism in Europe, and the politics of Russia and Ukraine.

Dr. Stadelmann's other publications include *The Dependent Ally — German Foreign Policy from 1949 to 1990*, *The Quest for Power — An Introduction To World Politics in the 21st Century*, *U.S. Presidents For Dummies*, *First Ladies For Dummies*, and *Political Science For Dummies*. In addition, Dr. Stadelmann has contributed chapters to many books and has published numerous academic articles.

Dedication

This book is dedicated to the people who had the most impact on my life, my parents Wolfgang and Heidi and my two daughters Katarina and Holly.

Author's Acknowledgments

Special thanks go to my parents and my two daughters Katarina and Holly, who kept me on track for the last months, supported me in this endeavor, and patiently waited until my work was done. Without their support, this work would not have been possible.

I would also like to express my gratitude to my editor, Christopher Morris, who did an excellent job working with me on the book. Without his input, this book would not have become what it is today.

Publisher's Acknowledgments

Executive Editor: Lindsay Berg
Project Editor: Christopher Morris
Copy Editor: Christopher Morris
Technical Editor: Jeff Swisher

Production Editor: Bharaneedharan Murthy
Cover Image: © Mehaniq/Shutterstock

Printed and bound by CPI Group (UK) Ltd, Croydon, CR0 4YY

07/12/2025

14785991-0002